PIAGET
for the
classroom
teacher

PIAGET
for the
classroom
teacher

**BARRY J.
WADSWORTH**
Mount Holyoke College

with drawings by the author

**Longman
New York and London**

PIAGET FOR THE CLASSROOM TEACHER

Longman Inc., New York

Associated companies, branches, and representatives
throughout the world.

Copyright © 1978 by Longman Inc.

Developmental Editor: Nicole Benevento
Design: Angela Foote
Manufacturing and Production Supervisor: Louis Gaber
Composition: Maryland Linotype Composition
Printing and Binding: Fairfield Graphics

Library of Congress Cataloging in Publication Data
Wadsworth, Barry J
Piaget for the classroom teacher.
Bibliography: p.
Includes index.
1. Learning, Psychology of. 2. Piaget, Jean.
1896–   3. Cognition (Child psychology) I. Title.
LB1067.W3   370.15′2   77–17655
ISBN 0–582–28012–5

Manufactured in the United States of America
Printing: 9 8 7 6 5 4 3 2   Year: 92 91 90 89 88 87 86 85

To Eva, Barn at Seven,
and Bonnie at Two

Acknowledgments

The author wishes to thank the following publishers for their kind permission to reprint:

Basic Books from Chapter 6, "Language and Thought," by Eleanor Duckworth in *Piaget in the Classroom*, edited by Milton Schwebel and Jane Raph, © 1973 by Basic Books, Inc., Publishers, New York; from Chapter 12, "The Having of Wonderful Ideas," by Eleanor Duckworth in *Piaget in the Classroom*, edited by Milton Schwebel and Jane Raph, © 1973 by Basic Books, Inc., Publishers, New York.

McGraw-Hill Book Company from *Measurement and Piaget*, edited by P. Green, M. Ford, and G. Flamer, "Developmental Theory and Diagnostic Procedures." © 1971 by McGraw-Hill Book Company, New York. Used with permission of McGraw-Hill Book Company.

The Viking Press from *To Understand Is to Invent* (pp. 50, 53–54, 95–96, 99–101, 103–104), by J. Piaget © 1973 by The Viking Press, New York; from *Science of Education and the Psychology of the Child* (pp. 24, 27–29, 34–35, 37–38, 44–45, 47, 89, 137, 171, 173, 174–175), by J. Piaget © 1969 by The Viking Press. Reprinted by permission of The Viking Press, New York.

Preface

My interest in Piaget and his theory began while I was in graduate school working on a doctorate in educational psychology at the State University of New York at Albany. Prior to that time I had been a seventh-grade teacher in a self-contained classroom on Long Island for seven years. Like many other teachers, over the years I began to feel that I was getting in a rut, that there must be better ways to teach. My approach to teaching was very conventional. I enjoyed working with the students, but I felt that I was just another cog in the wheel, not really accomplishing all that I could in the classroom. I had intuitive feelings about how to improve my teaching, but I found no support for these ideas among the school's administrators. I was fortunate at that point to be able to go to graduate school; there, I hoped, I would further my understanding of children and teaching.

After completing my doctoral work I became a college teacher, and for the past nine years I have been teaching courses in educational psychology, child development, psychological testing, and learning disabilities. When I started teaching in college I looked in vain for introductory readings on Piaget's theory for those of my students who were interested in teaching. Finding nothing suitable, I wrote a fifty-page outline of Piaget's theory specifically for use with my classes. Colleagues encouraged me to expand my outline into a full-length book, *Piaget's Theory of Cognitive Development*, which was published by David McKay in 1971. That book deals primarily with Piaget's theory and only generally with its applications to educational practice.

This book stems from my continued interest in Piaget's work and my efforts to apply Piagetian concepts in the classroom. Here I do apply Piagetian theory to educational practice. Theory is involved only to the extent necessary to provide a rationale for the teaching practices and principles presented. The major part of the book deals with teaching traditional subject and skill areas including reading, mathematics, science, and history as well as teaching in general. Two chapters are devoted to an assessment of cognitive development. The emphasis of the book is on application at the preschool and elementary levels, although a reader interested primarily in high school teaching will find relevant materials in most chapters.

Psychologists and educators have often considered Piaget's theory a "radical" approach to education. To the contrary, in most respects Piagetian theory is a conservative approach to educating children. Unquestionably it suggests teaching practices and curriculum that are not typically found in traditional schools. But the primary thrust of Piaget's theory is that educational practice should be as consistent as possible with what is known about how children develop cognitively, socially, and emotionally. This is hardly a radical notion. To my knowledge all Piagetian theorists believe that children should learn to read, write prose, solve arithmetic problems, and develop the assorted skills that schools traditionally set as objectives. In addition, Piagetian theory at its core deals with the acquisition of knowledge and *true comprehension* of what is acquired. In my opinion, Piagetian methods are a more efficient set of methods than traditional methods for acquiring skills and knowledge.

The reader should not assume that "open classroom" methods are synonymous with Piagetian methods. Much of the philosophy of the open classroom movement does rest on developmental psychology and, in part, on Piagetian theory. Indeed, *some* open classrooms that I have observed meet all the requirements for a good Piagetian classroom. But the label "open classroom" covers a great variety of schools and practices, both in the United States and abroad, and many of them *do not* meet Piagetian criteria. If I were asked to give an example of a fine school and an explicitly Piagetian school in philosophy and practice, I would cite The New School located in Norwalk, Connecticut.[1]

Some readers may think that a Piagetian approach is "unstructured" and undisciplined in relation to education because it incorporates elements of self-selection and encourages student interaction in the classroom. Nothing could be farther from the truth. In a Piagetian school, children *are not* set free to romp and play and do whatever they want in a chaotic and disorderly manner. A Piagetian

1. The New School of Mid-Fairfield County, Inc., 11 Allen Road, Norwalk, Connecticut 06851. The director of the school is Dr. Rose Park.

classroom, like a good Montessori or open classroom, is orderly even when it is very active. Bells do not ring every fifty minutes, and activities are not always started and dropped on a fixed time schedule. At times, each child may be working at individually selected activities. This does not have to be, and should not be, disorderly or unstructured.

One of the primary messages of Piagetian theory to educators and parents is that children acquire knowledge of objects and reasoning through activities that are purposeful to the child. Meaning and understanding are constructed from actions on objects and experiences with the things that are to be known. Meaning and understanding *cannot* be acquired through reading and listening alone. For this reason, a Piagetian classroom is active. Children *do* things; they do not work exclusively with symbols. There is a lot of manipulation and exploration of the objects that the teacher places in the child's environment. The emphasis is on experiencing the things to be known. Reading about and talking about things are not neglected, though they are not emphasized to the exclusion of anything else, as in traditional classrooms. From a Piagetian point of view, structure and freedom must always be kept in balance. The teacher imposes structure through the rules that are set forth and the materials that are placed in the environment. Children need sufficient freedom to permit *them* to construct knowledge.

It is appropriate to end by thanking the people who have made it possible for me to write this book and are responsible for making it better than it probably would have been if I had been without their criticisms and left entirely to my own devices. My wife, Eva, has provided unending support for this project and has spent many hours reading, editing, and typing the manuscript. Several colleagues at Mount Holyoke College have given generously of their time in criticizing parts of the manuscript: particularly Bob Shilkret, Barbara Jones, and Cathy Huntley. My thanks also to Beth Stephens at the University of Texas for her comments on the chapters on assessment. The Mount Holyoke College Faculty Grants Committee provided funds for preparation of the final manuscript. Their assistance has been appreciated. Lastly, my thanks to my editor at Longman, Nicole Benevento, who has encouraged the progress of this book over the past years.

The pages that follow reflect my construction of Piaget's theory and what it means for education. I hope that the ideas presented are helpful to the reader in understanding Piagetian theory and in conceptualizing ways that it can be used to improve teaching and other aspects of schooling.

BARRY J. WADSWORTH

Contents

PART IV   COGNITIVE-DEVELOPMENTAL ASSESSMENT   215

PIAGET
for the
classroom
teacher

BACKGROUND
PART I

Introduction

I

You believe you understand what Piaget is talking about. You are enthusiastic because what he says makes a lot of sense and because many of your intuitive feelings are confirmed by what you have read about Piaget. You believe that he is saying things that are relevant to educational practice, and you see in Piaget's conception of the child and development hope for revitalizing what happens in classrooms. But you cannot figure out how to implement in educational practice what Piaget and other developmental psychologists talk about as theory. You have sought out books and articles on the application of Piagetian theory but have not found much. You have listened to psychologists and educators talk about Piaget with enthusiasm—but with little practical application for the classroom. You are not alone; this need is shared by all of us who have recognized the potential for education in Piaget's work. Certainly professional psychologists and other educators have as many questions as classroom teachers have.

It is with a measure of uncertainty, but with a sincere feeling of challenge and urgency, that I set out to write a book that deals in large part with the application of Piaget's theory to educational practice. My uncertainty stems from the hazards of trying to apply, or suggest applications of, psychological theories to educational practice. This is never a flawless process. The transition from theory to practice is never a direct step.

The urgency of which I speak stems from my conviction that Piaget has much to say that can help to revolutionize (or evolutionize) educational practice. As a former elementary school teacher and now as an educational psychologist, I have a feeling of optimism. Also, Piaget has come into vogue in educational circles. An awareness of his ideas and concepts is important and is to be encouraged, although there is the ever-present danger that his ideas will be poorly understood, misapplied, and then rejected as *just another* useless psychological theory. This has happened to others; the history of educational innovation is replete with failures, many of them the result of a lack of understanding and misapplication. Dewey and his ideas suffered this fate.

The challenge in trying to write about the application to education of Piaget's ideas comes from an intuitive and professional awareness that Piaget is on the "right track" and from a desire to try to move some of his ideas into educational practice. Piaget does not have all the answers, but he does offer a rich framework for conceptualizing the development of children's thinking and the schooling process.

Piaget's theory is *primarily* a theory of intelligence or cognitive development—specifically of how knowledge is acquired and develops. How knowledge develops is obviously an important issue in education, but it is not everything. The child is not merely a cognitive being; he or she is also a social being, a member of a class, a family, a sex, a race, a social-economic status, a time, and a variety of other things. From the start teachers must be concerned with more than just cognitive development. Neisser (1967) writes:

> . . . a really satisfactory theory of higher mental processes can only come into being when we have theories of motivation, personality, and social interaction. The study of cognition is only one fraction of psychology, and it cannot stand alone. (p. 305)

And Hunt (1969b) cautions us:

> Despite the tremendous amount of observational evidence that Piaget and his collaborators have produced, despite the variety of theoretical conceptions for which the implications of their observations provide an intriguing and relevant dissonance, the work of Piaget is, I believe, but a beginning. His work leaves little fully established except probably that psychological development is much less an automatic unfolding with anatomical maturation than it is a joint product of that maturation of the infant continuously interacting with his circumstances and with even maturation in part a function of the interaction . . . because of their implications for other views, Piaget's observations and interpretations open doors. (p. 31)

Hunt's comment that Piaget's work "leaves little fully established" is a valid point. It is the nature of theory to be only theory. Theories are conceptions of how things are thought to work. They are, at best, imperfect in the fields of psychology, education, and all social sciences. If a theory did leave things "fully established," it would no longer be a theory; it would be a set of *laws*, the clear answers to questions. But in psychology (and other social sciences) there are no laws. Nothing about human behavior is predictable 100 percent of the time. The most useful means we have to explain human behavior are theories, imperfect as they are. The question worth asking is: What theory (or theories) best explains the question(s) about behavior I am asking?

Discussing educational application of Piagetian theory, Hamlyn (1971) writes:

> It seems to me that in practical terms the rather wholesale way that Piaget's theory has been taken up by many educationalists has its dangers. Piaget's psychology is a cognitive one and it is excusable that it leaves emotional development largely out of consideration, but this side of things must be remembered . . . it seems to me that the worst danger in the application of Piaget's theory of education is that details may be accepted as overly rigid, and teachers may argue that there is no point in trying to teach children certain things before certain ages. Such an attitude could be educationally disastrous. There is . . . [a] necessity within education of trying to teach people what they cannot understand. (p. 23)

Piaget *is* concerned in his writing with all aspects of development: cognitive, emotional, moral, and so forth.[1] The focus of his work, however, has been on cognitive development. One could gain the impression that the cognitive is of primary importance to Piaget. This would be misleading. Piaget has stated several times that all aspects of development are related and important:

> To educate is to adapt the child to an adult social environment, in other words, to change the individual's psychobiological constitution in terms of the totality of the collective realities to which the community consciously attributes a certain value. There are, therefore, two terms in the relation constituted by education: on the one hand the growing individual; on the other the social, intellectual, and moral

1. Some of Piaget's writing that deals with other than cognitive aspects of development are *The Moral Judgment of the Child* (1965) and *Will and Action* (1962).

values into which the educator is charged with initiating
that individual. (Piaget 1969a, p. 137)

Why is Piaget's work important to education and educators?
Primarily it is important because Piaget, more than any other psychologist, has provided us with a useful description of how the minds
of *children* develop; how knowledge develops during childhood.
What Piaget says about these things is not entirely new. Piaget has
much in common with Comenius, Rousseau, Pestalozzi, Montessori,
Dewey, and Wertheimer (Eson 1972). More than any other person,
though, Piaget has carefully researched his conceptions. He has been
studying how children's intelligence develops since 1919. He has
continuously revised his own thinking, although his basic assumptions
about mental development have remained substantially intact.

From the beginning of his work, Piaget has conceived of mental
development as a form of adaptation to the environment, intellectual
adaptation modeled upon concepts of biological adaptation. That is,
the development of intelligence in the child is defined and conceptualized as resulting in the child's progressively greater effectiveness in interacting with his environment. Piaget's work stands in
opposition to the assumption of the "innatism" of mental development as well as the behavioristic notion that the "environment"
alone determines mental development. Piaget states that both genetic
endowment and the child's *action* on the environment are necessary
for development, but that neither is sufficient in itself to ensure
development. For Piaget, the important thing is the *interaction* of
maturation, environmental experience, social experience, and equilibrium. For Piaget, the key to the child's development, as it relates
to educational practice, is the *activity* of the child: *his action* on
objects, events, and other people.

Application of psychological theory is always, in part, a speculative
affair. One cannot proceed from theory directly to application with
absolute certainty that it will "work." This would be an unrealistic
expectation. Also, education is an unusually complex operation. It
is one thing to train into a rat a specific behavior pattern through
reinforcement procedures; it is another thing to "educate" a child.
The first deals with behavior, the second with intelligence. Behavior
and intelligence are not the same. The aspects of the world that
make the child what he is are numerous and complex. Education is
clearly not merely something that the teacher does to the child in

the classroom, although what the teacher does in the classroom is important.

Each child is a unique individual. That is, each child *constructs* his own reality, rather than being a passive recipient. No child is like the "average" child. Sylvia Ashton-Warner (1972) summarizes some of her observations relevant to education:

> A style of teaching suiting one nation does not necessarily suit another. A look into schools, Asian and Western, is to see the subtle differences in children and the not always subtle differences. What my apprenticeship in our schools is reminding me, as I've said before, is that children differ not only from country to country, but from state to state; from city to city and from school to school. Nor is that all; from teacher to teacher and from child to child. (p. 172)

Thus the "cookbook" approach to education inevitably fails. When one plugs children indiscriminately into methods or curricula, or vice versa, the results are seldom optimal. It would be deceptive to present the reader with a set of teaching practices, materials, and curricula and say, "Do this and you will educate children as Piaget recommends." Such an approach is destined to fail, as the history of educational innovation shows. The goal of this book is limited to illustrating some of the educational procedures that are consistent with the ideas of Piaget and others in child development. The hope is to rattle some assumptions, shake up some ideas, and encourage experimenting with the products of the individual reader's (teacher's) thinking and activity. No one can "teach" anyone else how to teach. To develop one's concepts about children, about learning, about development, about teaching, one must be *active*. Without activity, a set of concepts or ideas remains meaningless. One must assimilate Piaget's ideas (or any other ideas) to put them into practice, and this cannot be done without genuine activity of one's own. This book, like any book, offers the reader only words. The meaning is not in the words themselves, but in the reader's past, present, and future active experiences.

One last word by way of introduction. This book assumes that the reader has some understanding of Piaget's basic concepts. This is not an introductory book designed to familiarize the reader with Piagetian theory, although what follows does contain a brief summary of Piaget's basic concepts. I have made an effort to avoid specialized language when possible. The reader who becomes lost in the vocabulary here is encouraged to read an introductory book on Piagetian theory and then return to this book.[2]

Three Theoretical Positions

A central thesis of this writing is that development[3] is a valid aim of education. Among recent works, this position was most clearly stated by Kohlberg and Mayer (1972). Development, as construed in the work of Piaget, his collaborators, and other developmental psychologists, is seen as a valid and "better" aim of education than other conceptions of what education is—or should be. There are three major "streams" of educational thinking (Langer 1969, Kohlberg and Mayer 1972), each forming a theoretical position, each resting on a different set of assumptions. The assumptions of each theory form the core around which each theory is constructed. Each evolves a different conception of the child. Each suggests different ways of "educating" the child. The three theoretical positions are referred to here as *romanticism-maturationism, cultural transmission-behaviorism,* and *progressivism-cognitive development* (Kohlberg and Mayer 1972).

Romanticism-maturationism

Romanticism has its roots in the writings of Rousseau. This is primarily a maturationist conception of development. Experience or the environment is important only insofar as it affects development by providing necessary nourishment for the "naturally" growing organism. Genetically predetermined stages are seen as unfolding "naturally." Stages can be *fixated,* or arrested by experience, but the *course* of development is assumed to be innate, inborn, inherited, or genetically predetermined.

2. Several introductions on Piagetian theory are *Piaget's Theory of Cognitive Development* (Wadsworth 1971), *The Origins of Intellect* (Phillips 1969), *Six Psychological Studies* (Piaget 1967), *The Psychology of the Child* (Piaget and Inhelder 1969), *Piaget's Theory of Intellectual Development* (Ginsburg and Opper 1969).
3. "Development" here includes all aspects of development, including intellectual or cognitive development, moral and social development.

Romantics hold that what comes from within the child is the most important aspect of development; therefore, the pedagogical (educational) environment should be permissive enough to allow the inner "good" (abilities and social virtues) to unfold and the inner "bad" to come under control (Kohlberg and Mayer 1972, p. 451). Thus, the child is conceptualized like a plant. It is begun from a seed, and all the characteristics that it can evolve and will evolve are predetermined and contained within the seed. The plant needs sunshine, air, and water (a good environment) in which to grow, but environmental factors do not have major effects on the characteristics of the plant beyond retarding or maximizing growth.

Cultural Transmission-behaviorism

The traditional education practiced in the United States and most Western societies is rooted in the conception that the job of education is the direct transmission of bodies of information, skills, and values of culture to the child. In the Soviet Union, this idea has been institutionalized as an explicit state policy.

The cultural transmission conception of development views the mind as a machine.[4] There are environmental "inputs" and behavioral "outputs," but it is implied that the organism has little to do with its own development. The environment is assumed to be responsible for development. Underlying this mechanistic conception of development are such associationistic concepts as *stimulus and response* and *reinforcement*, which have their roots in the works of John Locke and A. H. Thorndike, and most recently, B. F. Skinner. Development of the child's mind, moral values, and emotions is seen as a result of specifically acquired associations under control of the environment (via reinforcement).

Current educational innovations based on the cultural transmission

4. In my experience as a teacher in psychology and education I have found that many students reject the cultural transmission-behaviorism conception of man purely on emotional grounds. They are disturbed by the notion of considering themselves "machines" or even machinelike. Although the position of this book on Piaget's work lies in large part in opposition to the behavioristic conception of development, one must be cautioned against rejecting things for purely emotional reasons. One is, of course, free to do that, and from certain perspectives, it is perfectly valid to do. But such a rejection is not based on the psychological truth or falseness of the question of whether man is a "machine," a genetic map, or a unique organism playing a part in his or her own development.

rationale are *educational technology*[5] and *behavior modification*.[6] The most recent clear application of these principles to preschool education can be found in the writings of Bereiter and Engleman (1966). In these views, external experience (or reinforcement) is considered critical in shaping or determining the course of learning and development in this model. Maturation or genetic predeterminism is considered to be of little significance.

The cultural transmission-behaviorism model suggests that children can learn only through direct instruction. The teacher must teach the child. This is most efficiently carried out when the teacher (or parent) controls those reinforcers that work for a specific child and makes receipt of reinforcement contingent on learning desired responses.

Progressivism-Cognitive Development

Underlying the progressive-cognitive development conception of learning and development is the amalgamation of the significance of both maturation and the environment (though the importance of the environment and maturation is construed entirely differently from their construction in the other two models). This is the interactionist viewpoint. Mental development is seen as the product of the interaction of the organism (the child) and the environment. This position was first elaborated by Plato, and early in this century by John Dewey, and most recently by Jean Piaget.[7] In this conception the child is viewed neither as maturationally determined nor as a machine completely controlled by external agents. The child is a "scientist," an explorer, an inquirer, critically instrumental in con-

5. "Educational technology" sounds like it means something more than it does. Basically educational technology means the application of technological innovations to educational practice. This includes such things as computer-assisted instruction, teaching machines, programs, television, and other audiovisual devices. The assumptions underlying these techniques are generally the same as those of the cultural transmission conception of learning.

6. "Behavior modification" means the application of reinforcement techniques to educational or therapeutic practice. The name "behavior modification" is misleading because it refers to a specific technique among many techniques. Indeed, all people in education, regardless of what "techniques" they may be using, are involved in modifying behavior, whether they want to call it that or not.

7. Jean Piaget is obviously not the only person working in developmental psychology in this area. Literally hundreds of others have made important contributions in recent years. Piaget, though, with the possible exception of Hans Werner, stands alone in the magnitude of his research over fifty years and in having generated a cohesive theory.

structing and organizing the world and his own development.[8] The position elaborated in this book falls in the progressivism-cognitive development viewpoint.

This book is not a comparison of the three different viewpoints. Occasional comparisons will be made with other viewpoints, but these are made largely to clarify the Piagetian position by contrast to other possible positions. The reader interested in extended comparisons of the three major viewpoints is directed to Langer (1969), Kohlberg and Mayer (1972), Kohlberg (1969), and Maier (1969).

8. A caution was previously made regarding the rejection of psychological theories on emotional grounds. Similarly, one must caution against accepting psychological theories for emotional reasons. My experience has been that most people "like" Piagetian theory. They like the picture Piaget paints. Again, this is neither evidence for the correctness or incorrectness of assertions nor adequate logical grounds for the acceptance of a theory. No doubt it is important for teachers to *like* and feel comfortable with whatever they use.

How Piaget

2

Conceptualizes Development

Cognitive development is a continuous process that begins at birth. Piaget divides development into four broad periods (Wadsworth 1971). In order of their occurrence they are: (1) the sensorimotor period, 0–2 years; (2) the preoperational period, 2–7 years; (3) the period of concrete operations, 7–11 years; and (4) the period of formal operations, 11–15 years. These periods are not independent or unrelated. Development is *both* continuous and discontinuous. Continuous means that each subsequent development builds on and incorporates and transforms previous developments. Discontinuous in this case means that qualitative changes take place from stage to stage. Thus, the periods of development are functionally related and part of a continuous process. The age ranges for each period are the *average* ages at which children generally demonstrate the characteristics of thought of each period. Some children clearly enter or exit these periods earlier or later than the average ages. As a group, deaf children are on the average about a year behind normal children. Blind children trail normal children by about four years on the average. Severely retarded children may be even slower in their rates of development. But in all cases, all children (normal, deaf, blind, and retarded) appear to move through the Piagetian stages in the same order. Children do not skip stages. Within each of these groups and among all children, rates of development or rates of moving through stages vary considerably. One cannot assume that a child's age alone tells you his current level of conceptual development.

The periods of development outlined by Piaget are irreversible in the sense that once a child has developed the capacity for a particular type of thought, he does not normally lose that capability.

As all teachers and parents know, just because a child has a level of logical thought, he or she does not necessarily always think or act logically.[1] One's behavior is not always reflective of one's "best" thinking.

The Periods of Development

The four periods of development outlined by Piaget are summarized in table 1. This section briefly outlines each major period. The reader wishing greater detail in each of the stages of development should refer to Wadsworth (1971), Phillips (1969), Piaget and Inhelder (1969), and Flavell (1963).

Sensorimotor Period

By the time a child is born, development of the mind has already started. The nervous system and the sensory mechanisms are operating. Physiological development before birth is clearly necessary for the cognitive development, which will take place later.

Much of the behavior of the newborn infant is reflexive in nature. The baby can suck, grasp, cry, and otherwise respond on a reflexive level. At this point the child's "experiences," his motor and perceptual actions on the physical world surrounding him, begin to influence his development. Through maturation[2] and interaction with the environment, sensorimotor reflexes become modified, and

---

1. It is important to make a distinction between learning or development and behavior in general. Not all behavior reflects a child's highest level of development. Clearly much behavior reflects motivations other than the child's cognitive capability. The human mind is not always engaged at its highest level or always engaged at all! All people engage in irrational behaviors that clearly do not reflect their highest levels of thought. The fact that one has developed logical thought does not ensure that one will think logically at all times or behave accordingly. Indeed, one should make a clear distinction between behavior and thought. They are not the same thing. See "Development, Learning, and Behavior," p. 28.

2. "Maturation" here refers primarily to the physiological growth and development of the nervous system, including the brain. Maturation of the nervous system is relatively complete only by the age of 15 or 16 and thus is an important factor throughout development (Piaget 1969a, p. 36).

behaviors not present at birth begin to emerge. The hungry infant begins to differentiate via his sucking reflex between a milk-producing nipple and other objects that his mouth encounters. This is development, this is learning, this is sensorimotor intelligence in operation on the most primitive level.[3]

The infant's actions (sucking) have been *assimilated* into new behavior patterns (or *schemata*) after some *accommodation* on the part of the infant.[4] By the end of the sensorimotor period, typically sometime between eighteen months and two years, the young child begins internally to *represent* objects and events experienced in his environment. That is, the child begins to manipulate objects and events mentally through representation. At this time the capability for carrying out action sequences in the mind (i.e., without actually "performing" the overt movements) begins to develop. This is the beginning of a higher level of thought. The child begins to solve some of his older sensorimotor problems in a new way—through representing action sequences and trying out solutions covertly (in his head). Thus, instead of having to engage in trial-and-error movement to find solutions to problems, the child begins to solve problems through internal representation, or thinking.

With this new capability, the child can be seen to go directly to solutions to problems he has not dealt directly with before. Thus, the average child at eighteen months or two years is qualitatively different in his thought in a variety of ways from the younger infant. Intervening have been maturation, the child's *actions* on his environment (experience), and the processes of assimilation and accommodation continually working toward an increasingly more efficient organization or equilibrium. The most complete description of cognitive development during the first two years of life can be found in *The Origins of Intelligence* by Piaget (1952a). A briefer outline is found in my previous work (Wadsworth 1971).

3. The young child has a "practical" intelligence. The infant cannot internally represent events and think as such, but he does "think," so to speak, with his whole body and through his actions. Practical problems are solved, and these solutions imply a primitive if nonmentalistic form of intelligence. Sensorimotor intelligence is seen as a necessary precursor to later representational thought, or what is commonly called "thinking."

4. The constructs of assimilation, accommodation, and schemata are central to understanding Piaget's conceptualization of development. The reader who feels uncomfortable with these concepts is referred to one of the introductory books on Piagetian theory such as Wadsworth (1971) or Phillips (1969).

TABLE 1

Summary of the Periods of Cognitive Development

Period	Characteristics of the Period	Major Change of the Period
Sensorimotor (0–2 years)		Development proceeds from reflex activity to representation and sensorimotor solutions to problems
Stage 1 (0–1 months)	Reflex activity only; no differentiation	
Stage 2 (1–4 months)	Hand-mouth coordination; differentiation via sucking reflex	
Stage 3 (4–8 months)	Hand-eye coordination; repeats unusual events	
Stage 4 (8–12 months)	Coordination of two schemata; object permanence attained	
Stage 5 (12–18 months)	New means through experimentation—follows sequential displacements	
Stage 6 (18–24 months)	Internal representation; new means through mental combinations	
Preoperational (2–7 years)		Development proceeds from sensorimotor representation to prelogical thought and solutions to problems
Egocentric stage (2–4 years)	Problems solved through representation—language development (2–4 years); thought and language both egocentric	
Intuitive stage (5–7 years)	Cannot solve conservation problems; judgments based on perception rather than logic	
Concrete operational (7–11 years)	Reversability attained; can solve conservation problems—logical operations developed and applied to concrete problems; cannot solve complex verbal problems	Development proceeds from prelogical thought to logical solutions to concrete problems
Formal operations (11–15 years)	Logically solves all types of problems—thinks scientifically; solves complex verbal problems; cognitive structures mature	Development proceeds from logical solutions to concrete problems to logical solutions to all classes of problems

SOURCE: Adapted from B. Wadsworth, *Piaget's Theory of Cognitive Development* (New York: David McKay, 1971).

Preoperational Period

The development of internal representation permits the young child to begin to use symbols to represent objects. Piaget (1970) writes:

> Between the age of about 1½ years and the age of 7 or 8 years when the concrete operations appear, the practical logic of sensori-motor intelligence goes through a period of being internalized, of taking shape in thought at the level of representation rather than taking place only in the actual carrying out of actions. (p. 45)

During the first half of the preoperational period, from the ages of two to four, the extremely rapid development of spoken language occurs. By four years of age the average child in any culture has mastered much of his or her native language. Typically he or she understands and uses a great number of words and uses the main body of the language's grammar effectively. The learning of spoken language at these ages, without instruction, is an astounding event in which nearly every child succeeds.

Educationally it is interesting that *all* children learn their native language without any formal instruction. Also, if children are raised in a bilingual home, they learn two languages with little apparent difficulty. One cannot help but wonder how all children learn to speak so easily while reading poses a problem for so many children a few years later. This question is explored in detail in chapter 14.

According to Piaget, language development occurs only after the child becomes capable of internal representation. The "talking" of the younger child (before representation) is deceptive. While the child may be using words, the sounds used do not represent objects and events. Thus, the typical one-year-old who says "mama" is not using the sound to represent his mother but has learned that by using that sound he gets his mother's attention (reinforcement).

During the preoperational period the child internally represents objects and events and "thinks." His thinking, though, is *prelogical* or *partly logical*. Thought is dominated by perception. In the classical conservation of number problem, the child is shown two parallel and equally long rows of, say, eight pennies (see figure 1A). After agreement is attained that each row has the same number of pennies, one row is lengthened (i.e., the same elements are spread out). The child is asked again, after the transformation (figure 1B), to compare the two rows of pennies. Until about the age of five or six, children typically will insist that the longer row has more pennies. Their explanations clearly suggest that the row perceived as longer has a greater number. If this experiment is repeated with a row of nine pennies and a second, longer row of eight pennies, the *non-conserving* child maintains that the longer row of eight pennies has a greater number. The child may be able to tell you that nine is greater than eight if you remove the problem from his view, but when you return to the two rows of pennies, judgments are made on the basis of perception (which row "looks like" more) rather than on the basis of logic. Thus the child's thinking is prelogical.

Conservation problems are probably the best-known Piagetian items used for examining children's thinking. These items all have one thing in common. The interviewer presents a child with a problem such as the conservation of number problem. When equivalence is established (each row has the same number of elements) one set is transformed or displaced spatially (one row of elements is lengthened or shortened). The transformation is always in a dimension that is irrelevant to the quality being examined. Thus, in

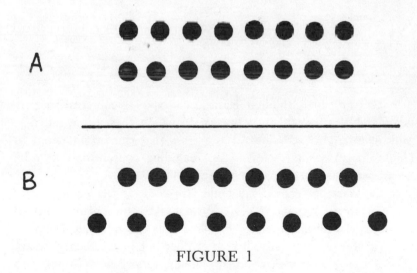

FIGURE 1

the conservation of number, one of two equal rows of elements is lengthened. In the conservation of length problem one of two equal lengths is made shorter (wire is bent into a ∿∿ shape) or is moved with respect to the second. In the conservation of liquid problem, a container of liquid is poured into a different diameter container. The child is asked to judge which has more, is longer, etc. The change is always in an irrelevant dimension, though a correspondence remains. The object is to see whether the child can hold constant the quality being considered (conserved) in the face of the transformation. This requires that the child recognize a correspondence between the original form and the transformed one.

The child with concrete operational thought has established the type of thinking necessary for conserving. He considers both the transformations and the correspondence. The ages at which different conservations typically emerge range through the preoperational and concrete operational periods. The structures permitting conservation are typically acquired at the following ages:

length	6–7
number	6–7
area	7–8
mass	7–8
liquid	7–8
weight	9–10
volume	11–12

The ages at which children learn each type of conservation vary considerably, although the sequence in which they are acquired is fairly constant. Descriptions of the tasks that can be presented to children in assessing logical skills, including conservation, can be found in the section on assessment (pp. 244–80).

If the young preoperational child is asked, "Is the moon alive?" he is likely to respond, "Yes." When asked to explain this, his reasoning usually incorporates movement as the rationale for what is living. If it moves, it is alive; if it does not move, then it is not alive. Thus, the moon as well as clouds, cars, candle flames, and trees (on windy days only) are all typically described as alive. The child's level of thinking is revealed not only through his answers to questions, but also through the reasoning behind the answers.

Another characteristic of preoperational thought is what Piaget calls *egocentrism*. The child thinks that everyone thinks the same way he does, that everyone thinks the same thing he does, and quite logically that everything he thinks is "right." Consequently, the preoperational child rarely questions his thinking and has difficulty assuming the viewpoints of others. He literally does not believe that there are viewpoints other than his own. Egocentrism of thought during the preoperational period diminishes slowly through the child's dealing with the thoughts of peers that conflict with his own thinking.

Concrete Operations

Around the age of seven the typical child begins to develop what Piaget calls *concrete operational thought*. One can no longer "trick" the child with concrete problems like the conservation problems, ones that involve a conflict between logic and perception. The child with concrete operations solves most of the *conservation* problems.[5] No longer is logic subordinate to perception in judgment when the child is confronted with concrete problems. In addition to conservation problems, the concrete operational child masters classification problems and seriation problems. He attends to all aspects of transformations (as in conservation problems) and sees correspondences between transformed states. The child's thought is reversible.[6] Generally, the child with concrete operations can use logic to arrive at solutions for most *concrete* problems.

But more development is still to come. The concrete operational child has difficulty applying his logic to nonconcrete problems. These include complex verbal problems, hypothetical problems, and problems dealing with the future (which are a type of hypothetical problem). Thus, thought is still bound to the concrete and tied to perception (but no longer dominated by perception). For example,

5. The logical solution to different types of conservation problems begins in the late part of the preoperational period, and some are not mastered until formal operations begin to develop.

6. Reversibility is the ability to carry a thought backward as well as forward in time, to reverse a thought. Unlike many of the learnings of young children, no models or examples of reversibility serve as guides for thinking. Events in life are not reversible. Piaget says that reversibility of thought is the most important aspect of thought that separates the concrete operational child from the preoperational child. Reversibility is necessary for operational solutions to problems and is the logical tool that permits logic to triumph over perception in thinking.

while the concrete operational child may give logically "correct" answers to the conservation problems, the quality of his reasoning is tied to the concrete aspects of the particular situation. There is no indication that the child yet thinks in more abstract formal rules independent of concrete objects.

Formal Operations

The last period in Piaget's conceptualization of development is the period of formal operations. This typically occurs between the years of eleven and fifteen.[7] During this period the child becomes capable of applying logical thought to all classes of problems: verbal problems, hypothetical problems, problems dealing with the future, and so on. If you will, the *structures* for logical thought become fully developed during this period. With the development of formal operations, the child is *capable* of thinking as logically as he ever will be. There are no further improvements with respect to the logicality of the thinking one is capable of. To avoid confusion, this does not mean that the adolescent (or the adult) always thinks logically. It merely means that the capacity for fully logical thought is present once formal operations are developed. Every parent of teen-agers knows that adolescents do not always think and behave logically. They also know that you cannot out-logic the typical adolescent when he or she wants to be logical. Also, the fact that capability for logical thought in a sense stops developing around age fifteen does not mean that adults do not or cannot continue to develop and change their thinking. Clearly, people continue to acquire new *contents* and elaborate old ones after formal operations are developed. What does not seem to improve is how logically one is *capable* of dealing with those contents.

As suggested elsewhere (Wadsworth 1971), an adolescent with formal operations is not yet an adult in thought. Initially his use of

7. The full development of formal operations can continue much beyond age fifteen. The variability in rate of development of formal operations is greater than that of the earlier stages. Acquisition of formal operations is the least "automatic" of the stages. Some people never develop formal thought; possibly as many as 50% of the American adult population (Kohlberg and Mayer 1972). In "primitive" cultures, formal operations are rarely seen as such reasoning has little adaptive value within such cultures (see chapter 7). Elkind (1962) and Schwebel (1975) found large numbers of college students who had not attained complete formal operations.

logic is egocentric (in a way different from preoperational ego-centrism) in a sense that the adolescent tends, when using logic, to use it as the sole criterion for what is "good," "right," "moral," and so on. He tries to reduce the world to what is logical. As yet he fails to differentiate between what is logical and what is "real." He fails to grasp the idea that the world and events are not always ordered logically. In this sense, the adolescent's thought is egocentric—logical but not yet fully realistic. Thus, many adolescents appear to be very idealistic in their thinking. Piaget's theory suggests that this is a temporary or "false" idealism and will change (adapt) when the adolescent confronts the "real" world. It should be understood that this period of false idealism is in no way a negative thing from the point of view of development. It is a *normal* and *necessary* part of development. False idealism is a *necessary prior-development* to realistic thought, whether one eventually retains idealism or not.

Thus, cognitive development as outlined by Piaget is a progressive process of *construction* of intellectual structures from birth through adolescence. Initially, these structures are evident on a motor and sensory level—later on a representation level. Each and every child *constructs* the world from his or her *actions* on it. The child must act on the environment for development to occur. These actions are the raw materials for assimilation and accommodation, and generate the development of mental structures or schemata. Each step in development makes the individual child more effective in dealing with his or her environment. Every new change in schemata results in a qualitative change in the thought of which the child is capable. Thus, development is a form of *adaptation* to the environment in the same way that all biological activity is adaptive.

The sequence of development is the same for all children, though rates of development vary considerably from child to child. There do not appear to be any major sex differences in development when viewed from a Piagetian perspective. Boys and girls, on the average, develop at about the same rate. Also, development of mental opera-tions does not appear to be related to schooling. Children who do not go to school seem to develop logical operations as quickly on the average as children who go to school, at least through concrete operations. Similarly, there are few cultural differences in cognitive development. Children of all cultures develop through the same stage sequence as described by Piaget, though there are some differ-ences in the acquisition of specific concepts.

The Relative Roles of

3

Genetic Factors and Experience

An important educational and psychological issue is the relative place of genetic factors and experience in development and learning. The issue cannot be resolved "scientifically" to everyone's satisfaction because that would require experiments that subjected similar children to different environments for long periods of time and then studied the effects of the different environments on the children's development. Such studies fall beyond ethical limits. How one conceptualizes the relationship between genetic (or maturational) factors and experience (or environmental factors), then, must rest on types of evidence and assumptions that are subject to interpretation and dispute. Examples are observational and correlational types of studies and experimental studies done with animals.

The types of evidence that are available can be interpreted in different ways. For example, typical black children perform less well than typical white children on school achievement and intelligence tests. (This is observational information.) Some people (Jensen 1969) argue that this supports the concept of genetic inferiority of blacks. Some argue that the poorer environment of blacks produces lower relative performance on achievement and intelligence measures and does not reflect genetic inferiority or superiority. The arguments, of course, are much more complex than this (see Kamin 1974), but the necessity for interpretation and making assumptions is always present. Similar interpretations are made about the observation that girls in elementary school outperform boys, Oriental-American children outperform children of all other groups, and so forth.

The conception that is most appealing has been suggested by Piaget (1971b) and Flavell (1971). In normal children the relative

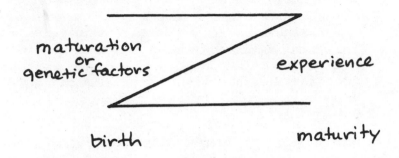

FIGURE 2
The Relative Contribution of Heredity and Experience
to Mental Development

influence of maturation or genetics (versus experience) on mental
development is viewed as greater than experience at birth and in the
early years, its relative influence diminishing with age. The relative
role of experience is viewed as the opposite of that of maturation. The
importance of experience (versus maturation) is seen at its least at
birth, with its relative importance increasing with age. The relationship can be visualized in figure 2.

Piaget (1971b) writes:

> The epigenesis [development] of the cognitive functions,
> like any other, does, in fact, presuppose an increasingly close
> collaboration between the factors of environment and genome
> [set of genes], the former [the environment] increasing in
> importance the larger the subject grows. (p. 21)

Flavell (1971) writes:

> I wonder if it may be that, in the course of development,
> the constraining role of maturation or endogenous [internal]
> factors actually decreases rather than increases. Now, we
> usually think that what's really important is the kind of
> stimulation a child gets in infancy, and that once that's
> taken care of, you don't have to worry so much about the
> rest of development. We think of infancy, in other words,

as the critical period of cognitive development. But if you actually look at the facts in the Piagetian domain, it turns out that it is far more certain, and I think more biologically guaranteed, that a child is going to achieve sensorimotor acquisitions than it is that he will acquire formal operations. The evidence suggests that whether or to what extent you get formal operations will depend much more upon the specific encounters the child has with his milieu than would be the case for sensorimotor actions or even concrete operations. (p. 190)

This conception argues that maturation is initially the major factor in development and becomes increasingly less a factor with age. This view also helps explain the fact that there is less variability in development during the first years of life than in later years. From Piaget's point of view, maturation (or experience) alone never ensures development; both are necessary:

> . . . maturation as regards cognitive functions—knowledge—simply determines the *range* of possibilities at a specific stage. It does not cause the actualization of the structures. Maturation simply indicates whether or not the construction of specific structures is possible at a specific stage. It does not itself contain a preformed structure, but simply opens up possibilities—the new reality still has to be constructed. (1971a, p. 193)

Thus Piaget's conception of development argues for the necessity of both maturation and experience in development. To construe that Piaget is a maturationist alone or a preformationist alone would be incorrect. The view presented here also suggests that development and related learning can be affected by education and other forms of experience; the *potential* effects of these are greater the older the child or the more advanced the development of the child.

Effects of Environmentally Induced Retardation

A strongly held belief among psychologists is that children raised in an unstimulating environment will be retarded in intellectual development and that the effects of the retardation will be permanent. That is, children raised in unstimulating environments will develop more slowly than children raised in stimulating environments, and their ultimate level of development will be lower than that of normal children. Children developing in this way are called *functionally retarded*; that is, their retardation is thought to be caused by environmental rather than organic (or physical) factors (e.g., brain damage).

Nothing in Piaget's theory directly supports the view that early environment-induced retardation will have effects that are not reversible. Piaget's theory certainly concurs that a lack of stimulation (active experience) during any period of development will hamper development during that period. The unfolding of genetic possibilities *is not* automatic. Active experience is always necessary for development, according to Piaget, and the quality of that experience affects development. There is little debate that experience affects development. Reasonable evidence upholds that the effects of *functional retardation* are reversible; once a child's rate of development has slowed down, it can speed up again. The secret lies with the environment. Skeels and Dye (1939) reported years ago that institutionalized children who were regarded as retarded made dramatic gains in intellectual development when they were moved from a setting where they were primarily with retarded children of the same ages to a setting where they were with older retarded children and adults. Hunt (1961), in reviewing the work of Skeels and Dye and other studies available at that time, concluded that in retarded children the change to a *more* stimulating environment produced the increase in rate of development.

Recent support for the reversibility of functional retardation comes from Jerome Kagan's work in Guatemala. He has been studying how children in non-Western cultures develop (see *Carnegie Quarterly*, Summer 1975). Kagan found in an isolated Indian village that

> . . . babies are raised in small, dark huts that lack even windows. Though loved and cared for, these infants are not allowed outside where, it is thought, the sun or dust might harm them. They have no toys, cannot roam about, and are rarely spoken to. In psychological terms, they lack experiential variety—and they must contend with malnutrition and disease which combine to retard their development as well.
> . . . At about 12 months, the San Marcos child leaves the dark hut and begins to play with other children and to encounter an interesting world. (p. 6)

According to Kagan, the San Marcos children are considerably slower than American children in intellectual development during their first and subsequent years, although the differences narrow with age. By the ages of ten or eleven, there are no differences between the two types of children. Kagan reasons that the initial slow rate of development is caused by the restricted environment during the first year. Subsequent recovery is brought about by the positive change in the children's environment. Kagan concludes that delayed development in children persists "only if the environment that causes the delay remains the same" (p. 6). Hunt (1969a) writes:

> Although the question of the permanence of the effects of experiential deprivation during infancy is far from answered, such evidence as I have been able to find, and as I have summarized here, would indicate that if the experiential deprivation does not persist too long, it is reversible to a substantial degree. (p. 40)

While it is difficult to detail specifically how to reverse functional or pseudo retardation, it is reasonable to conclude that such retardation is reversible in principle. The fact that many cases of retardation seem to persist tends to *reinforce selectively* the widely held belief that retardation is not reversible to any great degree. In many cases, a lack of improvement may reflect the fact that there may not have been qualitative improvement in the environment of the child.

Inhelder, in an interview in which she described some of her beliefs about retardation, said:

> They [retarded children] develop [conservation concepts] much later but they go through exactly the same steps normal children do. Using this developmental approach, it was relatively easy to distinguish between pseudo defective children and the truly retarded. . . . Often the [pseudo defective] children were socially deprived. Sometimes they would have specific defects like dyslexia or aphasia. Under the global approach, they had all been considered retarded. We found that such defects would respond to a specific kind of help. . . . If one succeeds in training our young patients to overcome their specific difficulty then it is likely that their potential was more or less normal. From the psychological point of view that's about the only thing we can do. In fact we did all kinds of training studies with a group of children with different difficulties who weren't able to go through normal

school training. As a result of our training method—which is an application of our fundamental studies in growth and development—they were able to gain a lot. But one or two of them did not gain at all, so it is highly probable that their potential was not high enough. You have to take each case individually and devote a lot of time to it. (Hall 1970, p. 54)

In principle, functional or pseudo retardation is reversible. This conclusion is reached by Hunt (1961) and Kagan and receives general support from Piaget's theory, specifically from the work of Baerbel Inhelder, Piaget's co-worker. Inhelder (1968, and in Hall 1970) speaks of her success using diagnostic and remedial methods that are consistent with what is known about growth and development (particularly Piaget's theory). Kagan's research efforts reveal the importance of general improvement of the environment of the "retarded" child.

Development, Learning,

4

and Behavior (Performance)

For Piaget, development, learning, and behavior are closely related and yet different. The distinctions between these terms and their relationship are frequently blurred in psychology and education.

Behavior is what people do. It may be any overt act such as walking or talking, or it may be a covert act such as thinking. All school performances are behaviors. From observations of behavior, inferences are made about learning and development. A child who has previously had difficulty opening a combination lock is observed opening the lock with little difficulty. We infer from this behavior that the child has learned to open the lock. Another child who has never solved a paper-and-pencil math problem begins to get correct solutions. We infer from this behavior that some learning has taken place. Behaviors are always the observable basis upon which inferences about development and learning are made.

Unlike behavior, cognitive development and learning can never be observed directly because they are *hypothetical constructs*, inferred to exist. In the extreme case, if there was never any behavior, we could not infer any development or learning. On the other hand, a person can be "behaving" quite regularly, yet we may not infer development or learning unless we see a change in behavior. The child who continues to make the same mistakes in division problems does not demonstrate any new learning.

The fact that development and learning are hypothetical constructs and are known only by inference from behaviors or performances creates some problems. There are different conceptions of development and learning and their relationship. For example, behaviorist psychologists frequently do not make a distinction between behavior,

28

learning, and development. The behaviorist-oriented psychologist or educator is frequently concerned only with observable behaviors and avoids inferences about or distinctions between learning and development. For Piaget and most other developmental psychologists, the distinctions between behavior, development, and learning are real and vital. Piaget (1964a) writes:

> First I would like to make clear the differences between two problems: the problem of *development* in general, and the problem of *learning*. I think these problems are very different, although some people do not make this distinction.
>
> The development of knowledge is a spontaneous process, tied to the whole process of embryogenesis. Embryogenesis concerns the development of the body, but is concerned as well with the development of the nervous system, and the development of mental functions. In the case of the development of knowledge in children, embryogenesis ends only in adulthood. It is a total developmental process which we must re-situate in its general biological and psychological context. In other words, development is a process which concerns the totality of the structures of knowledge.
>
> Learning presents the opposite case. In general, learning is provoked by situations—provoked by a . . . teacher, with respect to some didactic point; or by an external situation. It is provoked, in general, as opposed to spontaneous. In addition, it is a limited process—limited to a single problem, or a single structure. (pp. 7–8)

For Piagetians, cognitive development is the reorganization of mental structures, which occurs when a person spontaneously acts on the environment (transforms it), experiences disequilibrium, and assimilates and accommodates events. The subsequent result is structural reorganization, which permeates all aspects of the intellect. Such is the case when the young child develops representational abilities, acquires conservation abilities, or becomes capable of reasoning on the basis of hypothesis during the formal operational period.

Learning, as Piaget has indicated, has a less fundamental, but important, effect on the intellect. "Functionally, learning is the application of an intellectual structure to a wide variety of objects and events. That is, one learns rules about how to apply the structure, and, consequently, the structure becomes increasingly elaborated" (Strauss 1972, p. 331). Learning is the acquisition of a skill or of specific information based on current intellectual structures or development. Learning may otherwise be an association (or memorized acquisition) or a strictly verbal acquisition (rote learning).

The relationship between development and learning is a crucial one for education. The Piagetian view is that development determines to a large extent how learning can proceed. Inhelder (1971) writes:

> The central biological question concerning learning is whether it constitutes the source or result of development. It would certainly be the source were development to consist solely of an accumulation of acquisition of external origin, as empiricists suppose. On the contrary, if development consists of a continuous construction of operatory structures through interaction between the subjects' activities and the external data, then the assimilation of these data will determine and direct the learning process which depends on the developmental stages. Consequently, in our view, it is development that directs learning rather than vice versa. (pp. 152–53)

In the area of mathematics, if a child has developed fundamental concepts of number, then the child can learn with comprehension that $1 + 1 = 2, 1 + 2 = 3, 2 - 1 = 1, 3 - 2 = 1$, and so on. If the child has not developed fundamental concepts of number he can *memorize* $1 + 1 = 2, 1 + 2 = 3$, etc., but he cannot *learn* the arithmetic rules with comprehension. In the first case (learning with comprehension), the *learning is integrated* into mental structures and can be reproduced from those structures. In the second case (learning with memory), the *learning is essentially isolated* from mental structures and is dependent on recall and association to be produced.

The advantage of *learning with comprehension* over *learning with memory* (rote learning) is that it permits the child to apply the structural rules that he has developed to reason over a wider range of problems. The child who *comprehends* the rules of mathematics can theoretically solve all problems that require those rules. The child who has memorized some solutions is restricted to solving those particular problems and cannot truly reason about mathematics. Learning that proceeds from development results when the child transforms objects and events and discovers their correspondences. "To know is to transform" (Piaget 1976).

To make these distinctions does not belittle learning with memory and does not claim the all-importance of learning that proceeds from development. Educators should, however, be familiar with the differences because goals of education are often stated to suggest the desirability of learning with comprehension *when the practices result in learning with memory*. Teachers cannot maximize comprehension unless they understand learning and its relationship to development. School behavior, or performance—the observable aspects of mental activity—can reflect both developmental learning and learning from memory. Without making the distinction suggested here, one might assume that behavior reflects something it does not.

THEORETICAL
PART II
FOUNDATIONS

Knowledge—

5

A Construction of Reality

A theoretical and practical question central to learning and education is how knowledge develops. Is knowledge a copy of reality or is it an individual, unique construction? The notion that knowledge is a *directly* acquired copy of reality —that is, that the mind of the child "takes in" essentially a replication of the world beyond his body—has been around for a long time. Somehow, the child was thought sensorially (visually, auditorily) to incorporate accurate "images" of the real world directly. No longer is this conceptualization held to be valid by Piagetian scholars and workers in child development.

Neisser (1967) in his book *Cognitive Psychology* writes a classic statement that integrates the literature on sensory aspects of cognitive development:

> There certainly is a real real world of trees and people and cars and even books, and it has a great deal to do with our experiences of these objects. However, we have no direct, immediate access to the world, nor to any of its *eidoly*, which supposed that faint copies of objects can enter the mind directly, must be rejected. Whatever we know about reality has been *mediated,* not only by the organs of sense but by complex systems which interpret and reinterpret sensory information. (p. 3)

Clearly, the copy-of-reality conception of knowledge does not have a physiological base.

One of Piaget's major contentions is that each individual constructs reality. For each child this is a unique construction. That is, the child, having the same general types of experiences available as everyone else has, constructs what the world is to him. Based on sensory experience (visual, auditory, motor, kinesthetic), the child evolves schemata. The child's active assimilation of objects and events results in the development of structures (schemata) that reflect the child's concepts of the world or reality. As the child develops these structures, reality or his knowledge of the world changes. Clearly, a child's concept of "policeman" or "number" is not the same at age fifteen as it was at age three. The child's concept of an apple is the product of considerable experience with apples. The concept an older child has is typically more "adultlike" than the concept a younger child has, not because his eyes are better, but because his construction of the concept of "apple" is more advanced. Kamii (1973b) writes:

> When we come into contact with reality, we always transform it according to the network of concepts that we bring to the situation. The way a four year old transforms reality, or the stimuli in the environment, is much more static, egocentric, and deforming than the way adults transform the same stimuli. Our way corresponds much more closely to external reality because our logico-mathematical structures are more elaborate. . . . Piaget showed that we interact with reality not as it is "out there" but as our cognitive structures transform the stimuli coming through our senses. (pp. 219–20)

Reality for the child is *never* a mirror image of the real world. Children's conceptions develop from those initially based on limited information—unrefined, frequently inaccurate schemes—to increasingly more accurate and refined schemes. Regarding the issue of the acquisition of knowledge and reality, Piaget (1969a) writes:

> The essential functions of intelligence consist in understanding and inventing, in other words of building up structures by structuring reality. It increasingly appears, in fact, that these two functions are inseparable, since, in order to understand a phenomenon or an event, we must reconstitute the transformation of which they are the resultant. . . . The problem of intelligence, and with it the central problem of the pedagogy of teaching, has thus emerged as linked with the fundamental epistemological problem of the nature of knowledge: does the latter constitute a copy of reality, or on the contrary, an assimilation of reality into a structure of transformations? The ideas behind the knowledge-copy concept have not been abandoned by everyone, far from it, and

they continue to provide the inspiration for many educational methods[1] . . . many . . . continue to think that the formation of the intelligence obeys the laws of "learning," after the model of certain Anglo-Saxon theories of learning exemplified by those of Hull: repeated responses of the organism to external stimuli, consolidation of those repetitions by external reinforcements, constitution of chains of association or of a "hierarchy of habits" which produce a "functional copy" of the regular sequences of reality. . . . But the essential fact that contradicts these survivals of associationist empiricism . . . is that knowledge is derived from *action*, not in the sense of simple associative responses, but in the much deeper sense of the assimilation of reality into the necessary and general coordinations of action. To know an object is to act upon it and to transform it, in order to grasp the mechanism of that transformation as they function in connection with the transformative actions themselves. To know is therefore to assimilate reality into structures of transformation, and these are the structures that intelligence constructs as a direct extension of our actions.

   Intelligence, at all levels, is an assimilation of the datum into structures of transformations, from the structures of elementary actions to the higher operational structures, and that these structuralizations consist in an organization of reality, whether in act or thought, and not in simply making a copy of it. (pp. 27–29)

The question can be raised, If everyone constructs reality for himself, why do so many people see reality similarly and end up with similar conceptions of the world? The answer to this is that objects and events have certain physical characteristics and as the child acts on the objects, their characteristics are discovered. Ten different children acting on rocks are likely to develop similar conceptions of rocks. But each child's conception is a construction, not a copy, of reality. The similarity to reality is a consequence of the nature of objects and the constructive process. Adaptation is a process of changing one's self (accommodation) to more closely approximate reality.

   How and why does a child acquire a conception of an object? A child's concept of a tree evolves out of his actions on trees, but clearly

1. An assumption implicit in Behaviorism, stimulus-response, or operant psychology is that knowledge is a copy of reality. This appears to be an assumption of traditional and conventional educational practice.

his conception changes with increased experience. A child raised where only pine trees grow may have, early on, a concept of trees similar to an adult's conception of pine trees. Children raised exclusively in cities may conceive of trees as things that grow only in parks or in sidewalks. Eskimos living in a treeless world may conceive of trees as being without leaves—indeed, for them, a tree is essentially like a piece of driftwood: leafless, rootless, earthless. Without any direct experience with growing trees, Eskimos' conception of a tree is clearly inaccurate (relative to the conception of others), but it is accurate given the amount and type of information that they have to develop a conception of trees. Conversely, while Eskimos have a limited conception of "tree," their environment has generated many conceptions of "snow"; several dozen types of snow are differentiated and conceptualized by Eskimos. The Eskimo—more than most people—depends on knowledge of the environment for survival. Being able to conceptualize many different types of snow has clear adaptive value.

The Earth is a physical thing. Its objects and properties are governed by natural laws with which we all must cope. Children in similar environments are likely to end up with similar conceptions of most objects because the objects themselves provide common physical properties to be discovered. A hundred children playing with water are probably going to arrive at similar conceptions of water—not because they take into themselves a "copy" of water but because, as they evolve their constructions (schemata) from their active experience, the water places constraints on the conceptions they can evolve. Actions on the objects provide feedback from and about the object. It would be difficult for a child to evolve and maintain a conception of water as a solid because the feedback from the object argues to the contrary. Thus, objects themselves provide children with the information needed to correct any faulty concepts.

Kephart (1971a, p. 193) makes a useful distinction between what he calls *veridical* laws (of nature) and valid laws. Veridical laws are related to natural laws. Valid laws are those that reflect social (arbitrary) approval.

> In veridical tasks, the consequences of performances, be they success or failure, are immediate and unvarying. Since such tasks are related to natural laws, these same laws provide the consequences of the performance [feedback]. Natural law is characterized by complete predictability. Nature does not "repeal" the law of gravity because its application would be

inconvenient for the child or for the teacher. When balance is lost, the consequences are completely dependable [such as when children are learning to sit, crawl, walk, etc.].

The consequences of valid performances, on the other hand, are not thus predictable [i.e., all academic schoolwork such as reading, writing, etc.]. They are dependent on some external application by the teacher. Teachers, and all other social agents, are fallible. They sometimes fail to apply the consequences which they have set up or they permit "extenuating circumstances" to alter cases. Valid performances, therefore, have variable consequences. Learning is much easier and much more efficient when the consequences of the response are completely predictable. Veridical tasks lead to more efficient learning than do valid tasks. (p. 194)

Kephart's distinction between veridical and valid types of tasks and learning parallels the Piagetian conception of adaptation as it relates to physical knowledge and social-arbitrary knowledge (see pp. 48–56). Kephart's conception also supports Kamii's (1973a) belief that "reinforcement" from teachers is appropriate for encouraging social-arbitrary (valid) learning, but not for encouraging physical knowledge. Reinforcement can increase the consistency of feedback that is missing in social-arbitrary or valid learning. In physical (veridical) knowledge the natural laws of nature provide the most consistent type of feedback or reinforcement. A rock will tell you that it is not soft!

Physical (concrete) objects have physical structure. As children's concepts of objects begin to develop early in life, they are rarely correct by adult criteria. A young child's representation of a person is typically a large round head with a stick body. But the child's conception changes and improves with time and experience. A child's conception eventually more accurately approximates an adult's conception as a consequence of feedback from the object and increased differentiation. Thus, although the child's conception may look like a mirror image of the adult's, it is not obtained as a mirror image. The concept is constructed.

Operative and

6

Figurative Knowing

Piaget has stated repeatedly (1969a, 1970) that knowing an object requires acting on the object, transforming it, assimilating it, incorporating it into operational structures (schemata). Knowledge is not derived from perception directly. To know an object or event one must manipulate it with the senses and the mind. Knowledge is viewed by Piaget (1970) as a construction:

> . . . for the genetic epistemologist, knowledge results from continuous construction, since in each act of understanding, some degree of invention is involved; in development, the passage from one stage to the next is always characterized by the formation of new structures which did not exist before, either in the external world or in the subject's mind. (p. 77)

Piaget (1970) describes two aspects of thinking that are different but functionally related: the *figurative* aspect and the *operative* aspect, or figurative and operative thinking. The person looking at a tree "sees" it figuratively, but in his mind he also conceives it as alive, breathing, having roots, branches, and leaves, and as burnable, as a potential piece of furniture, and so on. These aspects are operative conceptions that go beyond the limitations of figurative knowledge. Figurative thoughts are perceptions, imitations, mental images (interiorized imitations), those aspects of thought that deal with states or successions of states as they appear in the senses. They are the thought that occurs at the time of perception of external objects and events—or at the perception of mental images (internal events). When we look at an object and our thought produces identification of that object, this is figurative thought or figurative recognition of a static event. A child looking at a tree sees leaves, branches, trunk, etc.; what he sees is figurative knowledge about the tree.

Operative thought is the product of perceptions (figurative) and intelligence (schemata). Operative knowing is the product of transformations of states resulting from the child's actions. Operative functioning is, in a sense, the organization, consolidation, and integration of figurative knowledge. Operative thought results in changes in schemata and is consequently tied to the process of assimilation and accommodation. Intellectual development can be characterized as the growth of operative knowledge.

Operative knowing and figurative knowing are functionally connected. Figurative knowledge "feeds" the development of operative knowledge and is its source. On the other hand, changes in operative knowing result in changes in subsequent figurative knowing. That is, changes in "concepts" or schemata derived from perceptions result in changes in subsequent perceptions. In this sense, figurative knowing is always subordinate to operative knowing, and operative knowing cannot "improve" without figurative information. Concepts cannot improve unless there are perceptions. The child looking at a tree who suddenly realizes that it is alive (operative knowledge) no longer gets the same *figurative* information from the tree. The new operative knowledge changes the child's perceptions, or the figurative knowledge that he gets.

The significance of the figurative and operative aspects of thought is that perceptions are not direct sources of information. We do not look, see, and therefore know. When we know determines what we "see," which in turn provides raw material for changes in what we know. Piaget (1969a, pp. 34–35) writes:

> Where perception is concerned . . . it is increasingly difficult to believe as we did once that ideas and operations are derived from perceptions by means of simple abstractions and generalizations . . . we have been able to show that sensorimotor causality does not derive from perceptive causality, and that, on the contrary, visual perceptive causality is based on tactico-kinesthetic causality that is itself dependent upon the activity proper as a whole, and is not exclusively upon perceptual factors. It follows from this that operational causality has its roots in sensorimotor causality and not in perceptive causality, since this latter is itself dependent on sensorimotor causality in its motor as well as its perceptual aspects.

Knowledge is not derived from perceptions directly. Schemata, or concepts, are the products of operative knowledge. Operative knowledge is derived from figurative knowledge, which includes perceptions. An intimate link exists between knowledge and perceptions—though not a direct link. One does not know because one sees. One sees, one assimilates and accommodates to what one sees, and the result is knowledge. Knowing involves both perception (experience) and the assimilation of experience. The process is a process of construction.

Cognitive Development

7

as Adaptation

Webster's (1956) defines *adaptation* as "adjustment to environmental conditions" and *biological adaptation* as "modification of an animal or plant (or of its parts or organs) fitting it more perfectly for existence under the conditions of its environment." Biologists tell us that when an environment changes, living organisms adapt accordingly—if they can. The giraffe presumably got its long neck through an adaptation of the species over many centuries. Living organisms moved from sea to land, and the survivors adapted successfully. The Eskimo developed a way of life suited to a harsh environment. All these are forms of biological adaptation. Piaget (1952a, 1971b) views cognitive development as a form of adaptation in the biological sense:

> . . . intelligence is adaptation in its highest form, the balance between a continuous assimilation of things to activity proper and the accommodation of those assimilative schemata to things themselves. . . . All intelligence is an adaptive process. . . . (Piaget 1969a, p. 158)

From the beginning of an infant's life the adaptive value of cognitive development can be seen. The hungry infant sucking on an object that does not satisfy hunger "learns" to cry when hungry. Learning to cry for food is an early and primitive intellectual act, a result of modifying the crying reflex with which the infant is born. Clearly this has adaptive value, as it results in the infant fitting a little more effectively into his environment.

Most children in all cultures learn to speak between the ages of two and four without any formal instruction. How does the two-year-old begin to learn language? Does speaking have adaptive value to the young child? Surely it does. Speech is a more efficient means of communicating and consequently solving problems than any of the skills that the young child has developed prior to that time. The toddler who is able to say "mama," "milk," "water," "food," or "hurt" gets his needs met much more quickly and efficiently than one who has to rely on crying or another less effective form of communication. Learning to use spoken language has genuine adaptive value from the beginning of that learning. The social environment continually reinforces the child for improved speech. Each new word a young child becomes able to use in a representational sense adds to his efficiency and is adaptive.[1] Learning is inherently or internally motivating when it has adaptive value to the individual.

In his book *Science of Education and the Psychology of the Child*, Piaget (1969a) writes: "To educate means to adapt the individual to the surrounding social environment" (p. 151). Piaget argues that educational methods should encourage this adaptation by making use of the "impulses inherent in childhood itself, allied with the spontaneous activity that is inseparable from mental development" (p. 151). Adaptation, as Piaget suggests, is most probable when the activity of the child is spontaneous. Spontaneous activity or active education does not mean that children should do whatever they want, but that adaptive learning will not occur unless the child comes to it with spontaneous activity.

Adaptation always requires activity on the part of the individual. One cannot adapt unless one acts. The child cannot learn to speak unless he listens and practices speaking. The child cannot comprehend the concept "square" unless he manipulates shapes (either overtly or covertly). Adaptation, like all aspects of development, is intimately tied to activity. Furth (1970) writes: "Adaptation always presupposes an interaction of the environment and the organism" (p. 180).

Education that is clearly adaptive can be seen in the training of

1. Not all children learn to speak between the ages of two and four. A few years ago I was contacted regarding a child who was three and one-half years old and lacked speech. After evaluation by eight specialists, the child had been diagnosed as retarded. In conversation with the boy's mother, it became apparent that she habitually anticipated everything the child wanted or needed. She hovered about the child so much that there was no reason why the child should learn to speak. He did not need to speak. The boy had what was for him a perfectly satisfactory communication system between himself and his mother. In this case learning to speak would not have had any adaptive value *to the child* at that particular time and in that particular situation. My evaluation did not rule out the possibility of retardation, but it was clear that the diagnosis of retardation was based largely on the child's lack of normal speech. Given the child's environment, there was no adaptive reason for him to develop speech.

children in primitive societies. In such societies education is typically very informal; it consists largely of children modeling their behavior after adults. There is constant imitation and role playing. The young boy watches his father hunting and imitates him in games and play. There is little doubt that these "educational" activities have adaptive value in the biological sense. What is learned may be necessary for biological survival. Education in such situations is "active." Children learn by doing—in games, through imitation, or by role playing. Few, if any, symbols other than spoken words are involved in their education. In addition, everything is closely tied to concrete aspects of the child's environment.

Clearly, a general implication of Piaget's work is that good education[2] is active and adaptive. A question that educators can ask themselves is whether the things they wish children to learn have any adaptive value in the biological sense. Obviously, learnings with adaptive value that can be perceived by the learner carry with them more inherent motivation to learn than things without such value. One can ask, "Is learning a particular thing going to make the child more effective in dealing with his environment?" With respect to spoken language the answer is, "Yes." Learning to speak has adaptive value; so much so that children usually acquire it with no formal instruction. What about reading? What is the adaptive value from a cognitive-development point of view of learning to read, as it is typically taught in schools? It is argued later in this book (see chapter 14) that, for the young child, initially there is no adaptive value to his school reading efforts. Before reading can be of much use to the child, the child has to learn to read quite proficiently. To be able to read a handful of words does not significantly improve the child's ability to communicate. The real adaptive value of reading is typically late in coming—when reading becomes fairly well established, probably for most children when formal operations have begun to develop, around the age of ten or eleven.

As one can ask, "What is the adaptive value of the child of learning to read?" so can one ask the same question of all other *contents* or skills to which a teacher might expose children. Another question that can be asked by the educator is, "Can things that we want children to learn that do not have adaptive value for the child be given

2. "Good education" is a value-laden statement. "Good," according to Piagetians, means consistent with development and/or aiding development.

adaptive value?" To some extent this seems possible. Let us return for a moment to the issue of reading. Reading instruction as typically handled has little adaptive value or significance to cognitive development before the child begins to develop formal operations. One can to some extent structure situations to increase the adaptive value of reading and writing (or other learning) for children, or increase the probability of these learning situations having adaptive value *to the child* before formal operations are developed. Lest there be some confusion, keep in mind that from a Piagetian perspective the child must always be active. The child must come to *any* task spontaneously for that task to be of optimum value. While we can structure situations to make them more adaptive, educators cannot *ensure* adaptive learning in this way. The child must adapt himself to the surrounding environment.[3]

The most efficient use of the adaptation value of learning is to match instruction to the child's developmental level, that is, not to require children to learn things before they have developed the specific capabilities for logical thought that are prerequisites to comprehending that particular learning. Children are inherently motivated to figure out the world. Assimilation and accommodation tend to perpetuate themselves. If the child encounters something that he does not comprehend, he will try to assimilate it. Of course, children cannot acquire learnings for which they do not have the prerequisite skills. The developmental sequence is rigid. Efforts to induce learning when it is not possible can have disastrous consequences.[4]

Before leaving the concept of adaptation, it should be mentioned that children raised in barren environments (children with little to "adapt" to) usually develop less rapidly and not as completely as persons raised in normal environments. Hunt (1961) has described the consequences of environmental deprivation on the development of

3. While I have not seen any formal evaluation of the things children learn outside of school, it is probably the case that outside learnings have more *adaptive* value *to the child* than many things "learned" in school.
4. The consequences of inappropriate instruction are well known. If comprehension is impossible, children can resort to memorization to convince others that they have learned something. The unfortunate result of this is that students often convince *themselves* that memorization is learning. Witness the number of college students who survived high school mathematics and have only limited mathematical comprehension. Another consequence of inappropriate instruction is failure—and the negative social consequences are great if failure becomes a habit. Such is likely to be the case for children who are developmentally behind their peers. Such children can learn to hate school, learning, teachers, and themselves.

intelligence in his classic book *Intelligence and Experience*. Institutionalized children typically exist in environments that do not place demands on them to adapt in a manner similar to children in normal environments. These environments would seem to preclude the possibility for normal development (normal adaptation) by the very structure of the surroundings they offer children. It could be argued that *all* children in institutions for the retarded have severe genetic or physiological problems and as a result a limited capacity for development (i.e., they would not develop "normally" even if they were not institutionalized); but it is probable that *not all* children enter such institutions with limited capacities for development. Equally probable is that virtually all children in institutions develop less well from an adaptive point of view than the average child in a normal environment. One wonders whether such institutions do not to some extent ensure retardation because their environments do not demand and are not adequate environments for "normal" adaptation (learning and development).

Piaget suggests that all cognitive development that occurs has some adaptive value to the child. Educators interested in learning and development can use the concept of adaptation to evaluate what they ask children to learn. Both the school curriculum and the day-to-day classroom activities can be evaluated in this way. Learning activities that are adaptive for the individual child are more likely than standardized classroom activities to capture the inherent motivation of the child (as his spontaneous interests do). To the extent that school and classroom activities can be truly adaptive, the development of the child and the learnings dependent on those developments will be effectively acquired.

Active Experience

8

and Cognitive Development

> To know an object is to act on it
> and transform it . . .
>
> Piaget, *Science of Education and*
> *the Psychology of the Child*

Piagetians separate knowledge into three types: physical knowledge, logical-mathematical knowledge, and social-arbitrary knowledge. Each type of knowledge is dependent on the actions of the child, although his actions affect the construction of the three types of knowledge differently. Physical knowledge is abstracted directly from objects. Logical-mathematical knowledge is abstracted from the child's *actions* on objects, not from the objects themselves. Social-arbitrary knowledge is abstracted from the child's interactions with other people. Piaget (1969a) writes:

> . . . we know today that experience is necessary for the development of intelligence, but that it is not sufficient in itself, and above all that it occurs in two very different forms between which classical empiricism failed to distinguish: physical experience and logico-mathematical experience. Physical experience consists of acting upon objects and in discovering properties by abstraction from those objects [concrete knowledge]: for example, weighing objects and observing that the heaviest are not always the largest. *Logico-mathematical experience* . . . also consists in acting upon objects, but the process of abstraction by which their properties are discovered is directed, not at the objects as such but at the actions that are brought to bear on the objects [abstract knowledge]: for example, placing pebbles in a row and discovering that their number is the same whether they move from left to right or

right to left (or in a circle, etc.); in this case, neither the order nor the numerical sum were properties of the pebbles before they were laid out or before they were counted, and the discovery that the sum is independent of the order consists in abstracting that observation from the actions of enumerating and ordering, even though the "reading" of the experiment was directed at the objects, since those properties of sum and order were in fact introduced into the objects by the actions. (pp. 37–38)

Physical Knowledge: Discovery

Physical knowledge is the result of actions on objects: touching, lifting, throwing, hitting, biting, smelling, tasting, looking at, listening to, and so forth. The knowledge is derived from the objects themselves and is a form of discovery. The five-year-old who drops objects into a container of water is "discovering" physical knowledge about those objects. The child will eventually "discover" that rocks sink, big ones and small ones; wood floats, big pieces and small ones; and only one brand of soap floats. To construct this knowledge the child must have repeated active experiences in which he carries out manipulations that *transform* objects and reveal their correspondences (Piaget 1975).[1]

Acquisition of physical knowledge *does not* require reinforcement from another person. When the child is actively constructing physical knowledge, the physical properties of the objects themselves correct or reinforce the child's learning. A young child may expect (predict) that a small stone may float when he drops it into water because the stone is small. His schemata tell him that small things float and big things sink. When he drops the small stone into the water, the stone itself (with the help of the water) will confirm or deny the child's expectation. The physical nature of the objects involved "corrects"

---

1. Knowledge always involves transformations *and* correspondences. Transformations involve a change in the form of objects; correspondences involve looking for what is common between two things. "First of all, they [children] have to realize that a change of form is a displacement—it is a moving of a part [transformation]. When the ball [of clay] is changed into a sausage, one part is moved from where it was and ends up somewhere else. Secondly, they have to realize that when a part is moved, what is added in one place *corresponds* with what is taken away from another place. The little children do not see that at all. They forget that what is added on the end came from somewhere."

the child and is a consistent source of feedback or reinforcement. The teacher cannot provide the consistency of reinforcement for physical knowledge that objects themselves provide. If the child's prediction about physical knowledge is incorrect (e.g., the small stone sinks), cognitive disequilibrium can occur, and the child must change or accommodate his available structures to fit the discrepancy.

The educational moral here is simple. Children acquire knowledge about the physical properties of objects by manipulating the objects. Implicit in Piaget's work is that all other ways of coming to "know" objects are qualitatively inferior. Reading about, or listening to someone talk about, an object cannot provide the quality of knowing (comprehension) that can be acquired by actively manipulating the object. Gagné (1970) writes:

> The great value of concepts as means of thinking and communicating is the fact that they have *concrete references*. The importance of this characteristic cannot be overemphasized. But since concepts are learned by the human being via language, there is often the danger of losing sight of this concreteness. Learning can become uneververbalized, which means that the concepts learned are highly inadequate in their reference to actual situations. The learner, one may note, "does not really know the meaning of the word," even though he can use it correctly in a sentence. Suppose, for example, a student has merely *read* that striated muscles are made up of bundles of long narrow cells. This verbal information is unlikely to provide him with the kind of concept of striated muscle he needs if he is a student of physiology or anatomy. (p. 187)

Logical-Mathematical Knowledge: Invention

Logical-mathematical knowledge, unlike physical knowledge, does not come from the objects themselves but is constructed from the child's *actions* on objects (Piaget 1969a, DeVries 1973b). For example, number and number-related concepts are logical-mathematical types of knowledge. Number *is not* a quality or characteristic of an object. Number is an invention of each child, derived from a child's actions on a set of objects. A child's awareness that a row of ten pennies can be made into a circle of pennies, a pile of pennies, or any other configuration of pennies, and that there always remain ten pennies, can be deduced only from the child's repeated manipulation of the pennies, which transforms the collection and reveals correspondences between the configurations. Number is not a property of pennies; the child invents this knowledge.[2]

As with physical knowledge, reinforcement from others is not needed for logical-mathematical knowledge to develop. The information the child gets from acting on objects is *always* truthful, and the child's constructions are always internally consistent. Thus it can be detrimental for the teacher to contradict the child regarding logical knowledge (Kamii and Radin 1970). Piaget (1970) states that logical-mathematical knowledge is *always* the result of a coordination of actions—several simultaneous actions rather than *a single* action. He believes that the roots of all logical thought are found in the coordinated actions that are the basis for logical-mathematical knowledge (pp. 18–19).

Physical knowledge and logical-mathematical knowledge are conceptualized as different and derived from different aspects of the child's actions. Physical knowledge is discovered by the child; logical-mathematical knowledge is invented by the child. Kamii (1973a) writes:

> Piaget makes a distinction between "discovery" and "invention." His favorite example of "discovery" is Columbus' discovery of America. Columbus did not invent America, he points out. America existed before Columbus discovered it. The airplane, on the other hand, was not discovered. It was invented because it did not exist before its invention.
>
> Corresponding to the distinction between discovery and invention is the distinction between how physical knowledge and how logico-mathematical knowledge are constructed. Physical knowledge can be built by discovery, but logico-mathematical knowledge cannot. It can be built only by the child's own invention. . . . By acting on objects, he can thus discover their properties. In logico-mathematical knowledge, on the other hand, the child cannot discover from the objects themselves whether there are more brown beads or more —— beads in a collection. All logico-mathematical structures have

2. The knowledge that one does not change the number of elements in a collection by changing the arrangement of the elements is called conservation of number. This knowledge is not developed typically until about age six or seven.

to be invented, or created, by the child's own activity rather than discovered from the reactions of objects. (pp. 207–8)

The development of physical knowledge and logical-mathematical knowledge is not entirely separate. Like many other things, we conceptualize them separately because it is usually easier to think about them that way. Kamii (1973c) writes:

> Neither physical knowledge nor logico-mathematical knowledge can exist without the other. Pure logic almost exists, but physical knowledge is involved even in the classical example of the child who always found 10 pebbles, whether he counted them from left to right, or from right to left. The fact that pebbles let themselves be ordered is an example of physical knowledge. Physical and logico-mathematical knowledge are thus almost indissociable. (pp. 214–15)

Thus, while it is useful for us to conceptualize a difference between types of knowledge, we must keep in mind how closely physical and logical-mathematical knowledge are tied together in their formation. A given transformation of an object by a child can involve the construction of both types of knowledge.

Social-Arbitrary Knowledge

Social experience, or social interaction, is one of the factors that Piaget includes in all his discussions of cognitive development (the other factors are maturation, equilibrium, and experience, which includes physical and logical-mathematical experience). Social experience is an *active* process in the same way that physical experience is an active process. The importance of social experience cannot be overlooked because it is instrumental in the developmental process.

Children learn many things, not from objects or from their actions on objects, but from other people—from *actions on* or interactions with other people. Language, values, rules, morality, and symbol systems are examples of *social-arbitrary knowledge*. Social-arbitrary knowledge is constructed while transforming what others "tell us." Children learn through social experience that blocks are for building and not for throwing, and that blocks are called "blocks" and not "blobs" (Kamii 1973b). Such knowledge is made by people and can only be learned from people (DeVries 1973b). The child in isolation cannot invent social knowledge; in part, it must be discovered through interactions with others. Piaget (1969a) writes:

> . . . the child is social almost from the day of its birth. It smiles at people in its second month and seeks to make contact with others. . . . But alongside these internal social tendencies there is also the society that is external to individuals, which is to say the totality of those relationships being established between them from the outside: language, intellectual exchanges, moral or legal action—in short, everything that is handed on from generation to generation and that constitutes the essential foundation of human society, as opposed to animal societies based upon instinct.
>
> From this point of view, and despite the fact that it possesses urges toward sympathy and imitation from the very first, the child has everything to learn. It starts, in effect, from a purely individual state—that of the first months of existence during which no exchange with others is possible—and ends by undergoing a progressive socialization that in fact never ends. At the start, it knows nothing of either rules or signs symbols and must therefore go through a process of gradual adaptation—composed both of assimilation of others to itself and of accommodation of itself to others that will enable it to master the essential properties of external society: mutual comprehension based on speech; and a communal discipline based on reciprocity. (pp. 174–75)

Social-arbitrary knowledge is specific to a culture or subcultural group. Social knowledge is not derived from concrete objects but from "actions" on people. Unlike physical knowledge and logical-mathematical knowledge, social-arbitrary knowledge requires people. Without interactions with people, it is impossible for a child to acquire social-arbitrary knowledge.[3]

Piaget has clearly illustrated the significance of children's actions in their mental development. Children can develop only by acting on objects and interacting with others. When we look back to our early school years we remember the things that we actively did and have difficulty remembering the things to which we passively submitted. I

3. Moral development is the most thoroughly investigated area of social-arbitrary knowledge. Piaget did some early research in moral development, which is reported in his book *The Moral Judgement of the Child* (1965). This work has been followed by people like Kohlberg (1969b). A close parallel exists between moral development and cognitive development.

still remember vividly when a whale became beached on the North Shore of Long Island. Our class teacher (of the combined fifth, sixth, seventh, and eighth grades) was also the principal of our three-room school. When she heard about the stranded whale she immediately arranged for a bus, and within an hour the whole school (about sixty children and three teachers) saw a whale: a real, live, fullblown whale sitting (and suffering, I am certain) on a beach. Unfortunate as the whale's condition was, it provided a feast for the eyes. We looked at it, we listened to it, we went up to it to touch it (it could not move much), we ran away from it when it opened its massive mouth, we threw water on it, we made faces at it—we did all sorts

of things. From that day on, we all knew exactly what a whale was! I do not remember what we were studying in class the week before our whale, but I know we did a lot of things relating to whales the week after. We talked about whales, we read everything we could about whales, we drew pictures of whales. We learned a lot about whales by being *active*, and that activity gave more *meaning* to what we later read and heard.

Knowledge is acquired not through the senses directly, but through the action and interaction of the child. The meaningfulness of written and spoken information to a child is dependent upon the actions he has had. Piaget and others (Dienes 1963, 1967; Dewey 1970; Montessori 1964) tell educators quite clearly that the key to intellectual

TABLE 2

Three Types of Knowledge

	Physical Knowledge	Logical-Mathematical Knowledge	Social-Arbitrary Knowledge
Defined	knowledge about the physical properties of objects	abstract knowledge	knowledge made by people
How acquired	discovered by actions on objects; objects are the source	invented from actions on ob jects; actions are the source	obtained from actions on and inter- actions with others; peo- ple are the source
Reinforcer	objects	objects	other people
Examples of areas of knowledge	size, color, texture, thick- ness, taste, sound, flexi- bility, density	number, mass, area, volume, length, class, order, time, speed, weight	language, moral rules, values, cul- ture, history, symbol systems

development as it pertains to teaching and learning is the activity of the child. In Piagetian terms, the child learns, constructs new mental structures or qualitatively modifies present ones (accommodation), when he or she spontaneously acts on the environment, resulting in the assimilation of objects and events. Internal reorganization of schemata is a product that results from the child's activity. Knowledge is an individual construction; each individual constructs reality. It is not the activity of the teacher or the parent that is important, but the activity of the child. The activity must also be spontaneous, not prescribed by some external agent.

Coordination of Actions

9

to Operations to Structures

Piaget argues that there is a functional relationship between a child's physical and mental actions and the development of logical thought. He asserts that *actions* lead to the development of *operations,* and operations in turn lead to the development of *structures.* All quotes in this chapter are from Piaget (1970).

Operations

Operations are mental acts, such as the various types of conservation. Operations have four main characteristics. First, operations are actions that are internalized; that is, operations can be carried out in thought as well as in action. Internalized actions begin to emerge around the age of two years, the end of the sensorimotor period, when the child becomes capable of internal representation. The second characteristic of operations is that they are reversible. For example, addition and subtraction are the same operation carried out in opposite directions: 2 can be added to 1 to get 3; or 1 can be subtracted from 3 to get 2. The third characteristic of an operation is that it always maintains some invariant (no change) although a transformation or change always occurs. In the process of addition, for example, pairs of numbers can be grouped in different ways (5-1, 4-2, 3-3), but the sum remains invariant. Similarly, in all conservation operations, quantities are conserved during change in irrelevant dimensions. The fourth characteristic of an operation is that no single operation exists alone. An operation is always related to a structure or network of operations. For example, the addition-subtraction operation is related to the operations of classifying, ordering, and conserving number. Each of these particular operations emerges in development at about the same time and has a common core of cognitive prerequisites. Each operation is necessary for the other operations to emerge fully.

An operation differs in specific ways from an action. An action can be an isolated event, such as a child manipulating an object. Actions can lead to the development of physical and logical-mathematical knowledge. Logical-mathematical knowledge eventually results in operations. Operations are mental activities that are internalized, reversible, conserved, and integrated with higher organizations (structures) and other operations. Thus the child who discovers through manipulation of objects that a particular collection of stones always has ten stones, regardless of how the collection is arranged, has or is constructing the mathematical operation of commutativity.[1] The raw materials for the operation are the child's actions.

Structures

Structures (schemata) are the highest-order mental organizations, one step higher than operations. Like operations, structures have certain characteristics. A structure is a totality in that certain laws apply to all the parts of the structure.

> The system of whole numbers is an example of a structure, since there are laws that apply to the series as such. Many different mathematical structures can be discovered in the series of whole numbers. One, for instance, is the additive group. The rules of associativity, commutativity, transitivity and closure for addition are all held within the series of whole numbers. (pp. 22–23)

The laws that govern a structure are also laws of transformation, so that in the case of addition of whole numbers, a number can be transformed into another by adding something to it. Also, structures are self-regulating in the sense that one need not go outside the

1. The principle that a sum is independent of the order of its elements. This is an example of logical-mathematical knowledge as constructed from the child's actions on objects, not from the objects themselves.

structure to find elements for transformations, and the result of a transformation stays within the system.

> Referring to the additive group once again, when we add one whole number to another, we do not have to go outside the series of whole numbers in search of any element that is not within the series. And, once we have added the two whole numbers together, our result still remains within the series. (p. 23)

While structures are the highest-order mental organizations, according to Piaget, it should be noted that structures are always related to other structures and that many structures are substructures of larger structures. For example, the structure of whole numbers is a part of a larger structure (all numbers), which includes fractional numbers, rational numbers, etc.

Classification Structure

An example of a structure is the classification structure. Elements of the classification structure emerge before the structure is complete. For example, children of four or five years of age can place objects of similar shape or color into collections based on their characteristics. This is simple classification. Children of this age typically do not comprehend the inclusion principle, i.e., that a total class must be as big or bigger than one of its subclasses.

> A child of this age will agree that all ducks are birds and that not all birds are ducks. But then, if he is asked whether out in the woods there are more birds or more ducks, he will say, "I don't know; I've never counted them." It is the relationship of class inclusion that gives rise to the operational structure of classification. (pp. 27–28)

Thus, classification does not have the characteristics of a structure before the inclusion principle is grasped.

Ordering or Seriation Structure

Similar in development to the classification structure is the ordering or seriation structure, which children typically develop around age seven. A child of four or five years is presented with a series of sticks varying in length by perceptually small differences (one-quarter inch). The child is asked to order the sticks from the smallest to the largest. Preoperational children perform this task without any structural framework. They may add a long one and a short one, another long and short one, and so forth; arrangements may be entirely random.

Around the end of the preoperational period, children typically manage with trial and error to arrange all the sticks in a series. Their approach is still not systematic. After age seven or so, children develop a systematic, coordinated method that reflects a completely developed seriation structure. They seek out and select the smallest stick (or they may begin with the largest stick), then the next smallest, and so on. The arrangement is made without trial and error.

> The reversibility implied here is one of reciprocity. When the child looks for the smallest stick of all those that remain, he understands at one and the same time that this stick is bigger than all the ones he has taken so far and smaller than all the ones that he will take later. He is coordinating here at the same time the relationship "bigger than" and the relationship "smaller than." (pp. 28–29)

The relationship between a child's actions on objects and the child's mental or intellectual development is made clear by Piaget. Actions lead to the development of operations; mental operations lead to the development of mental structures.

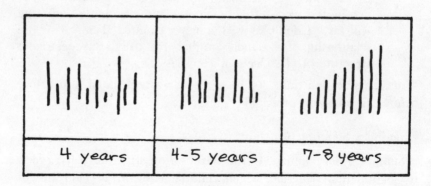

FIGURE 3
Typical Seriation Constructions

Mathematical Structures and Structures of Logical Thought

Throughout his writings, Piaget suggests a relationship or similarity between the logical structure of the mind and the logical structures of mathematics. Piaget (1970) outlines the relationship between the "mother" structures of mathematics and the structures of thought in children. Here, Piaget refers to the work of Bourbaki, a mathematician who derived three basic, or "mother," structures of mathematics that were not reducible and that independently or in combination could generate all other mathematical structures. The three structures are the *algebraic structure*, the *order structure*, and the *topological structure*. Piaget observes that young children have cognitive structures resembling these mother structures of mathematics. "Now these three types of [mathematical] structures appear to be highly abstract. Nonetheless, in the thinking of children as young as 6 or 7 years of age we find structures resembling each of these three types" (p. 26).

The prototype of the *algebraic structure* is the mathematical concept of a group. "Algebraic structures are characterized by their form of reversability" (p. 25).

> In children's thinking algebraic structures are to be found quite generally, but most readily in the logic of classes—in the logic of classification. . . . Children as young as 4 or 5 years can classify geometric shapes such as circles, squares, triangles on the basis of shape. . . . It is the relationship of class inclusion [developed around age 7 or 8] that gives rise to the operational structure of classification, *which is in fact analogous* to the algebraic structures of the mathematicians. (pp. 27–28)

Thus, in the thought of even very young children are structures analogous to the algebraic structures of mathematics.

Of the second mother structure, *order structure*, Piaget says: "This structure applies to relationships, whereas the algebraic structures applies essentially to classes and numbers . . . the form of reversibility characteristic of order structures is reciprocity" (p. 25). Piaget uses the structure of seriation as an example of an order structure in children's thinking.

Bourbaki's third mother structure, *topological structure*, includes ideas such as proximity, inclusion, and exclusion, and applies to geometry as well as to other areas of mathematics. The typical four-year-old understands and can represent topological relationships. When asked to copy drawings with topological properties, such as:

the parts of the drawings are usually placed in proper relationship to one another, demonstrating a comprehension of topological space. The same-age child typically can distinguish simple Euclidean shapes —circles, squares, triangles—but has difficulty drawing Euclidean shapes. This inability to represent Euclidean shapes does not seem to be the result of a lack of drawing skills. It is clear that children develop topological concepts and that they are developed prior to the development of Euclidean concepts.

Piaget has attempted to demonstrate that the three mother structures of mathematics appear spontaneously in the development of young children. Bourbaki has suggested that these structures can be combined to generate all the other structures of mathematics. Piaget says, similarly, that in children's thought additional structures evolve from a combination of two or more of the basic structures that have their natural roots in children's thinking.

> When we study the development of the notion of number in children's thinking, we find that it is not based on classifying operations alone but it is a synthesis of two different structures. We find that along with the classifying structures, which are an instance of the Bourbaki algebraic structures, number is also based on ordering structures, that is, a synthesis of these two different types of structures. It is certainly true that classification is involved in the notion of number. (p. 38)

Number, a synthesis of class inclusion and relationships of order, depends on two mother structures, the algebraic and the order, at the same time. Either structure alone is not adequate. All this evidence persuades Piaget and his co-workers that the logical aspects of the structures of thought are similar to the logical aspects of mathematics.

The Development of

10

Representational and Symbolic Abilities

One overriding characteristic of schooling is that it is dominated by spoken and graphic symbols. Letters, words, and numbers are used in instruction in reading, writing, spelling, and arithmetic and cannot be avoided in social studies and science. Little attention seems to be given to the need and desirability of introducing children, particularly young children, to graphic symbols (letters and numbers). Many seem to assume that teaching reading through the printed word and arithmetic through the printed number is always a reasonable practice. For most teachers and parents, the sooner children confront symbols, the better. There are some serious dangers in having children try to master graphic symbols before they are developmentally ready to do so. To understand the dangers, one needs to understand the development of what Piaget calls the "semiotic function" (Piaget and Inhelder 1969), which is referred to here as the *symbolic function*. Graphic symbols, whether they are letters, numbers, drawings, photographs, pictographs, street signs, or business motifs, are used to represent things. The use of arbitrary graphic symbols (letters, numbers) is but one form of representation. Developmentally, it is the most advanced use.

Representational activities in children are first observed in *deferred imitation*. A sensorimotor child (less than two years old) who imitates another person's behavior when that person is no longer present is representing another's behavior with his own behavior. The pre-operational three-year-old can be observed in *symbolic play*, a second and more developmentally advanced form of representation than deferred imitation. One might observe a child with a block of wood, playing with it as if it were a car and giving it all the attributes of a real toy car. This is a game of pretending and a type of representation not found during the sensorimotor period.

A third, and still more advanced form of representation, can be found in children's drawings, which are almost always realistic in intent, though until the age of eight or nine, children typically draw what they know rather than what they see.[1] A fourth aspect of the symbolic function is what Piaget calls mental *images*, i.e., internalized representations that are different from either perceptions or mental operations. Images form "a system of signifiers dealing not with concepts but with objects as such and with the whole past perceptual experience of the subject" (p. 70). Images are "pictures in the mind" with which children can carry out action sequences internally.

The fifth aspect of the symbolic function, *verbal evocation*, as Piaget calls it, is the ability to verbalize events not occurring at the time. "When the little girl says 'meow' after the cat has disappeared, verbal representation is added to imitation" (Piaget and Inhelder 1969, p. 54). Piaget and Inhelder (1969) add:

> In spite of the astonishing diversity of its manifestations, the semiotic function presents a remarkable unity. Whether it is a question of deferred imitation, symbolic play, drawing, mental images . . . or language, this function allows the representative evocation of objects and events not perceived at that particular moment. The semiotic function makes thought possible by providing it with an unlimited field of application, in contrast to the restricted boundaries of sensorimotor action and perception. (p. 91)

The use of graphic symbols is still another aspect of language and the representational act. Reading activities, writing activities, and mathematical activities require an understanding of the use of written or graphic materials. To state the obvious, the child must understand what symbols are before he will be able to use them. This obvious point is frequently overlooked in educational practice. The child's ability to use abstractions develops in an orderly and predictable way. One cannot assume that because a child shows some

1. Children's drawings are a rich source of information about the child and development. The developmental stages with respect to drawings from scribbling to visual realism are described by Piaget and Inhelder (1969). A major analysis of children's drawings is in Kellogg (1970).

capabilities for abstraction and representation that he or she is there- fore "ready" to deal with graphic symbols and activities such as reading, writing, and mathematical manipulation of written numbers.

Piaget (1962a, 1969a) describes three developmental levels of abstraction of graphic written materials. The earliest and most primitive type of abstraction are *cues*. When one sees part of an object and then identifies that object based on the part seen, one is using a cue. The part "represents" the whole. A cue is always part of an object. Thus we can identify trees by their silhouettes or leaf formations, a brand of car by its front grille, or people by their voices. This early type of abstraction does not really involve repre- sentation as such. It does involve an association of a part of the object with the whole of the object. The use of cues is a prerequisite to the use of further graphic representations.

The first true form of representation is the use of the *symbol*.[2] A symbol is more abstract than a cue but retains some relationship to the object it represents. Examples of symbols are maps, drawings, and road signs. These are not identical to, or part of, the object represented but are related in form. The degree of relationship can vary. Drawings may be very "realistic" in their representation of what they portray. A road map usually has an accurate relationship to the roadways it represents. Symbols, as described by Piaget, are not arbitrary. They are generally shared by other people although they may be unique and private to the individual child.

The third and most abstract level of graphic representation is the use of *signs*. Signs are abstractions that are entirely *arbitrary* in nature, such as letters, words, and numbers. Signs bear no relationship to the objects they represent. Letters, numbers, and words have no inherent meaning. Perceptually, they do not resemble what they represent. Signs are acquired from the culture one lives in and constitute a form of social-arbitrary knowledge. The ability to use the three graphic or written levels of abstraction—cues, symbols, and signs—develops in that order. The ability to use signs implies the

---

2. Webster defines *symbol* as "a sign by which one knows or infers a thing." The word is used popularly to cover *all* graphic representations. Piaget uses "symbol" to describe *one* type of graphic representation. Similarly, Piaget in recent years has used the term "semiotic function" to refer to the use of representations of all types rather than the term "symbolic function" because he differentiates between "symbols" and "signs" (Piaget and Inhelder 1969, p. 51). I have retained "symbolic function" here because "symbolic" is probably better known to readers than "semiotic."

ability to use symbols and cues; the ability to use symbols does *not* imply the ability to use signs.

When children enter school, they are asked to begin to use representations on the sign level. Any activities that involve number and letters presuppose that children have developed structures that permit the comprehension of signs. Comprehension of written language is available to the child only if he or she has developed the cognitive ability to use signs and has available "meaning" to attach to signs.[3] For a child who has not developed a cognitive ability to use signs, comprehension of the reading and writing process using signs is impossible. Many kindergarten and early elementary school children have not developed the ability to use signs or lack to some extent the experiential background that gives appropriate meaning to the signs with which they are asked to deal. A child operating on the symbol level of representation will not be able to "figure out" (construct schemata) what reading is all about. The efforts to attain what some peers are attaining can result in failure and discouragement with all the attendant complications. The child may resort to methods of "learning" (e.g., memorizing everything) that are inefficient and, once established, abandoned only with great difficulty.

Representational skills, aside from their importance in reading, writing, and arithmetic, are necessary for the acquisition of physical knowledge and logical-mathematical knowledge. As the child acts on physical objects, he must be able to evoke previous similar actions and their results in order to organize the results collectively into knowledge. This requires representation of the results of prior actions. In conservation (logical-mathematical knowledge) learning, the child must be able mentally to reverse a change. This cannot be done without representational skills (Kamii and Radin 1970, p. 97). Representational skills play a crucial role in cognitive development as well as in the acquisition of reading, writing, and arithmetic skills.

3. The capability for reading and mathematics is dependent not only on having the cognitive capability to comprehend signs as a form of representation, but also on having "meaning" to attach to particular signs. The child must "know" the objects represented. Meaning or knowing is derived by the child from his or her actions on the objects or events that the signs represent. Thus, the object dog represented by the sign *dog* can have meaning to the child only if the child can use signs and has an experiential source of meaning to bring to that sign. See chapter 14 for more details.

The Role of Language

II

in Cognitive Development

"... language does not constitute the source
of logic but is, on the contrary, structured by it."
Piaget and Inhelder, *The Psychology of the Child*

Possibly none of Piaget's views has
been as misunderstood as that of the relationship between language
and cognitive development. Basically, Piaget believes that spoken
language *is not necessary* for the development of intellectual functions; the mind can develop in a normal manner without spoken
language. While spoken language is not necessary for development,
representation, of which spoken language is one form, has an important facilitative effect on development.

It has been stated repeatedly that intellectual functions are constructions; they are not innate. Such functions begin to develop prior
to the acquisition of spoken language or any other form of symbolic
representation. Structural development from birth to two years of
age (the approximate age of onset of spoken language) is clearly
observed. The young child evolves sensorimotor action schemes for
the solution of simple problems. Representation does not appear until
after the child acquires certain mental structures (like object permanence). In Piaget's view, adequate development of logical skills is a
prerequisite to the development of representation in general and
spoken language in particular. Piaget (1970) writes:

> ... the decisive argument against the position that logical
> mathematical structures are derived uniquely from linguistic
> forms is that, in the course of intellectual development in
> any given individual, logical mathematical structures exist
> before the appearance of language. Language appears some-

what about the middle of the second year, but before this, about the end of the first year or the beginning of the second year, there is a sensori-motor intelligence that is a practical intelligence having its own logic of action. (pp. 41–42)

Language refers to the child's use of a symbol (a word) to *represent* an object. When the child says "mama" for the first time, he or she is typically using the sound not to represent an object (mother), but strictly in an imitative sense because the child has discovered that the sound gets attention. Not until eighteen months or two years of age do most children begin to represent objects and events internally and thus become capable of the use of sounds as representations.

Sensorimotor development is seen by Piaget as necessary for the development of preoperational thought, including the development of language and other forms of representation. There is additional evidence that language does not form the basis of, and is not necessary for, the development of logical operations (intelligence). One can look at the development of deaf and mute children who have not had language available to them.

Furth (1966) examined the mental development of deaf and mute children and concluded that they develop logical structures in the same sequence as Piaget's description of normal children, although their development is typically delayed by about one year. Development in blind children who have spoken language is usually delayed by three or four years. Piaget (1970) writes:

> This position is confirmed by the fact that in deaf and dumb children we find thought without language and logical structures without language. . . . Another interesting point is that, although deaf and dumb children are delayed with respect to normal children [about one year] they are delayed much less than children who have been blind from birth. Blind infants have the great disadvantage of not being able to make the same coordinations in space that normal children [and deaf and dumb children] are capable of during the first year or two, so that the development of sensori-motor intelligence and the coordination of actions at this level are seriously impeded in blind children. For this reason we find that there are even greater delays in their development at the level of representational thinking and that language is not enough to compensate for the deficiency in coordination

of actions. The delay is made up ultimately, of course, but
it is significant and much more considerable than the delay
in the development of logic in deaf and dumb children. (pp.
46–47)

Supporting Piaget's beliefs about the relationship between language
and cognitive development are studies in which people have tried
to teach logical thought to children through language. These studies
have met with little success. Sinclair (1969) found a relationship
between language development and logical thought but was un-
successful in training nonconservers to conserve by using language
training.

The evidence is that logical skills start to develop before children
begin to use language or symbols (representation). The logic of the
child less than two years of age is a logic of action. The development
of thought during the sensorimotor period forms the basis for development in the following years. Piaget (1970) maintains that the
development of sensorimotor logic is prerequisite to the acquisition of
symbolic or representational skills. This does not mean that language,
spoken language in particular, is not important; it means merely
that it is not necessary for the mental development of the child.
Mental or cognitive development is dependent on active experience.

Language and Thought

While, in Piaget's view, spoken language is not necessary for cognitive development to proceed during the preoperational years, the
development of representational skills, of which spoken language is
one form, is necessary. The child must develop capabilities for internal representation (images) to move beyond the sensorimotor stage.
In a very real sense, the sensorimotor child can be characterized as
prerepresentational.

Representation and language add significantly to, and are instrumental in, the development of the child's power of *thought*. Piaget
and Inhelder (1969) write:

> As to the increasing range and rapidity of thought thanks to
> language we observe in fact three differences between verbal
> and sensori-motor behavior. (1) Whereas sensori-motor pat-
> terns are obliged to follow events without being able to ex-

ceed the speed of the action, verbal patterns . . . can represent a long chain of actions very rapidly. (2) Sensori-motor adaptations are limited to immediate space and time, whereas language enables thought to range over vast stretches of time and space, liberating it from the immediate. (3) The third difference is a consequence of the other two. Whereas the sensori-motor intelligence proceeds by means of successive acts, step by step, thought, particularly through language, can represent simultaneously all the elements of an organized structure. (p. 86)

Language and representation help make preoperational thought much more efficient and powerful than it was during the sensorimotor period. Sensorimotor thought can proceed no more quickly than the actions that the child carries out. Preoperational thought, like adult thought, can represent in a fraction of a second what may have taken the sensorimotor child minutes to execute in action. Thinking through language takes less time than thinking through action. In addition, preoperational thought, because it is not restrained by actions, can simultaneously coordinate more elements at once in a thought than can sensorimotor thought restrained by action.

The characteristics of preoperational thought are due in part to the child's acquisition of symbolic processes (semiotic function), of which language is usually the most important. Piaget and Inhelder (1969) continue:

> The advantages of representative thought over sensori-motor schemes are in reality due to the semiotic function *as a whole*. The semiotic function detaches thought from action and is the source of representation. Language plays a particularly important role in this formative process. (p. 87)

The significance of language in the *development of thought* is central. It is safe to say that without the development of language or other representational skills, the child's development of thought and use of thought would be severely hampered.

To make such strong statements about the importance of language in thinking *should not* confuse the reader into believing that language is always desirable in education. While representational skills are necessary for, and facilitate, thought, verbal facility does *not* reflect superior thought or intelligence. It is *not* true that children best learn and acquire knowledge through language. It is *not usually* true that the best mode of instruction in school is through language. Educators and noneducators need to recognize the paradox of language. As crucial as representation and language are to the child in developing preoperational thought, they play *no direct role* in the *acquisition* of knowledge until formal operations are developed.[1] Language is *never* the source of knowledge. Physical knowledge and logical-mathematical knowledge *cannot* be acquired through language (reading, listening); they are acquired through active experience with objects. Social-arbitrary knowledge has a clear tie to language in many cases because it is acquired only from other people.[2] Language is frequently instrumental in the *communication* necessary for the child to acquire social-arbitrary knowledge, though language *is not the source* of the knowledge. Language is not knowledge except in the sense that it may be knowledge of language usage. Similarly, a lack of facility in language should not be automatically considered to reflect a knowledge deficit, although a deficit in knowledge is sometimes accompanied by a language deficit.

Language is rarely the most appropriate instructional medium for the acquisition of knowledge. Furth and Wachs (1974) write:

> The educational implication of Piaget's position on language is clear. In order to educate children so that they will one day be capable of using language in an intelligent manner, nothing is as important as developing the child's *intelligence*. To reach the intellectual stage where a person can function comfortably with verbal propositions stage of formal operations, the medium of actions and physical encounters is appropriate; whereas a *premature* emphasis on language as a prime medium for thinking is bound to result in low level activities that do not nourish intellectual development. (p. 21)

Most people would agree that it is desirable to have children develop verbal skills for purposes of communication. This is a goal of education that needs little justification. Education (and society) seem to

1. With the development of formal operations, usually *beginning* around age ten or eleven, children become capable of using representational material (written and spoken) to construct new knowledge.

2. Social-arbitrary knowledge is knowledge that people construct: history, cultural morals, values, norms for social relationships, what is "right and wrong," etc. Both spoken and written language are means by which these are frequently communicated, but not the only means. Children learn about values and what is right and wrong from what they observe people doing.

have put the cart before the horse in not taking into account the fact that actively acquired knowledge is the base upon which comprehension is built. Rather than set a goal of verbal competence (facility and comprehension) upon graduation from high school, education seems to have placed a premium on verbal facility at the beginning of schooling. Piagetians argue that this is an inappropriate priority. Emphasis should be placed on the development of thinking and knowledge, the only source from which comprehension and verbal competence can arise.

The Appropriate Use of Spoken Language

Piagetians are in favor of children developing verbal competence. Their view is merely that verbal competence must follow knowledge, not precede it. Verbal facility without knowledge is an empty shell. Piaget-influenced educators usually agree that the traditional classroom places too great an emphasis on verbal activity in instruction and learning. There is too much talking *at* students, and not enough active learning. Kamii and DeVries (1973b) write:

> We have nothing against encouraging children's development of representational ability, but the preoccupation with words . . . does seem to be at the expense of operative thinking [logical thinking]. (p. 10)

and Elkind (1972) writes:

> The implication for teaching is clear. Our teaching at the elementary school level is generally much too verbal and abstract because we have been misled by children's verbal prowess. (p. 48)

A preoccuption with language can be an obstacle to the development of thought and intelligence. Elementary school children, like many of their teachers and parents, can become persuaded that language is the key to knowledge and learning. Motivated to pursue language acquisition, children can come to ignore their normal "instincts" for active learning. Such preoccupations may, in the long run, inhibit the acquisition of knowledge through action.

Piaget, of course, never advocated a "silent" classroom. To the contrary, his statements suggest that he favors the open, spontaneous interaction of children with other children and adults. Language, particularly spoken language, is essential for communication. The educator needs to distinguish between the importance of language as it pertains to communication and the acquisition of knowledge.

Do's and Don'ts

A few rules for the appropriate and inappropriate uses of language in education are suggested by Piaget's theory.

1. *Do not* teach linguistic formulas. Duckworth (1973) writes:

> . . . teaching linguistic formulas is not likely to lead to clear logical thinking; it is by thinking people get better at thinking. If the logic [and knowledge] is there, a person will be able to find words adequate to represent it. If it is not there, having the words will not help. (p. 146)

The child who is taught a verbal rule like "To divide a fraction by a whole number, invert the second number and multiply" may be able to repeat the rule and carry out the appropriate numerical operations. But without the knowledge underlying the principle, there will be no comprehension. Time is better spent in active learning experiences that can affect comprehension. Piaget says:

> If you spend one year studying something verbally that requires two years of active study, then you have actually lost a year. If we were willing to lose a bit more time and let the child be active, let them use trial and error on different things, then the time we seem to have lost we may have actually gained. (Hall 1970, p. 31)

2. *Do not* interrupt children's thinking. Kamii and DeVries (1973b) write:

> . . . we certainly do not object to the presence of a rich language in the preschool classroom. What we do object to is language which is unnecessary for meaningful communication (such as telling the child what he is doing), language which interrupts the child's thinking (such as stopping the child when he is halfway down the slide to ask him to tell the teacher what he is doing), and language which prevents the child from pursuing his own problems. . . . (pp. 13–14)

When children are actively engaged in spontaneous learning (going down a slide *can be* a case in point), it is generally not productive to break their concentration and divert them with conversation. Verbal activities related to learning can be encouraged *after* a child completes or ends a period of spontaneous activity. Generally, it is better to ask, "Tell us what you did," than interrupt to ask, "Tell us what you are doing."

3. *Do* question children's reasoning and make suggestions *at the right time*. Although it is not desirable to interrupt children's spontaneous learning *while* it is in progress, questions from the teacher (or other students) can result in actions and subsequent learning that might otherwise not occur *at that time*. Duckworth (1973) writes:

> . . . the right question at the right time can move children to peaks in their thinking that result in significant steps forward and real intellectual excitement: and . . . although it is almost impossible for an adult to know exactly the right time to ask a specific question of a specific child—especially for a teacher who is concerned with 30 or more children—children can raise the right question for themselves if the setting is right. Once the right question is raised, they are moved to tax themselves to the fullest to find an answer. (p. 264)

Duckworth (1973) provides an example of the impact questions can have:

> Hank was an energetic and not very scholarly fifth grader. His class had been learning about electric circuits with flashlight batteries, bulbs, and various wires. After the children had developed considerable familiarity with these materials, the teacher made a number of mystery boxes. Two wires protruded from each box, but inside, unseen, each box had a different way of making contact between the wires. In one box the wires were attached to a battery; in another they were attached to a bulb; in a third, to a certain length of resistance wire; in a fourth box they were not attached at all; etc. By trying to complete the circuit on the outside of the box, the children were able to figure out what made the connection inside the box. Like many other children, Hank attached a battery and a bulb to the wire outside the box. Because the bulb lit, he knew at least that the wires inside the box were connected in some way. But, because it [the bulb] was some-

what dimmer than usual, he also knew that the wires inside were not connected directly to each other and that they were not connected by a piece of ordinary copper wire. Along with many of the children, he knew that the degree of dimness of the bulb meant that the wires inside were connected either by another bulb of the same kind or by a certain kind of resistance wire.

The teacher expected them to go only this far. However, in order to push the children to think a little further, she asked them if they could tell whether it was a bulb or a piece of wire inside the box. She herself thought there was no way to tell. After some thought, Hank had an idea. He undid the battery and bulb that he had already attached on the outside of the box. In their place, using additional copper wire, he attached six batteries in series. He had already experimented enough to know that six batteries would burn out a bulb, if it was a bulb inside the box. He also knew that once a bulb is burned out, it no longer completes the circuit. He then attached the original battery and bulb again. This time he found that the bulb on the outside of the box did not light. So he reasoned, with justice, that there had been a bulb inside the box and that now it was burned out. If there had been a wire inside, it would not have burned through and the bulb on the outside would still light. (pp. 265–66)

This is an example of the right question at the right time, for this child. Duckworth (1973) points out that the teacher had to be willing to accept the destruction of a light bulb: "Without these kinds of acceptance, Hank would not have been able to pursue his idea" (p. 266). Also, Hank had known a lot (content) about the materials he was using.

4. *Do* relate words to objects. It is important for children to know the proper words or names for things, but it is more important for them to *know* the things to which the words refer. Generally, teachers should avoid using words when children have no knowledge of the objects referred to by the words. Or the teacher should provide opportunities for children to come to know (through active learning) the objects referred to.

Many subjects that children are asked to "learn" in school are presented entirely at the verbal and pictorial level. An example is most "social studies" for elementary school children. Children are asked to listen to lectures, read books, or look at pictures, maps, movies, film-strips, and the like on such topics as American history, world history, politics, and economics. For preoperational and concrete operational children these experiences are basically meaningless. Children at these levels of development generally do not have the experiential back-ground to bring much "meaning" to such activities. The words and representations are not related to objects they have experienced.[3] According to Piaget, not until children develop formal operations do they become capable of constructing knowledge from words and pictures.

Studies of phenomena that elementary school children cannot understand are essentially a waste of time. When children cannot bring meaning to verbal or pictorial materials, what is acquired at best is some verbal association or, in the case of pictures, a limited, if not distorted, conception of objects and events. To comprehend words *without distortions* of meaning, children must be able to experience or have experienced the appropriate objects.

A special language interpretation problem exists for the bilingual child, particularly for a child who comes from a background where English is essentially a second language or an "imposed" new lan-guage. Many Mexican-American, Puerto Rican, and black children (who have been raised on black English) are examples. These chil-dren, on the average, *perform* below the average native English-speak-ing white child on school tasks and tests. This is frequently interpreted to mean that the lower-performing children are less "intelligent" than the higher-performing children. There are many arguments against this interpretation. Clearly there is a difference between the ability to communicate in a particular language and reasoning, thinking, or "intelligence." The child who used standard English as a second language rarely can communicate through English as effectively as through his or her primary language. Such children invariably have communication problems when they have to deal with

3. Pictures do not help children *construct* knowledge of objects. One cannot come to know what a horse or a typewriter is from a picture, except in a very limited sense. A picture is a static representation (symbol) which reveals only what a single case of the class of objects *looks like*. The dynamic and generaliz-able qualities of objects cannot be learned through nonexperiential methods at the preoperational and concrete operational levels. From a Piagetian point of view, this is a major criticism of the use of all verbal and audiovisual techniques before formal operations, including such heralded children's television programs as "Sesame Street." These methods *can* prompt the child to active learning. If, and only if, these methods yield spontaneous activity is their use justified.

school performance tasks, such as tests, through standard English. Many children for whom English is not their primary language are *always performing* under a communication handicap when compared to native English-speaking children.

Summary

Spoken and written language are forms of representation that develop during the preoperational period. The development of forms of representation, the semiotic or symbolic function, is instrumental in the development of preoperational thought. Spoken language is not necessary for the development of thought. Language facility is not the same thing as knowledge or intelligence. Children can become persuaded that verbal skills are more important than active learning, which can have a negative effect on cognitive development.

Language is important for communication. This is different from the acquisition of knowledge. Traditional preschool and elementary school classrooms are too verbal, too dominated by teachers talking. Children in classrooms at all levels should be free to interact spontaneously within reasonable guidelines. Teachers should avoid teaching linguistic formulas and should avoid verbally interrupting children's active learning. Questions from the teacher or classmates, posed at the right time, can prompt children to move further in their thinking than they might otherwise. Teachers should not intentionally expose children to language they cannot comprehend, unless children are given opportunities actively to explore the objects or events in question.

Motivation for Development

12

and Learning

The child must be active to develop and learn. The child must perceive materials and social activities as interesting to him or her in order to become effectively active. The motivation for substantive learning, according to Piaget, is *intrinsic* motivation. That is, the child "sees" the importance of the activity relative to himself or herself.[1] Intrinsic motivation is in the child, not in the materials of the classroom or in the teacher. Elkind (1971) writes:

> Educators . . . in their efforts to capitalize upon this intrinsic motivation seem to have missed the point of what Montessori and Piaget had in mind. To maximize intrinsic motivation and to accelerate mental growth we have recently had an emphasis upon "learning by discovery" and upon "interesting reading materials" and so on. These approaches miss the point because they assume that intrinsic motivation can be built into materials and procedures which will in turn maximize mental growth. But as Piaget and Montessori pointed out (Elkind 1967), intrinsic motivation resides in the child and not in methods and procedures [or materials]. It is the child who must, at any given point in time, choose the method of learning and the materials that are reinforcing to *him*. Without the opportunity for student choice and the provision of large blocks of time, in which the child can totally engross himself in an activity, the values of intrinsic motivation will not be realized. . . .

1. Young children, of course, do not "see the importance" of learning. They are aroused by certain things but do not have a mental awareness of their importance in an adult sense.

> . . . the education practice which would best foster in-
> trinsically motivated children in the Piagetian and Montessori
> sense would be the production of "interest areas" where chil-
> dren could go on their own and for long periods of time.
> Only when the child can choose an activity and persist at it
> until he is satisfied, can we speak of truly intrinsically moti-
> vated behavior. (pp. 25–26)

And Tuddenham (1971) adds:

> As Elkind pointed out—and as Montessori and Piaget have
> pointed out before him—intrinsic motivation resides in the
> child and not in methods or procedures of instruction. At-
> tempts to seduce him into being interested in what the adult
> values are really just the same old shell game. (p. 31)

Children of all ages need to have opportunities to select activities that
"interest" them. Technically, what is desirable is that children experience disequilibrium; to put it another way, *they must come to realize*
that their conception(s) is(are) no longer adequate in some sense.
The child's natural response to this will be to try to reestablish
equilibrium. Equilibrium occurs only after more active experience
with the objects that relate to the conception(s) in question. Disequilibrium is internal motivation. At a given point, the child is
going to be particularly "interested" in those activities that are going
to help him reestablish cognitive equilibrium. There is a need to
act further on and assimilate and accommodate to objects.

Equilibrium

The singular importance of *intrinsic motivation* in cognitive development—the necessity for the child to perceive the importance of
activity—rests largely on Piaget's concepts of equilibrium and equilibration. Furth (1971) writes: ". . . it is quite clear that the fact of
equilibration constitutes the most basic motivational factor in development" (p. 25). Equilibrium can be thought of as a more or less
temporary state of balance or stability between the processes of
assimilation and accommodation in the child's cognitive system.[2]

2. Assimilation and accommodation must both occur for optimal development.
Simply stated, if a child *only* assimilated, few schemata would develop, and
subsequently little differentiation. On the other hand, if a child only accommodated, there would be an overabundance of schemata, with little generality.

Equilibrium's primary function is to permit change in schemata while providing continuity and stability as they are changing (Stephens 1972, p. 71). Equilibrium is a *self-regulating factor* in the development of the child's knowledge. An event can be assimilated or accommodated to an existing structure without eliminating the old structure. In the case of assimilation, the structure's form remains essentially the same. In the case of accommodation, structure changes, but the old is merely modified and not lost. Thus equilibrium can be characterized as self-regulating, mobile, and active, with both a stability and a change component. Aspects of both a closed and an open system are involved. The closed aspect maintains the integrity of existing structures as the open aspect permits qualitative change. The child is constantly seeking a better *equilibrium*. Piaget (1971b) calls this searching process *equilibration*. He writes:

> Where I speak of equilibrium, it is not at all in the sense of a definitive state that cognitive functioning would be able to attain. Attained equilibrium is limited and restrained, and there is a tendency to go beyond it to a better equilibrium. . . . So, simply stated, there is a continual search for a better equilibrium. In other words, equilibration is the search for a better and better equilibrium in the sense of an extended field, in the sense of an increase in the number of possible compositions, and in the sense of a growth in coherence. (p. 18)

With an understanding of equilibration and equilibrium in mind, the next question is, What makes a child respond *actively* to a certain stimulus, or what causes disequilibrium and the gearing up of the equilibration process, the search for equilibrium? Piaget (1971b) most recently uses the concept of competence to try to clarify his ideas on this question:

> The organism is sensitive to a given stimulus only when it [the organism] possesses a certain competence. . . . A subject is sensitive to a stimulus only when he possesses the scheme [structure(s)] which will permit the response. In other words, the sensitivity to the stimulus is the capacity for response, and this capacity for response supposes a scheme of assimilation. We again have to create an equilibrium between assimilation, on the one hand, and accommodation to a given or an external stimulus, on the other hand. The stimulus-response scheme must be understood as a reciprocal. The stimulus

unleashes the response, and the possibility of the response is necessary for the sensitivity to the stimulus. (pp. 5–6)

Competence, in the biological sense, or capability for a response, must exist before the child can respond to a particular stimulus or event. Competence relative to a particular stimulus is the child's current level of conceptual development in the general sense; thus development or competence must precede further development or "learning" (in the strict sense) with respect to a particular stimulus. The stimulus, or external event, is necessary for development to proceed; competence, or sensitivity to the stimulus, is necessary to permit effective interaction with the stimulus. If the stimulus is present before the child has the *competence* to respond to it, the stimulus will have no value at all and will not contribute to accommodation and modification of structure (equilibrium).

Functionally, disequilibrium is an event or object (or thought) experienced by the child that does not readily fit into his existing schemata. The child cannot assimilate or fit the experience into his schemata. Such could be the case when a child with a limited set of animal concepts sees a giraffe for the first time. If the giraffe does not fit into any of his current concepts, disequilibrium may be created. The child will try to attain equilibrium—in this case he will make some change in his network of schemata (accommodation) so that the giraffe will "fit." This bit of accommodation is cognitive development in its clearest form. The child has moved from a state of equilibrium to a state of disequilibrium back to a state of equilibrium. This development depended on the level of conceptual development that the child had attained at the time with respect to the particular object (giraffe) and the activity of the child. A teacher could have presented the event, but the disequilibrating consequences of the event and accommodation depend on the child's perception of discrepancy with his available concepts, not on the event or on any external aspect of the situation (such as the teacher).

Internal motivation in its clearest sense has just been described. The motivation comes from being in a state of disequilibrium and "desiring" to return to equilibrium. According to Piaget, the question of whether a child is developmentally ready to learn a particular thing depends on whether the appropriate competence or sensitivity to that thing is present in the child's cognitive structures. If the competence exists, then the stimulus can potentially cause disequilibrium and initiate equilibration—the search for equilibrium.

Assessing Competence: Disequilibrium

Whether a child has a specific competence or is developmentally ready to "learn" a specific event may be very difficult to determine, but with training and experience one can assess a child's general level of competence or cognitive development by using Piagetian tasks. One can assess what stage of development children are in, and one can determine the nature of a child's specific conceptions. To make formal determinations of competence on a much finer level is possible, desirable, and sometimes necessary; but it is time-consuming and frequently impractical with thirty children in a class. It is helpful to know other ways to get an idea of what a child is ready to do.

One way, as Montessori has demonstrated and Dewey advocated, is to let the child decide what "stimuli" he is ready to deal with. In a very real sense, the child "knows" what competence he has. The child's interests and desires with respect to "learning" and what tasks he wishes to undertake can be viewed as reflecting the internal competence and sensitivities available to him.[3] The child's system for developing schemata is self-regulating and accurate from a developmental point of view. The child is always adapting to his physical and social environment, and his adaptations always make sense when viewed through his system. This does not mean that every time a child selects a task, he has the competence to master it. Children select tasks for a number of reasons (e.g., imitation of others). But one reason they select tasks is intrinsic motivation or disequilibrium.

Clearly, according to Piaget, motivation is an intrinsic affair. Competence must exist for disequilibrium to be activated by an external event. Equilibration is internal. This does not deny the necessity of external stimuli or events, for without them there would be no experience. When a discrepancy is perceived by the child, disequilibrium is created. An object or event cannot be assimilated directly. Disequilibrium *is* intrinsic motivation. To the child, the state of equilibrium is always desirable, and its attainment results in a "better" adaptation. The child always strives to attain cognitive equilibrium through further assimilation and accommodation. Materials or events never have the capacity to create disequilibrium in and of themselves.

3. This does not advocate allowing children to do whatever they want, but rather that one uses indicators or signals from the child in a diagnostic sense. The child tells what he "can do" and how he thinks. Obviously there is a difference between a signal that says, "I'm ready to deal with butterflies (Can't we do the butterflies now, teacher?)", and an evasion tactic.

Disequilibrium is always a state of imbalance with respect to the individual's cognitive structure and to the event. Clearly, a particular object or event can result in disequilibrium for one child and not for another.

How a Teacher Can Create Disequilibrium

According to Piaget, the teacher (or any other person) cannot ensure generating disequilibrium with respect to a particular learning within the child. In addition, *if* a disequilibrium occurs, the direction of disequilibration and the results of the subsequent equilibrium *cannot* be externally controlled. In simple terms, the teacher cannot control the course of cognitive development directly. The mechanism for control resides within the child.[4] Even though the teacher cannot control the results of disequilibrium, equilibration moves in the "correct" direction. The child's constructions become progressively more like those of objective reality because of the nature of the objects on which the child acts, as well as the nature of the social environment. A child acting on water is going to construct physical knowledge of water and eventually evolve a concept that approximates that of an adult. There is generally no reason for teachers to be concerned with the direction or outcome of disequilibrium.

Disequilibrium Training

Inhelder (1972, 1971) describes some of the learning studies Piagetians conducted in Geneva. These particular studies resulted in changes in children's cognitive structures. The studies were designed to determine the mechanisms for transition from one level of thought to another and were not concerned with acceleration as such.

One study was run with each child individually over six sessions for a few weeks, using children who had conservation of number (conservation of discontinuous quantities), but did not have conservation of length (conservation of continuous quantities). These two types of conservations are acquired on the average at around ages six and nine respectively. The child and the experimenter each had a collection of matches. The experimenter's matches were longer than the child's; it

---

4. The teacher can demand that a child "learn" a particular skill such as $1 + 1 = 2$. The child can memorize this. Such rote learning should not be confused with or assumed to reflect spontaneous learning. Memorization does not result in the reorganization of mental structures.

took seven of the child's matches to make a length equal to five of the experimenter's matches. In the training part of the study the child was presented with three problems. In the first problem (figure 4A), the most complex one, the experimenter laid out five matches. The child was required to make a line as long as the experimenter's beneath that of the experimenter, using the shorter matches. In the second problem (B), four experimenter matches were laid out as shown; the child again had to make a row of the same length, this time at some distance from the model.

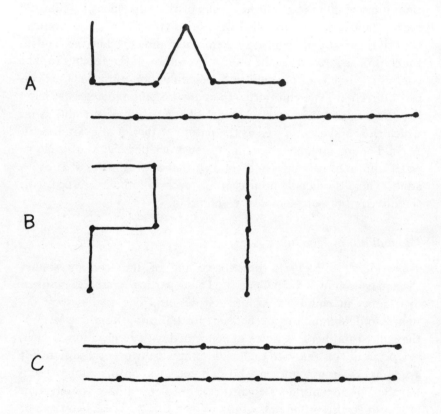

FIGURE 4
Matchstick Constructions: I

In the third and easiest problem (C), the experimenter laid out a straight line of five matches and the child was required to make one of the same length directly under the model. After completing his constructions, the child was encouraged to explain his solutions and reconsider his constructions (while the constructions remained in his view). The following reactions are typical of the subjects' behavior during the training (learning) sessions:

> In the first situation, the most elementary solution is to construct a straight line with its extremities congruent with those of the experimenter's zig-zag line [figure 5A]. The child is convinced that the two lines are the same length, although his line is made up of four small matches and the experimenter's of five long matches.
>
> In the second situation (B), the child has no ordinal or topological point of reference since he has to construct his line at some distance from that of the experimenter, and he has no difficulty in using the numerical reference: he constructs his line using the same number of matches as the experimenter, regardless of the fact that his matches are

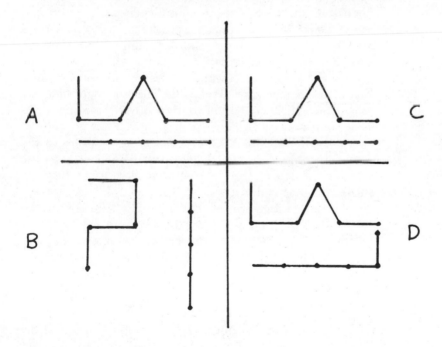

FIGURE 5
Matchstick Constructions: II

shorter [figure 5B]. When the experimenter now goes back to the first situation (A), the child notices, with some embarrassment, that the line he previously considered of equal length does not contain the same number of matches as that constructed by the experimeter [see figure 5A].

At this point, we often see amusing compromise solutions: In the first situation, the child may break one of his matches in two, thus creating a line with the same number of elements, without destroying the ordinal correspondence [figure 5C]. Another solution, again clearly indicating the conflict between topological, ordinal, and numerical references, consists of adding one match, but putting it vertically instead of horizontally [figure 5D]. When the child is then asked to construct his line in the third situation (C), he starts by using the same number of matches (five), as in the experimenter's line. Since this time both lines are straight and the second [child's construction] is directly under the model line, he sees immediately that this does not give the right solution; because his matches are shorter, his line does not reach as far as the model. Many children are perplexed at this point, and announce: "I can't do it; the red [child's] matches are smaller, it is impossible to get a road [line] as long as the other." However, after a while, the child will usually realize that he can compensate for the difference in length by using more match sticks, and add two, thus giving the correct solution. He is now on the way to grasping the relationship between length and number of elements. Going back to the second situation, he immediately says: "I will have to use more red matches to get the same road, because they are smaller." Those children who really acquire the concept will go even further; they will use the knowledge gained from the third situation (that seven red matches are equivalent in length to five green ones) in the first situation and will place their seven matches in a straight line without falling into the error of paying attention only to the ordinal aspects. (Inhelder 1971, pp. 155–56)

An experimental replication and extension of the above study (Wadsworth, Banks, and Kraemer 1975) recently confirmed the changes Inhelder reported. Children who received the same type of disequilibrium training described by Inhelder acquired conservation of length significantly more readily than children who did not receive the disequilibrium training. Both children with and without discontinuous quantity were trained; both types of children acquired conservation of length readily.[5] These experimental results clearly support Inhelder's conclusions.

Wadsworth, Banks, and Kraemer (1975) completed a follow-up of the same group of children one year after they had completed the training in order to determine if the differences between trained and untrained children were maintained. After the year there were no statistically significant differences between the trained and untrained children regarding where they were developmentally with respect to conservation concepts. Many of the trained children had "regressed" over the year's time while many of the untrained children had advanced "spontaneously." These one-year-later results suggest that the effect of the training was not permanent. In the only other study with a long-term follow-up, Bearison (1969) found that training effects were maintained after seven months.

In these short-term studies carried out with a number of children over a few weeks, qualitative changes in children's reasoning clearly occurred. The teacher-experimenter was instrumental in creating situations that we can say created a discrepancy (a form of disequilibrium) in the child's thinking and eventually led to a resolution and equilibrium. Inhelder (1971) writes:

> . . . we seem justified in concluding that it is indeed possible to make use of already acquired numerical operations to lead the child to spatial operations of measurement. However, even in the case of total acquisition, progress is slow, many obstacles are encountered in fitting the number concept to conservation of length problems. In some situations, the ordinal and topological references are misleading, and before the two operational structures can strengthen each other, there is a period of conflict which can be overcome only through constructive effort on *the part of the child*, who has to discover compensatory and coordinating actions. It is the feedback from these actions themselves which finally results in the acquisition of a structure of a higher order, and not the passive reading-off of a result. (p. 156)

5. According to Inhelder (1971, 1972) and Piagetian theory, conservation of discontinuous quantity is a necessary prerequisite for acquisition of conservation of length. It was unclear whether the children who did not have discontinuous quantity at the beginning of the study acquired it before acquiring conservation of length. All children who acquired length conservation also acquired conservation of discontinuous quantity.

Although these studies were designed to analyze the child's reasoning and integration of conflicts, it is clear that subjects made progress during the "learning" sessions.

Inhelder (1971, 1972) reports a second "learning" study, which dealt with training in class inclusion concepts with students not having the class inclusion concepts and conservation of liquid and substance, but having conservation of number. Half these students were given training in conservation of liquid and substance, and half were given training in class inclusion. In both groups, the subjects made progress in the concepts exercised. Interestingly, the children who received training in class inclusion concepts made substantial gains on the conservation concepts, while the children who receiverd training in conservation concepts did not make gains on class inclusion concepts despite their gains on conservation concepts (Inhelder 1971, p. 158). In addition, the amount of progress for both groups was very dependent on the "level" that the children were at when training began. This strongly suggests that progress in logical areas (class inclusion, for example) influences progress in more physical problems (conservation), but training in physical problems does not affect logical problems.

These studies suggest that the "teacher" can have an impact on a child's cognitive development when children's levels are carefully analyzed and programs for individuals are carefully designed with the disequilibrium principle in mind. One can accelerate the acquisition of concepts, but there may be no permanent advantages of short-term training in doing so. Children trained with carefully constructed techniques do move ahead. Of those who move ahead, there is evidence that many regress temporarily. Children who do not receive this specialized training seem to "catch up" in time. Thus it is unclear whether attempts at short-term training for acceleration have any advantage for the child. Piaget's statement still seems the most reasonable: "Perhaps a certain slowness is useful in developing the capacity to assimilate new concepts . . ." (Hall 1970, p. 31).

Borderline Children

To say that a child has developed a type of logical thought is not to say that he can apply it to all areas or contents. A child may be able successfully to apply classification thinking to the multiple-classification problem involving wooden beads but not be able to arrange the animal world in a hierarchy. In other words, a particular class of reasoning is not necessarily generalizable to all contents. Generally, the objects and events with which the child has had the most direct experience submit themselves to advances in his thinking before those objects and events with which he has had little experience.

Attainment of a concept is gradual and not an "either you have it or you don't" situation. There is clearly an intervening period, a borderline period, when the child sometimes conserves (makes reason-based decisions) and sometimes does not (makes perception-based decisions); there is a great deal of fluctuation in his responses. The child appears unable to make up his mind whether to obey reasoning or perception (Wadsworth 1968, 1971).

Children in the borderline status typically "learn" to conserve much more quickly than children who are nonconservers. The suggestion is that children who are borderline or "on the brink" of attaining a higher level of thought can fairly easily be nudged over the brink by experience. Vascillation in the borderline child's thinking is much more than inconsistency. It is clearly an indication that the child has moved from a lower type of thought (i.e., nonconserver) to a higher level (i.e., borderline conserver) and is struggling with a state of disequilibrium. In this case, the vascillation serves a functional purpose in moving on to the higher level of thought (i.e., conservation). This vascillation is a period of exploration and testing —a clear indication that equilibration is at work. What may appear to be inconsistency in the child is the child's actively moving to a higher level of thought. This type of inconsistency should not be discouraged. The teacher can, of course, provide experiences and questions that stimulate advances (as indicated by Inhelder's 1971, 1972 studies) if he or she recognizes a child's borderline status.

Surprise and Cognitive Development

Hunt (1969b) and Charlesworth (1969) argue for the importance of *surprise* as a key element in cognitive development. Surprise here describes the state of mind that a person arrives at when an expectation is not confirmed. We are all constantly making predictions. When things happen differently from the way we expect, the reaction is surprise, and frequently *overt* surprise.

Surprise is different from seemingly similar phenomena such as startle, amazement, or astonishment. If one hears a gun fired close at hand, one may be startled. This is an involuntary reaction. If one sees a ten-foot-high tomato plant, one may be amazed. If one finds an 1870 twenty-dollar gold piece, one may be astonished. Surprise can include all these reactions, but surprise always contains, in addition, a cognitive element of prediction or expectancy that is *not confirmed*.[6]

Surprise has several characteristics (Charlesworth 1969). Surprise is activated by an incorrect prediction about "known" things. It results in rapid attempts to assimilate or make sense out of the surprise. There is intense attention to the surprise, which lasts for a relatively long period of time. There is either slow accommodation or rapid assimilation of the surprise event. The ultimate result can be either a slight or a drastic modification of some parts of the child's cognitive structures. The reactions under a surprise situation are substantially different from those under a situation where a prediction about known events is confirmed (see table 3).

Piaget first suggested the importance of surprise in *The Origins of Intelligence*, published in 1952. While observing one of his own children, Piaget noticed that Laurent (3 months of age) was "surprised" when a string around his wrist activated a group of rattles over his head. Movement of his wrist produced movement of the rattles and sounds. This new discovery was repeated over and over by Laurent until he had assimilated the event and the rattles were under intentional control (Piaget 1952a, pp. 160–62). Surprise is seen here as part of a disequilibrating event that led to attempts to assimilate and accommodate to the event (Laurent continued to move his wrist to move the string to move the rattles).

Surprise as a concept is very close to the concept of disequilibrium. Charlesworth (1969) writes:

> . . . the surprise reaction can be viewed as consisting of a number of complex stimulus-producing responses that may serve to mediate, cue, arouse, instigate, "illuminate," and reinforce a variety of other responses that ultimately contribute to changes in existing cognitive structures . . . the surprise reactions themselves, especially the OR [orienting reflex] component, can be viewed as multi-functional, hyperstable properties of the organism that help to insure that the

6. See Charlesworth (1969) for a more theoretical and extensive treatment of surprise as a construct and its relationship to cognitive development.

TABLE 3

Dimensions Along Which Surprise and Familiar Events or
Situations Can Be Distinguished When Dealing with
Cognitive Development

	Surprise	*Familiar*
Initial event that activates child and produces expectancy	a known event	a known event
Outcome of event	was mis-expected; high information value	was expected; no information value
Surprise reaction	intense orienting	no reaction
Surprise reaction decay	slow	—
Accommodation-assimilation phase	very slow accommodation or rapid assimilation	rapid assimilation
Outcome	drastic or slight modification of original structure	no modification of original structure

SOURCE. Adapted from Charlesworth (1969, p. 285, table 1).

> organism behaves in such a way as to produce new knowledge about problematic properties of the environment . . . under normal environmental conditions surprise reaction and subsequent attentional and curiosity behaviors are very hard to suppress, and that for this reason they seem to be good candidates for the mechanisms that insure that most individuals make the progression from sensorimotor intelligence to formal thought. (p. 308)

The potential for surprise, or making incorrect predictions, is highest during the sensorimotor, preoperational, and concrete operational periods, prior to the development of formal operations. Only after the child is capable of considering all logical possibilities is surprise, as a consequence of thought, reduced, though it is never eliminated. Charlesworth (1969):

> When we compare the preoperational or concrete operational child with the mature adolescent, there is little question that the latter faces less uncertainty in his everyday contacts with his environment. (p. 268)

During the preoperational period, the child's egocentric thought and lack of operational thought make the possibilities for surprise greater than after formal operations are developed. During the preoperational and concrete operational periods, thought is constrained by perception, and the likelihood of making false predictions continues to be high. The child is constantly assimilating events in order to reduce environmental uncertainty or to make the environment more predictable. Thus the significance of surprise in cognitive development would seem to be at its *greatest* roughly from shortly after birth through age fifteen (or whenever formal operations are developed). Surprise continues to play the same role after formal operations are developed though it probably occurs less frequently.

Using Surprise in Teaching

The use of surprise in education has considerable potential for encouraging the acquisition of knowledge in the school-age child. Piaget states:

> . . . the element of surprise is an essential motor in education and in scientific research in general. What distinguishes a good scientist is that he is amazed by things which seem natural to others. Surprise plays an important role: We might try to develop an aptitude for surprise. (Duckworth 1964, p. 5)

Just as there is educational value in permitting the child to explore his or her spontaneous interests, so there is value in permitting the child to respond to surprise. Both surprise and spontaneous interests reflect high motivation to act on objects and events. Charlesworth (1969) writes:

> Under natural conditions where structural changes develop spontaneously, surprises occur as often as the environment creates expectancies and violates them. It seems to me, then, one task of the teacher would be to accelerate this process by judiciously choosing and applying both kinds of events in a learning situation. This requires that the teacher be aware

of what information the child has at the moment, i.e., what his cognitive predisposition towards the subject matter is. This may be a strenuous requirement, however, I would not be surprised if good teachers do just this most of the time anyway. (p. 91)

Surprise is an internal cognitive event that frequently has overt signs. For example, one can frequently see the surprise on a person's face. To function as a force in cognitive development, surprise must be surprise *to the individual child*. There is no assurance that what is surprising to one child or to an adult will be surprising to other children. Surprise occurs only when an individual child makes a prediction that *is not* confirmed. The child must actively predict before he or she can be surprised.

Some children will not experience surprise because their reasoning has not developed sufficiently. Inhelder et al. (1974) writes:

> . . . as was demonstrated by the learning studies, the "surprise" element has no effect if the child does not yet possess the cognitive equipment which enables him to fit the unforeseen phenomenon into a deductive or inferential framework. (p. 267)

For example, a child observing two rows of checkers, one longer than the other, may not be surprised when he counts the number in each row and finds them identical. The child can experience surprise only if his numerical concepts are developed to a point where both length *and* absolute number influence his judgments about quantities.

Children can and do encounter surprise on their own. Surprise, at least in part, accounts for disequilibrium and spontaneous interest. As children act on the objects around them, they develop expectations about how objects behave. For example, the preoperational child dropping objects into water may expect that large things will float and small things will sink, or vice versa. At some point the child is going to be surprised by a large object that sinks or a small object that floats. The lack of confirmation of a prediction is likely to motivate the child to try to make sense out of (assimilate) the experience.

One advantage of using surprise is that the " 'surprise' element can be introduced into training procedures in more varied situations and in more rapid succession than the child is likely to encounter in his usual occupations" (Inhelder et al. 1974, p. 267). Teachers can arrange what they believe to be surprising events to motivate children. For example, the teacher could ask children who have advanced but not complete conceptions of floating and sinking objects to make predictions about what would happen if a needle were placed on the water; if a metal box were placed on the water; if a wooden boat, full of water and with a rock in it, were placed on the water. Children who make incorrect predictions may be motivated to experiment on their own. Demonstrations like those mentioned before a class of students may surprise and motivate only a few students in the class. Demonstrations in science classes are sometimes fatal from a motivational point of view. Students may be bored, interested in something else rather than the demonstration at hand, or may not make predictions.

The optimal time for a teacher to interject surprising events is when a group of children is engaging in activities related to the surprise the teacher had in mind. If children are playing with floating and sinking objects, and it is apparent that the children's conceptions are that heavy things sink and light things float, then the floating needle or floating wooden boat should be surprising to the children. It is essential that children be given the opportunity to be active with the surprising objects rather than remain passive observers. Hall (1970), interviewing Piaget, reports his comments on teacher demonstrations:

> HALL: What if the teacher were to demonstrate this experiment to a class?
> PIAGET: It would be completely useless. The child must discover the method for himself through his own activity. (p. 30)

Observation of demonstrations by the child is never enough to activate cognitive change.[7] This can occur only if the child is active. But the use of surprise may generate activity and cognitive change that the child might not come to spontaneously for some time or might never encounter outside the school experience.

---

7. After formal operations are developed, children become capable of assimilating observational information into *new* schemes. Of course, they continue to benefit from active experience as much as they did before the development of formal operations.

TEACHING PRINCIPLES
PART III
AND PRACTICES

The Developing Learner

13

and the Teacher

Teaching means creating situations where
structure can be discovered.
Duckworth, *Piaget Rediscovered*

Piaget has said that teachers can-
not understand his methods unless they understand four points:
(1) the significance of childhood, (2) the laws of development, (3)
the structure of the child's thought, and (4) the mechanisms of
children's social life (1969a). Once these aspects of the child and
his development are understood, one can begin to interpret and
apply educational implications of Piagetian theory.

Piaget has evolved a useful theory to explain how and why children
develop and learn. The theory provides a frame of reference by
which the teacher can analyze behaviors of students and plan educational activities consistent with development. Piagetians *have not*
evolved a teaching method. There *is not* a set of teaching practices
that constitute a Piagetian approach to teaching. The universals of
education that can be derived from Piaget's theory are general
principles, not specific in-classroom teaching practices. The teacher
who feels that Piaget's conceptions of how children develop and
learn should be integrated into his or her classroom may feel at a
loss without any rigid guidelines. There are guidelines, but not the
type that tell the teacher what to do every step of the way. The main
guideline is Piaget's theory.

A burgeoning number of psychologists and educators, reputed to
be interpreters of Piagetian theory, are working directly in early
childhood education either in research or practice. There are substantial differences in their interpretations of Piagetian theory. This
is predictable because serious attempts to apply Piagetian and other

recent findings in developmental theories have begun to take place only recently. Also, in talking about a Piagetian or developmentally based educational program, there are no rules for interpretation that all must follow. As Millie Almy (1975) has pointed out, the difference between a Piagetian-based educational program and *some* traditional classrooms is not necessarily in the activities in the classroom but in the teacher's understanding what he or she is doing. There are certainly classrooms whose teachers have never heard of Piaget but whose programs are perfectly compatible with Piagetian theory. But some practices in traditional classrooms are not compatible with Piagetian theory, and many teaching practices compatible with Piagetian theory are not found in traditional classrooms.

My effort here is to make strict interpretation of Piaget's theory as it applies to education and to present those principles and examples of practices that are consistent with Piagetian theory. The remainder of this chapter presents my interpretations of Piaget's theory concerning:

1. What the long-term and short-term objectives of education "should be"
2. Principles of teaching
3. General teaching considerations
4. The similarities and differences between Piagetian and traditional classrooms

These interpretations are general and do not pertain to specific content areas. The chapters following this one deal with the acquisition of knowledge and skills in particular content areas.

Long-term Objectives

Piagetian theory does not reject the traditional long-term objectives of education. All educators and parents want children to leave high school with certain skills and adequate knowledge to carry them forward into adult life and work. These objectives are preserved in any interpretation of Piaget's theory. It is desirable to have students learn to read and be able to *comprehend* what they read. It is desirable to have children learn to solve mathematical problems and *understand* their solutions. It is desirable to have children learn to express themselves and communicate through both written and spoken language. It is desirable to have children develop social skills and *understand* social knowledge.

Piagetian theory recognizes the traditional goals of education but does not agree with all the traditional methods. These goals, according to any interpretation of Piagetian theory, can best be attained through educational methods and curricula that are consistent with how children develop.

Another long-term educational objective according to Piaget's theory is the complete "development" of the child. For Piaget, strictly in terms of cognitive development, this means the eventual development of formal operations and the development of the ability to apply formal thought to real problems. Piaget (1964a) writes:

> The principal goal of education is to create men who are capable of doing new things, not simply of repeating what other generations have done—men who are creative, inventive, and discoverers. The second goal of education is to form minds which can be critical, can verify, and not accept everything they are offered. The great danger today is of slogans, collective opinions, ready-made trends of thought. We have to be able to resist individually, to criticize, to distinguish between what is proven and what is not. So we need pupils who are active, who learn early to find out by themselves, partly by their own spontaneous activity and partly through materials we set up for them: who learn early to tell what is verifiable and what is simply the first idea to come to them. (p. 5)

This is clearly a statement that one of the goals of education is to help develop the mind of the child so that he can *think* and reason logically. As an objective, learning to think has been much talked about in the past but rarely conceptualized in any useful way. Learning to think goes beyond much of what goes on in education today, and is counter to many of the practices current in education. Piaget says nothing about filling the head of the child with facts, various contents, and rote-memorized information.[1] Kohlberg and Mayer

---

1. There are many things that one may legitimately wish children to learn that have nothing to do with development as such. Memorized information has nothing to do with development, as is the case with many skill learnings. Reading, writing, and arithmetic skills can be forced on children and acquired primarily through memorization or can be acquired in ways that are more consistent with the child's mental development.

(1972) provide a rationale and a discussion of why development in and of itself can be considered the primary goal, and a valid one, of education.

While the focus of Piaget's work has been on cognitive development, this does not mean that he ignores social development, emotional development, moral development, and ego development. He considers them important, and he feels that all aspects of development are inseparable in the long run as components of the whole personality. The development of each affects the other and is dependent on the other (Piaget 1972).

Piagetian theory suggests that the long-term objectives of education include the acquisition of traditional intellectual and social skills and comprehension of the use of those skills. In addition, the theory suggests a valid objective of education is to maximize the development of the child.

Short-term Objectives

As Kamii and DeVries (1973a) state, short-term goals of education should be conceptualized within the context of long-term goals. How do current goals help to maximize the development of formal operations and maximize the personality integration that can occur during late adolescence? In the most all-inclusive and general sense, the short-term goal of education during the early childhood education years should be to maximize preoperational development and assist the child in the transition into concrete operational thought with adequate development in all attendant personality dimensions.

More specifically, the statement of short-term objectives by Kamii and DeVries (1973a) is:

1. *Socioemotional development:* for the child
   a. to feel secure in his relationship with teachers;
   b. to respect the feelings and rights of others and begin to coordinate different points of view (decentering and cooperating [overcoming preoperational egocentrism, to argue openly about differences, and recognize differences]);
   c. to be mentally active and curious and to use initiative in pursuing curiosity;

    d. to have confidence in his ability to figure things out for himself and speak his mind with conviction;

    e. to enjoy both companionship and play with others and playing alone;

    f. to cope constructively with fears and anxieties and not to be easily traumatized.

2. *Cognitive development:* for the child actively to use his intelligence

    a. to figure out means to achieve desired ends and to think about (eventually coordinate) similarities, differences, and relationships;

    b. to come up with problems and questions of his own.

What is the teacher's role in a system of education patterned after Piagetian principles? Clearly, the teacher is not a full-time lecturer, or giver of information, or drillmaster, as is frequently the case in traditional education. Piagetian conceptualizations tell us that mental development is a form of adaptation to the environments—both the experiential and social environments. The child is the primary agent in his own development; it is the child who must *act on* the environment, who must assimilate the world into his structures and organize it internally. The child's construction of the world (as reflected in his developing structures) is largely a spontaneous process. Development is an individual affair, a unique creation in every sense of the word. The child's construction of reality is not a copy of what is out there in the environment but a constantly changing picture painted by the child. The child's constructions tend to become increasingly *similar* to a "copy of reality" as the child develops. As constructions become more refined, they become more truthful.

Any child with adequate inherited endowment and an adequate physical and social environment will in a progressive manner reconstruct the world and his or her own reality along the lines of "objective" reality. There is a built-in incentive to encourage this. Given time, most children in our Western culture will develop the capability to think logically (formal operations) and will develop adequate fundamental concepts of time, space, causality, morality, and so on. The child typically will learn and develop along these lines because of the way the world is, physically and socially, and because there is adaptive value to learning certain things. Coming to understand gravity on a sensorimotor level (sitting up, crawling, walking) and learning to talk both make the child more efficient in dealing with his physical and social environment.

Six Principles of Teaching

According to Piaget, teaching at all levels of education must be founded on the activity of the learner. Concepts cannot be effectively taught (learned) through verbal methods alone. Piaget says:

> If you spend one year studying something verbally that requires two years of active study, then you have actually lost a year. If we were willing to lose a bit more time and let children be active, let them use trial and error on different things, then the time we seem to have lost we may have actually gained. Children may develop a general method they can use on other subjects. (Hall 1970)

Cognitive development *does not* proceed as a consequence of the child talking, listening to others talk, reading, or watching television.[2] Cognitive development arises out of the activity of the child. Thus the best methods of education for development are those that foster the activity or active learning of the child. Duckworth (1964) writes:

> As far as education is concerned, the chief outcome of his (Piaget's) theory of intellectual development is a plea that children be allowed to do their own learning. Piaget is not saying that intellectual development proceeds at its own pace no matter what you try to do. He is saying that what schools usually try to do is ineffectual. You cannot further understanding in a child simply by talking to him. (p. 20)

The child receives valid information about objects and events when he acts on them (touches, tastes, looks at, listens to, and "thinks" about them). The child assimilates these actions and constructs knowledge in the process. Spoken or written symbols cannot replace the child's actions in the construction of knowledge. The source of all meaning is in the objects themselves and in the child's actions on objects, not in symbols.[3]

2. After formal operations are developed, the child becomes capable of using verbal and written information to form new concepts. Of course, active learning remains an important part of learning and development.

3. Symbols are objects. The child can obtain knowledge of symbols only from acting on symbols and interacting with others.

The activity of the child must be *spontaneous*. The motivation and initiation must flow from the child. If the child acts *merely* because someone suggests he do so (teacher, parent), it is unlikely that the child's actions will have the same effects in an assimilation and accommodation sense as the child's spontaneous activity. Kamii and DeVries (1973b) write:

> External direction of a child's action prevents the spontaneous mental action which Piaget finds in child initiated actions. . . . In our curriculum, the teacher does not direct the child's actions, but, instead, does everything she can think of to encourage the child's initiative. (p. 6)

If one puts children through physical actions, the desired mental actions (assimilation and accommodation) do not follow automatically. Such teacher-directed activities may be physical actions without mental actions. Without true disequilibrium there can be no true development and learning.

1. *Create an environment and atmospere in which children will be active and initiate and complete their own activities. Provide time to spare and materials to complete self-initiated activities.*[4] A classroom should permit a child to develop and carry out spontaneous interests and discover structures. The quality of the environment not only includes the physical aspects of space, materials, and so forth, but also the teacher-child and child-child relationships. In some respects, a standard Montessori classroom is a useful environmental model even though it is a "structured environment," typically restricted in the range of activities available to the child. Montessori materials used alone are too structured according to Piaget (1969a) and are limited to perceptual training in their usefulness. The Montessori spirit of self-initiated activity and the notion of a nurturant teacher-child relationship are very appropriate, however.

In a Piagetian classroom, to the extent possible there should be no formal periods or time blocks. Children should be permitted to complete the activities they start and maintain interest in the activities even if interest is maintained for several days or longer. I am reminded of an incident described by a third-grade teacher. A student in her class decided that he wanted to write out all the numbers from zero to infinity. In a very conventional manner, the teacher insisted that this would be impossible and would be a waste of time.

4. Partially taken from Kamii and DeVries (1973a).

She argued at length with the student; the student persisted, and the teacher relented. The student got a few sheets of paper and started writing numbers. Soon his few sheets of paper were covered with numbers. The teacher recommended that he use a long roll of paper. The student spent several hours writing numbers, one after another. Shortly after he began, the rest of the class became aware of what he was up to, and some other students became interested in his project. Eventually, the boy became tired and let one of his friends fill in for him while he rested. Soon, four or five students in the class were working in shifts on the writing-to-infinity project. The students kept at this for part of several days. After tens of thousands of numbers, they decided that infinity was still a long way down the roll of paper (and something they were no longer certain that they could get to), and they abandoned the project.

These third-grade students came away from this active experience with a much better concept of infinity than the verbal definition they had previously heard. They attached improved meaning to the word "infinity" after this activity. The intensity of the children's motivation was impressive. In addition, their understanding of numbers was probably enhanced. This intense spontaneous activity would have been precluded by rigorous class periods. And most important, the project was self-initiated (spontaneous), an active experience, and carried to "completion."[5]

2. *With regard to social-arbitrary knowledge, tell the child the right answer (give him feedback about his answers) and reinforce social-arbitrary knowledge. In physical knowledge, encourage the child to find the answer directly from activity on objects. In logical-mathematical knowledge, refrain from telling the right answer and reinforcing it.*

As stated, Piagetians make a distinction between three types of knowledge: physical knowledge, logical-mathematical knowledge, and what Kamii and DeVries (1973a) call social-arbitrary knowledge. The source of physical knowledge is *objects themselves*, which children construct by activity on objects. For example, the child learns what wood is and what the properties of wood are by manipulating wood. The source of logical-mathematical knowledge does not

5. This example does not mean that I am in favor of getting children involved with symbols early. An activity is seen as perfectly consistent with Piagetian principles if it comes from the spontaneous interests of the child. The children in this instance were not dealing with the arithmetic aspects of numbers, only with their sequence.

come from the objects themselves, but from the child's *actions* imposed on objects. For example, number is not a property of objects, but a product of the child's actions on collections of objects. Social-arbitrary knowledge is knowledge specific to a culture, knowledge that is made by people (e.g., language, values). Reinforcement about social-arbitrary knowledge (but not physical and logical-mathematical knowledge) is desirable because the only source of social-arbitrary knowledge is other people. Stable knowledge requires consistency. The child can know he is "right" only if others tell him so.

Reinforcement or verbal correcting of the child's physical and logical-mathematical knowledge is not desirable because these forms of knowledge are constructions of the child and the child must construct them. Direct verbal reinforcement of physical and logical-mathematical knowledge can divert the child from objects and his actions on objects. For logical-mathematical knowledge, the "reinforcement" comes from the action of the child. It is appropriate to encourage the child to be active, but not to direct or reinforce specific actions. The child's "comprehension" is best if based on his constructions, not on the verbal information he receives. Reinforcement

and verbal feedback tend to confuse the child where physical and logical-mathematical knowledge are concerned (Kamii and DeVries 1973a). The reinforcement for physical knowledge is inherent in the object; the object will correct the child. A child places wood in a fire; he places a stone in the fire. He does this repeatedly, and each time the stone does not burn. The object itself provides "feedback." No external reinforcement is needed. To *do* is to understand. The child who attends to verbal feedback from others for anything but social-arbitrary knowledge may be persuaded to disregard his natural disequilibrium. Anything that interferes with the spontaneity of the child's actions can limit the extent of their effect.

3. *Let the preoperational child go through stages of being "wrong."* Knowledge progresses gradually from a less-accurate state to a more-accurate state. There is no shortcut for this process. "If we want children to achieve formal operations, we must let them construct their own preoperational knowledge rather than trying to give them our ready-made, adult knowledge" (Kamii and DeVries 1973a, p. 6). This pertains to all three types of knowledge. In a sense, the young child's concepts (schemata) are usually always "wrong." Their concepts are never quite fully developed. Before the development of formal operations, children are naturally and *necessarily* going to make "mistakes." A young child who predicts that a small metal can *will* sink when placed in water has not necessarily made a mistake. His structures may tell him that metal sinks in water. Thus, for him, at this point in development of related schemata, the *logically consistent* prediction is that the metal can will sink. This is not a mistake in the usual sense of the word. The child's prediction provides useful (diagnostic) information about the child's structure.

A teacher or parent might be tempted to "correct" the child and tell him that solid metal things usually sink in water and that hollow metal things usually float. The child could memorize this verbal response and use it subsequently *in place of* thinking and further experimentation. The use of this type of response by the child would be largely devoid of meaning (knowledge) although the memorized statement may please a teacher or a parent better than the child's intuitive but incorrect response. A serious danger here is that children *do* listen to adults. They tend to believe that adults know what they are talking about. It is *not difficult* to persuade children that verbal fluency is highly valued (in place of knowledge). There is considerable social reinforcement for this belief. Children can come to believe that words are more important than things and that knowledge resides in words rather than in actions. A child who verbalizes an idea may have comprehension of that idea, *but he may not*. Similarly, children who *cannot* verbalize an idea *may have* comprehension of that idea based on their actions. Kamii (1973b) writes:

> The reason that it is important for us to let the child go from one stage after another of being *wrong*, is that *wrong* notions usually contain a certain amount of correctness. For example, to predict whether something will sink or float, it is not entirely wrong to consider heaviness as the determining factor. The reasoning is not entirely wrong; it is only incomplete. The preoperational child needs time to construct gross structures that will later be differentiated and coordinated into more adequate structures.
>
> We have a habit of thinking in terms of right and wrong answers and equating intelligence with the ability to pass or to fail specific test items. As Piaget points out, however, knowledge does not develop from "all wrong" to "perfectly correct." All children have *some* knowledge about whatever we try to teach them, and their knowledge always contains some elements of truth. Therefore, if we honestly want to meet preoperational children where they are, we have to figure out how *they* think and to interact with them in terms of how *they* reason. (p. 226)

4. *Some types of knowledge are best learned (and motivated) from interaction with other children.* One of the major characteristics of the preoperational child's thinking is egocentrism of thought, believing that one's thoughts are always "right," not questioning one's thinking and not being able to assume the perspective of others. Piaget says that egocentrism is gradually broken down during the preoperational period *primarily* by interaction with peers and other children (Wadsworth 1971). Thus, where logical-mathematical thought and social-arbitrary thought are concerned, the peer group becomes an increasingly important factor in (1) disequilibrating or shaking up the egocentric conceptualizations of the child and (2) providing information or feedback to the child about the validity of his social and logical constructions. These two consequences of peer interaction are used as raw materials in helping the child move beyond egocentric thought.

Preoperational Egocentrism

From a communication point of view, the child may be better equipped to communicate with his peers than with his parents and other adults. Conceptually, if a child has an idea which he wishes to communicate, he translates it into symbols (spoken words, writing, actions) and presents it. The meaning of the idea presented by the child rests on the configuration of structures that the child has available at that time. Similarly, a child's interpretation of a presented idea is based on the structures *he* has at that moment. Piaget (1964b) writes:

> . . . the child can receive valuable information via language or via education directed by an adult *only* if he is in a state where he can understand this information. That is, to receive the information he must have a structure which enables him to assimilate this information. (p. 3)

It is probable that any given preoperational child's structures are going to be *more* like the structures of other preoperational children than they are like the structures of an adult or of a child at a different developmental level. On a thinking and reasoning level, this leads one to the conclusion that communication about logical-mathematical

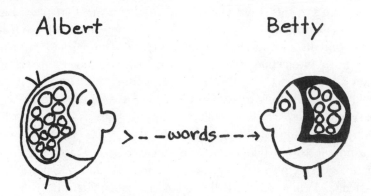

Albert   Betty

> - -words- - →

og = structures, Schemata, or concepts

Figure 6. Child B (Betty) hears Child A's (Albert) words.
Child B processes the words (symbols) through her schemata
to derive their meaning. Now it would seem that whether
Child B can end up with the *same meaning* that Child A
wished to communicate depends, in part, on whether they
both have schemata that permit this. If their structures are
vastly different, then the probability of their "understanding"
each other seems low. If they have the "same" or similar
structures, then their capacity for meaningful understanding
seems considerably greater.

and social-arbitrary knowledge should be more efficient between
children of the same developmental level than between children and
adults. Also it suggests that children may be better able to *understand*
the reasoning of other children than adults are. For this reason,
children, from a structural point of view, may be better able to
"teach" other children than adults are.

Using children to teach other children has always been a successful procedure. As all teachers know, there is a dual benefit in children
teaching children: benefit to the child being taught and benefit to
the child teaching. All teachers know—or should know—that the
best way to learn something is to teach it. It is probable that students
remain by far the largest source of untapped teaching talent in
schools at *all* educational levels. In spontaneous situations outside
school children "learn" from each other and "teach" each other.
This is a natural outcome of children's spontaneous interactions.

Needless to say, this is not encouraged in classrooms that place high value on silence and regimented order. It is suggested that extensive use of students as teachers be made both in a formal and informal sense. Such interaction was common in the old one-room schoolhouses. One advantage of the "open classroom" model is that it can encourage exactly this type of interaction between children.

5. *View all aspects of knowledge as inseparable.* Much of what we do as educators or psychologists is for our own ease of conceptualizing the things that interest us. So it is that Piagetians differentiate between physical, logical-mathematical, and social-arbitrary knowledge. While conceptually separable, psychologically they are not. In the mind and actions of the child, knowledge exists as an inseparable whole (Kamii and DeVries 1973a). A child actively playing with and trying to order a set of sticks of irregular length may be activating both his physical and logical-mathematical structures. He is deriving physical information directly from the sticks and logical-mathematical information from his actions on the objects (ordering). These sources of information are not separate in the child's thoughts or behavior. It is difficult to think of a "learning" situation during the preoperational period where a child could exclusively invoke one type of thinking. Throughout the sensorimotor, preoperational, and concrete operational periods, the child's acquisition of knowledge is based directly on his manipulation of concrete objects. These manipulations always have two potential sources of information: the objects themselves and the actions of the child on the objects. Thus, for practical purposes, physical knowledge and logical-mathematical knowledge are inseparable.

6. *If you want a child to acquire a specific fact or piece of content that is not available to him, teach it directly and reinforce the learning.* Piaget's theory suggests that the child will learn when there is some adaptive value to the learning and when the child is psychologically "ready." Now, we all recognize certain things that we want children to "know," at least on a verbal level. Common sense tells us that the adaptive route is not necessarily best in all cases, particularly with young children—especially where safety is concerned (e.g., moving cars on the road are dangerous; from the point of view of adaptation, the best way to "learn" this may be fatal). Teachers and parents want or do not want children to do certain things for justifiable reasons. These things should be taught directly to the child without any concern for the child's compre-

hension. In such cases, it is appropriate to have children memorize or "learn" a particular response and reinforce that learning. This method of "learning" does not contribute to the cognitive development of the child because it is not founded on the activity of the child. Nonetheless, it can obviously be justified.

Direct teaching using reinforcement (e.g., in behavior modification, token earnings) is frequently a desirable approach and the most efficient way to change a person's *behavior*. Care must be taken not to confuse *behavior* with *development*, or *learning as a consequence of reinforcement* (reinforcement produced learning) with *learning as a consequence of development* (developmental learning). A child who learns through reinforcement to say "Columbus" when someone asks "Who discovered America?" has undergone a behavior change. This does not require reasoning or logic. It merely requires a specific memorized association. There is value in being able to know this type of response, but it should not be confused with thinking, reasoning, or intelligence.[6] Behaviors acquired as a consequence of reinforcement or punishment do not affect the development of the mind per se. Indeed, content and skill learnings such as reading, writing, and arithmetic depend on certain levels of development to be optimally meaningful. When possible, the learning should be founded on the activity of the learner. When this is unrealistic, or if a behavior must be acquired quickly, memorization and reinforcement are appropriate.

Other General Teaching Considerations

The fact that the child's cognitive structures develop more or less independently of schooling must be considered by educators. The development of the child's intelligence and his ability to think logically follows a course well documented by Piaget and others who have done research in this area. Every step in development involves qualitative as well as quantitative changes. While each point represents an advance, the advance may not be on "all fronts" equally. Piaget (1969a) writes:

6. Many *intelligence tests* are based in large part on the child's having acquired specific verbal associations. Conceptually, these tests can be construed as largely testing acquired associations, not reasoning or logic. The above question is found on the WISC information subscale.

. . . there are all sorts of overlaps when one passes from one particular test [of development] to another: a child that belongs to one particular stage as far as one particular question of causality is concerned may well have moved on to the next stage with regard to some neighboring causal question. . . . (p. 171)

From the point of view of schooling . . . we must recognize the existence of a process of mental development; that all intellectual raw material is not invariably assimilable [or learned] at all ages; that we should take into account the particular interests and needs of each stage. It also means, in the second place, that environment [including education] can play a decisive role in the development of the mind; that the thought content of the stages and the ages at which they occur are not immutably fixed; that sound methods can therefore increase the students' efficiency and even accelerate their spiritual growth without making it any the less sound. (p. 173)

Cognitive development proceeds in an orderly manner for all children.[7] Rates of development vary in any culture, and the average rates of development vary somewhat between cultural or subcultural groups, though there seems to be less variation in rates of development between cultural groups than there is within cultural groups.

The Teacher as Organizer of the Learning Environment

The concern of many teachers and parents about progressive methods of teaching such as the "open classroom" and the "integrated day" programs is that the classroom becomes a place of chaos where little learning takes place. Few educators would suggest that chaos is in any way educationally beneficial. The teacher who implements Piagetian ideas in the classroom does not abandon control and order. School experience must be planned, organized, and controlled. The teacher requires management skills more under a Piagetian approach to teaching than under a traditional approach. Organization and control do not mean that children must sit most of the day at their desks, lined up in rows, working quietly or listening to the

7. Many children develop in ways that appear not to be orderly. The development of children with learning problems is typically consistent with the Piagetian principles of adaptation and development, although aspects of a child's development may be inefficient from an educational point of view (see chapter 18).

teacher talk. Control does not necessarily require telling students what to do and making sure that they do it. Control and planning effectively for children's spontaneous interest can be compatible.

The classroom atmosphere should be "conducive to learning." This means that, when appropriate, the individual child can spontaneously get involved with objects and activities that interest him. It is "an atmosphere in which the child uses his own initiative in pursuing his interests, says exactly what he thinks, asks questions, experiments, and comes up with a variety of ideas" (Kamii and DeVries 1973a, p. 6). Such an environment does not come prepackaged and ready-made. One cannot buy it from a manufacturer of school materials. Effective learning environments may require constant reorganization of classroom space to permit flow of students, access to materials, and practical use of space. The teacher must be active in creating an environment that works for the teacher and the students.

I am not an expert on classroom organization and do not wish to dwell on the need for organization. Many fine books make suggestions for teachers; a few are described here:[8]

> *Organizing the Open Classroom* by Joy Taylor. A small paperback (111 pages) that deals with organizing the classroom. There are excellent suggestions on all aspects of the topic. Included are specific suggestions on making a transition from a traditional program to a more open program. The book is very readable and practical.
> *Informal Teaching in the Open Classroom* by Virgil Howes. This deals with the open classroom model of education but is primarily a practical book on classroom organization. Topics include setting up learning centers, daily planning, keeping records, and moving toward the open format. It is well illustrated with many examples of useful materials. 220 pages.
> *Invitation to Learning 1: The Learning Center Handbook* by Ralph Voight. A practical book for teachers who want to know how to set up learning centers as an aid to individualizing learning and instruction. The values of learning centers are described. Other sections cover how to set up learning centers, "child tested" learning centers, and

8. Complete references for these books are found in the bibliography.

the most frequently asked questions about learning centers. 150 pages.

Arranging the Informal Classroom by Brenda Engel. An 88-page, large-format paperback that contains many practical ideas on the organization of space and materials in the classroom. Emphasis is on materials for different content areas that are easily obtainable and classroom furniture that is easily constructed. The book is liberally illustrated and includes several different floor plans that make sense.

Change for Children: Ideas and Activities for Individualizing Learning by Sandra Kaplan, JoAnn Kaplan, Sheila Madsen, and Bette Taylor. Short on "why" and long on "how." There are valuable ideas on classroom organization, learning centers, planning, recordkeeping, and independent study; a good reference book for ideas. 200 pages.

Moving from a traditional classroom to a more open and activity-oriented classroom is a demanding task. Teachers with large classes may need help. Paid aides are ideal if they are available; usually they are not. The largest and most reliable source of supervisory and instructional help for the teacher are the students themselves, either students within the teacher's class or students from other classrooms. These can be either students who are older than those in the teacher's class, or same-age peers. Teachers are encouraged to organize and make use of student help. The benefits to the student as both teacher and learner have been presented elsewhere (see p. 109).

The Teacher as Assessor of the Child's Thinking

Part of the teacher's role is to figure out what the child already knows and how he reasons in order to be able to suggest activities and ask questions at the right time so that the child can build his own knowledge (Kamii 1973a). "By watching what the child does and says, a teacher well acquainted with the child and with Piaget's theory can gain many insights which are not otherwise possible" (Kamii and DeVries 1973a, p. 7). Teachers familiar with Piagetian observational and interview procedures can find this approach to evaluation no more difficult than that of making judgments about children on the basis of test results. The formal use of Piagetian assessment procedures is presented in chapter 20; examples of assessment tasks can also be found in chapter 20. The teacher who has actively assimilated Piagetian theory, or arrived at the same position intuitively, will constantly be watching and listening to children and interpreting their observations with regard to their significance for children's thinking. From such observations, judgments about what children are capable of learning can be made. Not all evaluation requires formal testing.

What children say and do can tell the teacher much about a child's thinking and intelligence. What children do not do, or cannot do, can tell the teacher much about the child's capabilities as well. The child who avoids simple puzzles and cannot put them together when he does try them may be providing diagnostic information regarding his visual and/or motor skills. Similarly, the child who never engages in any activity requiring balance may indicate a lack of motor-kinesthetic development.

The Teacher as Initiator of Group Activities

In a Piagetian-oriented classroom, one is clearly concerned with the development and learning of the individual child. Many types of group activities are perfectly consistent with Piagetian principles. The normal open interaction of children, discussions between teachers and groups of students, field trips, games, sports activities are all activities that permit children to interact in valuable ways. Kamii and DeVries (1973a) write: "Group games help preoperational children to coordinate different points of view, and to compare outcomes" (p. 5). One of the major characteristics of preoperational thought is egocentrism, the inability to assume the point of view of others. Interaction with other children is the main mechanism through which egocentrism is broken down. In addition, interaction with others is necessary to acquire social-arbitrary knowledge.

Materials

Two types of knowledge are derived from the child's actions on or manipulation of concrete objects: physical knowledge and logical-mathematical knowledge. Physical knowledge is acquired from objects themselves, so the object must be available to the child. Logical-mathematical knowledge is derived from the child's *actions* on objects and does not require specific objects. A child can evolve number concepts from acting on stones, bottle caps, blocks, or any objects that can be manipulated and ordered.

Materials do not have to be elaborate and expensive. For pre-operational children, a set of blocks made of different shapes and sizes from scrap wood is *more* useful than a set of purchased blocks; there is virtue in their irregularity. Metal, glass, and plastic containers, which are usually discarded after their use, have many uses in the classroom. The inquisitive child does not require a factory-made toy to learn, and such purchased materials will not ensure that learning occurs. Teachers should be encouraged to use readily available materials that are easily collected. Few schools have budgets that permit purchasing a wide range of materials. The "science room" in the three-room school I attended could not have been equipped as it was if the materials had to be purchased (see p. 177). In addition, it is important for children to see that learning materials are not limited to manufactured items purchased for a specific purpose.

Development Is Not Automatic

Development does not occur automatically or is it inevitable. A child placed in a sterile environment where experience is limited will not develop cognitively at a normal rate according to Piagetian principles (Hunt 1961). People in "primitive" cultures rarely develop formal operations, though they develop through the Piagetian states up to formal operations in the manner of other children. This is to be expected given their very *concrete* life. What is there in primitive environments to encourage the development of formal operations? What adaptations are demanded by the physical and social environment? According to Kohlberg (Kohlberg and Mayer 1972) only one-half of the American adult population fully develop formal operations and only 5 percent attain the highest stages of moral thought.

In addition, a large quantity of literature has been largely ignored by the child development and Piagetian theoreticians. This is the literature on learning disabilities and on special education. People like Frostig (1970), Kephart (1971), Cruickshank (1966), and Barsch (1967) have been working with children with learning problems. Many of the problems can be viewed primarily as developmental problems. Kephart (1971) has outlined the class of visual, auditory, motor, kinesthetic, spatial, and time problems that *can* occur in "normal" children and has offered a rationale for their remediation. This orientation is primarily developmental (see chapter 18).

Thus development, while spontaneous, is not inevitable. It is becoming increasingly clear from a Piagetian perspective that a teacher (or parent) can be instrumental in encouraging and fostering development. Only a few years ago, research on Piaget's theory was interpreted by most Piagetians to mean not to hold out much hope for altering a child's development (Wadsworth 1971). This is no longer the case. Teachers can control the physical environments in which children have to act. They can control the social environments. They can *monitor* the development of individual children. Teachers and parents are part of the child's social environment upon which the child can act. The physical and social environment the child lives in is the only one to which he can adapt.

Accelerations

The function of the teacher *is not* to accelerate the development of the child or speed up the *rate* of movement from stage to stage. The function of the teacher is to ensure that development within each stage is thoroughly integrated and complete. In response to a question about speeding up the learning of conservation concepts, Piaget replied:

> Is it a good thing to accelerate the learning of these concepts? Acceleration is certainly possible but first we must find out whether it is desirable or harmful. Take the concept of object permanence—the realization that a ball, a rattle or a person continues to exist when it no longer can be seen. A kitten develops this concept at four months, a human baby at nine months; but the kitten stops right there while the baby goes on to learn more advanced concepts. Perhaps a certain slowness is useful in developing the capacity to assimilate new concepts. . . . We know the average speed of development of the children we have studied in our Swiss culture but there is nothing that says that the average speed is the optimum. But blindly to accelerate the learning of conservation concepts could be even worse than doing nothing. (Hall 1970, p. 31)

Little attention has been paid to the consequences of encouraging the child to *adapt* to certain things. What are the consequences of encouraging children to read before they are ready? Can one produce children who are word readers but end up as adults with very little *comprehension* of what they read? Can we produce students of mathematics who perform well on math tests but do not *understand* arithmetic? This is clearly possible, and as I look at many of the college students I have worked with, this is an explanation for the symbol-bound state in which many find themselves. Elkind (1971) writes that ". . . the longer we delay formal instruction, up to certain limits, the greater the period of plasticity and the higher the ultimate level of achievement" (p. 23).

Elkind's statement argues that teachers should not try to get children to learn things before they have acquired the mental structures prerequisite to comprehending those things. Inhelder (1971) states:

> It is very striking to see that when in learning situations we seek to make use of the many factors already observed in spontaneous development (i.e., to reproduce spontaneous development as closely as possible), we obtain proof of the importance of the selection of a learning procedure. It is quite impossible to gain positive results through the use of a learning procedure involving strategies of which the child, at his particular stage, is incapable. There are boundaries, or limits, which cannot be crossed. (p. 211)

Blind attempts at acceleration seem fraught with a variety of potential problems that can make children less efficient in the long run than if children were not encouraged to try to make adaptations before they were optimally "ready" to make that adaptation.

Reading provides a good example. Learning to read is a form of symbolic manipulation. Ideally the symbols as they are "learned" should be meaningful to the child. Children should have appropriate schemata or concepts that are evoked when they read or process written words. The "meaningfulness" of symbols to the individual child is not automatically ensured. Schemata, the source of symbolic meaning, are built up over time and experience. If a child tries to adapt to symbols at too early a point in development, he or she may construct a system for dealing with symbols that is *devoid of meaning* or less meaningful than if the child had not made such attempts until later.

An extreme case is the child who may read words without their conveying any meaning to him. He may say all the words that appear on the page (word-calling) and possibly even be able to pass some written comprehension tests, but he may not be able to use written information in a meaningful way. A detailed example is presented on page 133.

The teacher's function should be primarily as an arranger of the physical and social environments of the classroom and arranger of school experiences outside the immediate classroom. Cognitive development of the child proceeds when the child is active, not when the teacher is active. The environment should be arranged to encourage the activity of the child. Inhelder (1971) writes:

> It is obvious that if you try to teach too much at the pre-school level and thus to accelerate development greatly by making a child acquire knowledge normally gained only after the age of 8 or 9 years, then you will fail. It is clear that this type of education is not ideal. . . . Even if we do not teach directly what will be taught later on, we can pave the way by means of preparation that may later be extremely useful for the child's further development. For example, we are not going to start teaching a 5 or 6 year-old numerical structures since the child has not by then acquired conservation of number. But if we prepare him fairly early on, using exercises in handling materials of classification and ordering, etc., then it is not impossible that we shall have helped the construction of number at a later stage. (p. 212)

Similarities and Differences Between Classrooms

At some point the reader may have noticed a similarity between the practices in some traditional nursery school programs and some of the practices described here. Many traditional nursery schools have been doing for years things that Piaget's theory suggests, although many schools have not always had a clear theoretical rationale. The emphasis on play and concrete experience and the deemphasis on symbolic activities are examples. Kamii and DeVries (1973a) write:

> Generally, the kind of classroom which maximally enables all of these factors [of development] to play a part seems to us to be the traditional child-development classroom. The experience of traditional nursery school teachers in working

closely with young children brought them to the conclusion that good activities are those in which children spontaneously involve themselves intensely, such as socio-dramatic play, art, block building, music, games, stories, and raising animals. However, in our opinion, these educators have not been able to explain in a precise way *why* these activities contribute so ideally to children's socioemotional and cognitive development. Piaget's theory provides a theoretical rationale for the child-development curriculum which has been defended heretofore mostly for intuitive and socioemotional reasons. (p. 4)

In several important ways, the educational suggestions from Piaget's theory go beyond and are different from the traditional child development classroom practices:

1. A Piagetian-oriented program for preoperational children covers a range from preschool through grades two or three. This extends well into the elementary years the attitudes and orientation traditionally found only in some preschool and kindergarten programs. Today it is not uncommon to find kindergartens in which the students receive formal instruction very similar to what first graders received twenty years ago. From a Piagetian point of view, this is a step backward.

2. A Piagetian-oriented program should emphasize "thinking" (Furth 1970a; Kamii and DeVries 1973a, 1973b). The focus is clearly on the necessity of the child's spontaneous activity for developing thinking. Activity on objects is emphasized. The development of verbal skills is encouraged, not because they have a role in cognitive development, but because of language's ultimate utility in communication.

3. The role of the teacher is clearly viewed as different. The Piagetian-oriented teacher is a facilitator of learning and rarely a source of knowledge (except social-arbitrary knowledge) for students.

4. The Piagetian-oriented teacher takes into account the type of knowledge that the child is explaining when she interacts with the child. Social-arbitrary knowledge is responded to with reinforcement and feedback, while physical knowl-

edge and logical-mathematical knowledge are not. In these, the teacher questions reasoning and uses countersuggestions[9] as the main interactive devices.

5. In many cases, traditional reading instruction begins in kindergarten. Traditional instruction in the use of symbols in a Piagetian school is not *universally* encouraged until children are eight or nine years of age.

6. Piagetian principles can be applied to *all* levels of education rather than just the preschool and early primary years, thus allowing for a continuity in rationale for instructional practices throughout the years of schooling. A rationale for traditional classroom practices across grade levels has never been very clear.

The traditional child development classroom typically contains many practices that are consistent with Piagetian principles. This is not a reason for early childhood educators to be complacent about all their practices, unless they are consistent with the principles that have been outlined.

This chapter has presented my interpretation of Piaget's theory with respect to objectives of education, principles of teaching, and other general teaching considerations. In addition, the similarities and differences between a Piagetian and traditional classroom have been outlined. The next several chapters deal with children's acquisition of knowledge and skills in particular content areas: reading, science, mathematics, social studies, and history. The objectives, principles, and considerations described in this chapter underlie the discussions in the following chapters.

9. Countersuggestions are questions or statements that the teacher can use to determine the resistance of children's reasoning to change. See page 226 for a complete description of countersuggestions and how they can be used.

Cognitive Development

14

and Reading

A five, meeting words for the first time and
finding they have intense meaning for him,
at once loves reading.

Ashton-Warner, *Teacher*

Everyone agrees that reading is an important skill. It is essential that an adult read well, and learning to read is obviously necessary for the academic survival of the child. A child who does not learn to read sees the wrath of the educational system descend on his or her head.

Reading has been the subject of seemingly endless educational and psychological research. Yet in schools across the country an alarming number of children read below grade level. Teachers in elementary schools find children who do not like to read. Junior high schools and high schools have students who are completely "turned off" by reading. Standardized reading scores predict school dropout rates as well as any other criterion.

The lack of success met by educators in dealing with the instruction of reading is symptomatic of our poor understanding of how children learn in general, and learn to read in particular. How does one best learn to read?

What Is Reading?

Reading is a process of deriving meaning from written symbols. The words printed on these pages were organized so as to convey a meaning that I wished to express. You perceive the symbols and try to determine what they mean, either while perceiving them or shortly thereafter. For the reader there are functionally related aspects to reading. One aspect is perceiving written symbols, a visual activity; the other is ascribing a meaning to, or comprehending, the collection of symbols.

The study of child development by Piaget, among others, and the relatively new field of psycholinguistics[1] in combination suggest that teachers who use traditional reading methods have been "barking up the wrong tree" for a long time. Traditional methods of reading instruction may do more to interfere with learning to read than they help in accomplishing that task. Indeed, in many cases school reading instruction probably has helped to produce nonreaders.

It has typically been assumed that children must be taught to read; without instruction children will not learn to read, or if they do learn, they will not read well. But Piaget has demonstrated that children, largely on their own, do develop the necessary intellectual skills to master reading.[2]

Children are capable of complex learning. Without instruction, they master much of spoken language between the ages of two and four. They know how to learn. Instruction is not needed for children to learn how to read. What children need are the cognitive and perceptual capabilities to learn to read and a reason to learn to read. Given this motivation and the cognitive and perceptual prerequisites, children will go about solving the problem of reading in the same manner that they solve other problems.[3]

A second assumption underlying most traditional reading instruction is that the identification of individual letters is a prerequisite to word identification. Thus children will not learn to identify words

1. Psycholinguistics lies at the intersection of psychology and linguistics. Linguists are concerned with the nature of language as a system that is available to users. Psychology is concerned with behavior and the conditions under which it is learned. (Smith 1973)

2. These intellectual skills include use of language, symbolic representation (of which language is a form), perceptual skills, and logical operations. Each of these is described in greater detail elsewhere in this book (see Index).

3. I am *not* asserting that reading instruction is a waste of time. Children must (and do) develop the capabilities for reading—and with proper motivation can learn to read on their own. Some children learn to read spontaneously without formal instruction. Regardless, teachers and parents *are essential agents* in developing a desire to read and in facilitating the child's acquisition of reading and writing skills.

unless they learn to identify letters first. Most parents can demonstrate that this notion is incorrect. Many young children recognize some words before they recognize any letters. *Shell, Mobil, Exxon, Stop, Go,* and *Exit* are examples of words children frequently learn quite early.

Obviously, written words consist of letters and letter identification plays a major role in most methods of reading instruction. I have never seen any kindergartens where the alphabet is not taught. It is also true that most children learn to read to some level of competence. Nevertheless, the relationship between one variable (instruction in letter identification) and another variable (learning to read) does not demonstrate that one causes the other any more than we would be willing to conclude that increases in weight (experienced by most growing children) are the cause of learning to read. In any event, psycholinguistic theory and Piagetian theory do not support the proposition that instruction in letter identification is necessary to learn how to identify words and to read. It is even possible that emphasis on letter identification as the initial step in reading instruction may interfere with learning to read. Certainly an adult who identified every letter or even every word while reading would be regarded as a "poor reader." Further, much research has demonstrated that even for moderate rates of reading, identification of every word, much less every letter, is a visual impossibility. Thus, we may have a situation where we teach children a skill (letter identification) that we soon expect them to abandon.

A third assumption that seems to underlie traditional methods of reading instruction is that word identification is a prerequisite for comprehension. Obviously, one must be able to identify words to read, but word identification does not ensure word comprehension. Meaning cannot be obtained from words. Words, as arbitrary symbols, have no meaning of their own. Meaning can only be given to written symbols by the reader. A child who cannot identify the word *baseball* cannot learn the meaning of the word by learning to identify the symbols and calling them "baseball." If a child does not have a concept or cognitive structure that includes the notion of baseball, then meaning and comprehension of the symbols, *baseball,* are not possible.

A fourth assumption of traditional reading methods seems to be that reading is primarily a visual activity. Again, a questionable assumption. The view that psycholinguistics brings to reading is that fluent reading is primarily a process of cognitively anticipating, or predicting, word-sentence meaning using syntax and contextual clues (Smith 1975, 1973, 1971). Little time is spent "looking" at words except to gain information when predictions about word meaning falter or seem incorrect to the reader. According to some psycholinguists, vision is used in reading much less than people believed in the past (Smith 1975).

When they are learning to read, children reverse the relationship between vision and cognition. They spend a lot of time looking and less time predicting meaning than do fluent readers. But one finds in the development of young children acquisition of word meaning before the development of many visual skills required for reading. Most young children can relate the meaning of a story before they can identify any words (oral comprehension).

The previous statement does not mean that teachers should not be concerned with the visual aspects of reading. After all, you cannot read in the dark. An efficient visual system is necessary for efficient reading and for learning to read. The point is that there is more to reading than "looking." Predicting sentence meaning and word meaning is the major task in reading. Visual skills are needed largely to support the process of predicting word meaning.

A last notion that needs consideration is the relationship of the spoken and written aspects of language.[4] A common belief in reading instruction is that the learner has to learn to translate written language into spoken language, as if there are two languages. Spoken language and written language are aspects of one language. If one insists on translating from the written aspects of language to the spoken aspects of language, however, the task is as if there were two separate languages.

Assuming that there is one language, the meaning of the spoken aspects of language and the written aspects of language both reside in the same cognitive structures. The difference is not in the language but in the symbol system used to express (represent) the meaning that both aspects have in common. Spoken language uses sound. Written language uses written letters. Both express the same language. Both derive meaning from the same source. The meaning of written

4. The phrase "aspects of language" belongs to Smith (1975). He uses this phrase to make the point that there is but one language.

aspects of language does not arise out of the spoken aspects of language (Smith 1975).

The importance of reading as a skill and as a desirable educational goal cannot be disputed. Even though reading, according to Piagetian theory, cannot play a major role in the development of "thinking" until the development of formal operations, it can play a role in communication once reading skills are fairly well developed. A concrete operational child who wants to know what television channel "Sesame Street" is on may be able to look at a program guide and figure it out by reading. The same child will not be able to comprehend fairy tales or science fiction until formal operations are acquired.

Reading is an important skill, but it is not a necessary skill for cognitive development to proceed. Children can attain the development of formal operations without learning to read. Development during the preoperational and concrete operational periods depends on the child's actions on objects and events in his environment. These actions are the materials from which mental structures evolve. Reading, writing, or arithmetic skills do not contribute to this process. The child's actions are still central. When formal operations are developed, the child becomes capable of using reading skills in constructing mental structures.

While reading is not a vehicle for change in development (before formal operations), development is a necessary agent in reading. A child's level of conceptual development places certain constraints on whether he or she can learn to read, and how. Kohlberg and Mayer (1972) write:

> It seems obvious that many changes or forms of learning are of value which are not universals in development. As an example, while many unschooled persons have learned to read, the capacity and motivation to read does not define a developmental universal; nonetheless, it seems to us a basic educational objective. We cannot dispose of "growth of reading" as an educational objective . . . simply because it is not a universal in development. But we argue that the ultimate importance of learning to read can only be understood in the context of more universal forms of development. Increased capacity to read is not itself a development, although it is an attainment reflecting various aspects of development. The value or importance of reading lies in its

potential contribution to further cognitive, social, and aesthetic development. (p. 487)

Piaget does not support any established position with respect to reading instruction. He himself has never done any research on reading and, except for stressing motivation, has no opinion.[5] Nevertheless, Piaget's theory clearly suggests several considerations.

Within a Piagetian framework, one can conceptualize the child as approaching the task of learning how to read in the same manner in which the child intuitively approaches any situation. The child confronted with graphic symbols that do not make sense to him tries to assimilate and accommodate these symbols in an effort to make sense out of the written aspects of language. The child tries to "break the code" that words and sentences present. The child tries to organize and integrate into his cognitive structures the reading process. As with other learnings, learning to read is a process of construction. The child internally gives increasingly more accurate structure to the written aspects of representation. External structures (instruction) cannot *replace* the child's active efforts to figure out what the printed aspects of language are all about. Reading instruction is optimized when it is consistent with children's "natural" ways of learning and permits the child actively to organize the reading process.

Comprehension, Meaning, and Reading

Reading should be meaningful to the child. Without meaning, comprehension is by definition impossible. A child who cannot give meaning to words and sentences cannot comprehend the meaning of a written message. The consideration that written materials must be meaningful to the individual child is critical while the child is trying to learn to read. Without meaning and comprehension, the child is not learning to read, and he may be learning *not to read*.

What is "meaning"? For the purposes of this discussion, meaning refers to whether or not a child has cognitive structures that relate

5. Statement made by Piaget on May 6, 1974, at Conference on Special Education, Hingham, Massachusetts.

to particular written words. Cognitive structures are the reservoirs of meaning. If a child has a cognitive structure that he can relate to a written word, then the child can attach meaning to that word.

The written word *county* may have as little meaning to a young child as the word *shikari* has to most adults. Of what value is the reading process if it does not yield comprehension? How does the young child figure out that reading is supposed to produce comprehension if the written materials he tries to read do not have any meaning for him?

Typically, the spoken words that children use are meaningful to them. How does meaning develop? We know from Piaget's work that the sensorimotor child understands things in particular ways and has an awareness of his immediate environment. The child's awareness and understanding (meaning) at this time are largely perceptual and motor. As the infant moves about and actively explores his world, the world becomes increasingly more predictable for him. The child assimilates experience and accommodates in response to it. Cognitive structures (schemata) evolve. The meaning evoked by a spoken or printed word has its source in these cognitive structures. If the child hears the word "cat," and if the child has prior experience with the word, the meaning that will be evoked for the child is extracted from the child's schemata, which define the child's conception of a cat. This is true for all spoken words and for all written words.[6]

Somewhere around the end of the second year of life the typical child starts to use spoken words as symbols. He begins to make sounds that represent objects or events. The spoken words that children acquire and begin to use, by their very nature, have meaning to the child. Indeed, normally the meaning or cognitive structures exist before the child learns the spoken words. Thus, a child's initial spoken vocabulary is likely to be meaningful to him.

I believe it is *crucial* that, very early on in the process of learning to read, children become aware that printed words have meaning and that the written aspects of language can convey meaning in

6. Of course, schemata change. As the child assimilates new experiences, modification of structures takes place. Concepts change. As a result, meaning changes. A child at age three may include in his cat structure: cats, small dogs, raccoons, and beavers. This same child at age five may include just "cats" in this structure. The same child at age ten may include: cats, lions, tigers, etc. The spoken word "cat" would elicit three distinctly different meanings for the same child at different points in his life.

the same way as the spoken aspects of language. How can children come to this awareness? It is not something an adult can explain to a child. The only way a child can understand that written words have meaning is if the printed words and sentences he tries to master *are* meaningful to him. If the child has schemata that he can identify with the written word, the potential for meaning exists. Possibly the most important concern of the reading teacher (and all teachers) should be to ensure that any written language experience is meaningful *to the individual child*. This does not mean selecting an appropriate-grade-level reading book.

Conventional elementary reading books (as well as all textbooks) are written for and manufactured by publishing companies. There is no reason to believe that the words and sentences in these texts will be "meaningful" to the individual child. Indeed, an introduction to reading through such materials, if they are not generally meaningful to the individual child, results in children learning that reading *means nothing*.[7] Children persuaded to try to assimilate printed words that are not meaningful to them have two fates: (1) they can, through memorization, recognize words that have no meaning for them; or (2) they can fail to learn to recognize the words that have no meaning to them. Either way, the process must be a struggle.

Children must discover that written words have meaning in order to be successful. Who knows what words are meaningful to the individual child? The child knows! And the child's everyday vocabulary is a source of language that is meaningful to the child.

The classroom teacher may balk and say that the implications of this are that reading materials should be custom-tailored to each individual child, otherwise the meaningfulness of material cannot be ensured. This is the correct implication. The teacher will probably say that this is impossible for one normal teacher to accomplish. I disagree. I contend that it is possible for a teacher to accomplish this, though aides of some sort are a great help and in some situations essential. The end of chapter 15 discusses an example of how one can ensure that a child's initial reading program is completely meaningful to the individual child without being an impossible task for

7. "Word callers" are frequently children who have "learned" that reading means nothing. Word calling usually develops when children cannot comprehend what they are doing and resort to memorization. This permits them to give the appearance of reading.

the teacher. An important component of such a program must be placing the emphasis on letting *the child learn* to read and removing the emphasis from *the teacher teaching* the child to read. This does not suggest that the teaching role is eliminated, only that the teacher's role changes to one where the teacher facilitates children's learning to read.

Motivation and Reading

Reading requires certain logical and perceptual skills. In addition, there must be some motivation for learning to occur. The *child* must have a reason for learning to read. In terms of Piagetian theory, there should be from the outset of learning to read some *adaptive* value to learning to read *for the child*. Furth (1970) writes: ". . . it is not IQ but motivation that really counts in the business of learning to read" (p. 14).

Why should a child learn to read? Because his parents and teachers say it is a good idea? Educationally, this can be a poor reason, although this is the type of motivation that gets many children to try to read. From a Piagetian point of view, children should learn to read because it has some adaptive value to them. The written aspects of language may be spontaneously viewed by the child as a problem and create a general state of disequilibrium. The child finds the world of written words is not readily assimilated into existing schemes. As with all other problems the child encounters, there is an inclination to resolve it through normal assimilation and accommodation. All children strive to resolve what *they* perceive as problems; this tendency is evident from the beginning of life. Once set in motion, the assimilation mechanism responds to the child's experience and tries to make sense out of that experience. Thus, a child normally will perceive reading as a problem to be solved at some point, and will spontaneously pursue learning to read.

Why do children who learn to speak without any formal instruction struggle with reading instruction over many years, some never developing even limited competency? Several possible Piagetian conceptions help explain these questions. One is that speech, unlike reading, has genuine adaptive value to the child during the period of acquisition. Even a one-word vocabulary ("mama," for example) has instant value to the child. The child acts a bit more effectively with respect to the environment than he or she could through crying or using some other nonspecific sound. In addition, the child typically has readily available models from whom to learn speech sounds. The family surrounding the child typically is an excellent feedback system, constantly providing the child with information about the effectiveness of his speech. From a communication point of view, a little speech is more efficient than no speech. As the child's vocabulary increases, the rewards or payoffs increase accordingly. Thus the child's motivation to learn to speak and to improve speech is very strong.

Learning to read is different because typically the child has no models for reading in the same sense that he has models for speech. Reading is not something the child can model or imitate as easily as speech. Also, the rewards for learning to read a little bit are negligible (unlike the rewards for learning to speak a little bit). The child must learn to read quite a bit before he can find it useful in a communication sense. Furth (1970) suggests that spoken language develops in a concrete reference system while written language does not. The words that children learn to speak are typically more directly related to real objects they are familiar with (more meaningful) than the written words with which children are typically asked to deal.

Children receive very strong social reinforcement from teachers and parents for recognizing letters and words and trying to read. One difficulty with this is that children may come to believe that reading is merely recognizing written words. The child may not discover that reading can be meaningful and can be used in communication.

Motivation, from a Piagetian perspective, is best viewed through the spontaneous interests of the child and the concept of adaptation. The spontaneous interests of the child reveal to the observer what the child cognitively sees as a "problem" for him. The child's cognitive system is pointing out the things into which he would really like to sink his assimilatory teeth. This is a state of high motivation. The general implication of this for reading instruction is to wait for the child to show spontaneous interest in reading before getting the child into reading activities. Furth (1970a) writes: "When the child shows interest in reading he's probably ready to discover the coding rules" (p. 149).

A child should not be pressured into reading before his spontaneous interest is clear. When the child's interest is clear, the teacher or parent, aware of the child's high motivation, can begin to expose the child to reading experiences.[8] It may be that a child wants to learn to read but is not "ready" to learn to read. When essential perceptual and cognitive skills are missing, progress will be very slow even though motivation is very high.

Each child must break the code of reading. He must organize the world of written language so that his internal organization is progressively more consistent with that of others. Only through organizing written language himself can the child develop rules that he can comprehend and which are effective. The child who tries to assimilate an external structure (which many children try to do in an effort to do what is desired of them by adults) runs the risk of resorting to memorizing. Smith (1975) writes: ". . . conscious effort to memorize always interferes with comprehension; the more we try to remember, the less we are likely to understand" (p. 80). Memorization can be inefficient and stifling. John Dewey (1898) wrote: "No one can estimate the benumbing effects of continued drill in reading as mere form" (p. 29).

Will all children spontaneously develop an interest in reading at some point before age nine or ten? In all probability, most children will, if reading is an activity they see their parents, siblings, and peers engaged in, and if they have opportunities to explore letters and words. A major reason why children do not develop an interest in reading, or lose their interest in conventional schools, is the debilitating effect of trying to learn to read and failing to do so. Kindergarten and first-grade children try like crazy to do whatever their teachers suggest. Desire to please the teacher (or parent) may create a form of motivation to try to learn to read. Young children who are not ready cognitively or perceptually to begin formal reading instruction may strain to achieve what they are persuaded is important. In many instances, they will not meet with success. Branded as

8. The first objective of learning to read should be for the *child* to "figure out" that written words have meaning. This is something the child must do essentially on his own. Anything, including reinforcement, that tries *directly to shape* reading behavior can be counterproductive. If a child pays attention to directions, it may act to divert the assimilatory and accommodative functions from where they would go naturally. Piaget's work tells us that the child's system of organization is a better guide for him than an external guide (teacher or parent). Reading (all learning) provides its own reinforcement. This does not mean that the adult should not do anything. What it does mean is that there are dangers in formal instruction. Children can be persuaded that reading is something it should not be. Instruction can lead to confusion for the child and/or inefficient learning.

failures, they will come to view themselves as incapable of learning to read. The consequences of initial failure can be permanently debilitating.[9]

Reading does not become an agent in the child's thinking—an operative instead of a figurative activity—until formal operations are established. Until such time, children have difficulty solving complex verbal problems (although they have no difficulty applying logical thought to *concrete* problems at an earlier age). Furth (1970a) states that propositional thinking does not typically develop until the ages of eleven or twelve, not permitting the joining of reading and thinking until that time. It is during the period of formal operations that reading can play a part in expanding the intellect of the child and can become a challenging operative activity. Prior to the attainment of formal operations, reading is of little direct value to the development of the mind.

Most conventional reading programs are incompatible with Piagetian theory and developmental readiness as discussed in this chapter. Any blanket application of a reading program to children before formal operations begin to emerge (ages 9–10) is to be discouraged. The only clear and certain benefits of many traditional methods go to book publishers, who make money, and to those teachers who do not understand reading and gain some security working with an accepted method. The goal of reading instruction *should not* be to produce a six-year-old child who reads at first-grade level, or a seven-year-old child who reads at second-grade level. The goal is to produce adults who can read fluently, can enjoy reading, and can see some value in it.

All this is not to say that early reading programs cannot be compatible with Piagetian theory. One program described in the next chapter can be instituted in kindergarten and takes into account

9. Children can work out bizarre systems for dealing with reading problems. An example that illustrates the extreme is a fourteen-year-old boy who was brought to a reading clinic. He was able to sight-read and recall perfectly what he read. He could "read" through a college text and recall any passage almost perfectly. The educational therapist working with the boy at one point put a book on the floor and wrote on a piece of paper "pick the book up off the floor." He handed the boy the piece of paper and said, "Read what the paper says and then do what it says." The boy read what was on the paper but did not pick up the book. Further probing indicated that the boy was incapable of translating the written word into action. While he could sight-read with ease, what he read had absolutely no meaning for him. He had never discovered that written words could be used to represent objects.

the individual child: his motivation, his rate and level of development, and his spontaneous interest. It is also a method that can ensure "meaning" and can preclude failure.

Prerequisites to Learning to Read

A term regularly encountered in books on reading instruction is "reading readiness." Frequently, this is taken to mean that if a child passes a reading-readiness test he is ready to learn how to read. Unfortunately, this is too simplistic an approach to a very complex issue.

Reading involves perceptual processes (both visual and auditory), cognitive processes, motivation, and meaning. Educators must understand all these processes in their complex relationship if "learning to read" is to be understood. Piaget (1969a) writes regarding psychology and any efforts to understand learning to read:

> . . . it [psychology] will have to possess detailed information in fields of visual perception, and the perception of words, letters, and sentences; it will have to know exactly what the relations are between total perception and the "perceptual activities," as well as the laws of symbolic function, the relationships between word perception and symbolism, etc. (p. 24)

Reading readiness refers to whether the child has acquired the cognitive competencies and perceptual skills necessary to learn to read: to start attaching meaning to written words and sentences. But readiness to read includes much more. It is probably illusory to talk about reading readiness as if it were a particular state of being.

This section deals with the cognitive skills that a child needs to begin the reading process with some degree of efficiency. The two sections that follow deal with the mechanics of reading (perception) and the issue of motivation and reading. Collectively, these three sections address the reading-readiness question: What capabilities does a child need to start making sense out of the printed aspects of language?

Cognitive Prerequisites

Reading does not directly contribute to cognitive development at the elementary school level; reading is not a necessary skill to have for cognitive development to proceed.[10] On the other hand, certain cognitive capabilities seem to be prerequisites for the efficient acquisition of reading skills.

In written languages with fewer irregularities than English, such as Japanese, children typically learn to read earlier and more easily than American children. Makita (1968) reports that reading disabilities are rare in Japan: less than one percent of all children. In Japanese there are no symbols in mirror opposition (p-q, b-d, M-W); in English, these can result in perceptual or logical difficulties in reading. In Japanese, each letter has only one pronunciation and consonants are always tied to a vowel. Learning to read English requires certain prerequisites of logical thought that are not necessary for learning to read Japanese and other written languages more "regular" than English.[11]

Mastery of written language may be viewed as requiring a mastery of class inclusion operations.[12] Each vowel has a number of different pronunciations. For example, the letter a has a class of regular pronunciations (able) and a class of not regular pronunciations (father,

10. Being a "good student" in almost any subject area demands reading skills. Also, reading is useful in other tasks, such as identifying words on labels. Thus, reading can have some communicative value to young children. Certainly reading, or trying to read, can be a source of pleasure to young children, as they try to re-create, through "reading," stories that have been read to them. But the ongoing process of development of logical thought is not facilitated by reading proficiency. Furth (1970) writes: "Not knowing how to read becomes of no particular consequence for the developing intelligence at earlier ages" (p. 149). A fact that appears to be contradictory to this is that students who are good readers also seem to be good students. This relationship might be construed to mean that reading does affect abilities. The argument against this is that students who are both good readers and good students probably had developed prerequisite skills for both reading and general learning at a rate in advance of most other students their age.

11. The concern for irregularities in the written aspects of the English language prompted Sir James Pitman to devise the Initial Teaching Alphabet (ITA). ITA contains 44 characters, which makes it correspond more closely to the sounds of the English language. ITA was intended to be used only in the beginning stages of reading. When children become fluent reading ITA, they are then transferred to reading traditional materials. From a cognitive point of view, ITA makes considerably more sense than using the standard alphabet when reading instruction is begun in grade 1 or 2. ITA has never attained wide acceptance in the United States and its use is probably on the decline.

12. Class inclusion involves a comprehension of the relationships between classes and subclasses of objects. For example, roses are a subclass of flowers. If one has three marigolds and ten roses, one has more flowers than roses. Children under the ages of seven or eight typically do not understand this basic type of class. An extensive discussion of class inclusion and related concepts is found in Inhelder and Piaget (1969).

*a*ny, sen*a*te). In addition, the "long *a*" sound (as in *a*ble) is written by letter patterns other than *a* (v*ei*n, th*ey*, and br*ea*k). In written English many letters have a variety of possible pronunciations, and a given sound can be written with a number of different letter patterns. The child's ability to comprehend and organize this confusion depends on his having certain capabilities for logical thought. The problem for the child is a logical problem and not a reading problem as such. These necessary capabilities include the same logical skills that are necessary in multiple classification and class inclusion problems. Without these logical operations, the irregularities of written language must remain pure confusion for the young child.

Logical capabilities are developmental in nature. They cannot be taught directly to the child unless he is on the brink of discovering them spontaneously. Without an awareness provided by such cognitive capabilities, the child may attempt to memorize everything. Needless to say, memorization is not an efficient procedure for learning to read.

The preoperational child, up until age seven or so, has difficulty attending to the logical aspects of problems. Conflicts between perception and thought are typically resolved in favor of perception (as in children's responses to conservation problems). The preoperational child tends to attend primarily to limited aspects of objects.

Written words are what Piaget has called signs. *Signs,* unlike symbols, bear no relationship to what they represent. The ability to use signs develops after the ability to use symbols. Obviously, in order to begin to read successfully, children must be able to comprehend the use of signs. (The development of representational capabilities is presented in detail on pages 63–66.)

From a Piagetian perspective, the average child does not have some of the necessary logical operations to deal efficiently with written language before age nine or so, although children vary greatly in this respect. Furth (1970) suggests that not until the fourth grade will children typically have the cognitive abilities necessary to master reading. Thus reading instruction as it is traditionally introduced to children (in kindergarten or first grade) requires logical skills that most children *do not have.*

Mechanics of Reading

The rest of this section deals with what might be called the *mechanics of reading*.[13] The word "mechanics" can be misleading because it can be interpreted to mean "not affected by learning or development." This meaning is not intended. All perceptual activities are under the control of the brain, and the brain is first and foremost a learner.

VISUAL DISCRIMINATION

Written words are composed of spatial elements perceived visually. The child who is attempting to read must be able to discriminate visually in a consistent manner all written symbols that form letters and words. Discrimination of the distinctive features of shapes, letters, and words is *a learned skill*; the child is not born with a ready-developed and functioning capability for such discrimination. Normally one is born with physiologically complete and functioning visual and auditory systems. During the early months of life, however, perceptions are largely undifferentiated. The ability to discriminate visually and auditorily improves gradually with experience. Visually, the child learns to discriminate only those spatial objects he finds in his environment. Thus, a six-year-old child who has had considerable experience with letters may discriminate the letters of the alphabet. On the other hand, a six-year old who has little experience with letters will be less able to distinguish between the letters of the alphabet. Without experience, the child cannot "see" the differences between shapes. The child is in the same situation as an adult who cannot tell the difference between a Ford and a Chevrolet.

Studies have shown that persons blind from birth who at some later time gain vision (e.g., by an operation) are initially unable to differentiate visually between simple shapes (Senden 1960). When presented with blocks in shapes such as circles, squares, and triangles, they are unable to discriminate among them visually, but are able to identify each by touch (tactually).[14] Thus, visual discrimination is learned; it is not a capability with which one is born. The develop-

13. The format of this part of this section and much of the content was adapted from a series of lectures given by Newel Kephart at the Glen Haven Achievement Center, Fort Collins, Colorado, during the summer of 1971.

14. While adults who acquire vision have difficulty using it at first, they typically acquire visual skills much more quickly than children with vision do.

ment of visual skills is part of the brain's adaptation to the physical environment. The visual discriminations the child or adult *can* learn to make are those that are available in his particular environment. The young child will not learn to make discriminations that are not available to him, and there is no guaranty that he will be able to make them just because they are available to him.[15]

A common observation among teachers is that many children of ages six and seven (and some older) have difficulty differentiating between letters that have similar distinctive features, such as p-q (reversals), b-p, d-q, M-W (inversions), and e- e- ω (rotations). Inadequate visual discrimination may make learning to read difficult and can contribute to a reading-disabled child. While a child with such a problem may be called a "reading problem," the child's difficulty may not be with reading per se, but with visual discrimination. The child may have *seeing* difficulty, not reading difficulty.

SPACE

Written language signs are spatial. They occupy space and have distinctive shapes and forms. The young infant begins life without any spatial concepts. For the young infant, knowledge about space is always a second-order sensory datum. That is, one never gets direct information about space through the senses. Knowledge of space is always organized in the brain (Kephart 1971). For the infant, symbols and other shapes cannot be differentiated visually, and in a sense, everything "looks alike."[16] As the child acts on the environment and exercises vision, the capacity for differentiation increases.

Piaget and his co-workers have traced the development of the child's concept of space (Piaget and Inhelder 1967; Piaget, Inhelder, and Szeminska 1964). Briefly outlined, children's spatial concepts as they relate to reading develop in the following way. Before the end of the first year of life, children typically are able to differentiate most objects in their immediate environment (e.g., toys, parents). About this time they develop an awareness that objects they have seen still

15. Most children who have been exposed to letters and words in the home enter kindergarten able to make many of the visual discriminations necessary in reading. This is valuable preparatory experience.

16. According to Kephart (1971) differentiation of space typically begins on the kinesthetic level. Piaget refers to this as the sensorimotor level. It is probably that some kinesthetic-motor learning occurs before birth. This is probably limited by the nature of the preborn's physical situation. Nonetheless, some input into the central nervous system and subsequent organization certainly does occur.

exist even when they are hidden from their view. Prior to this development, objects that were removed from the child's view no longer existed in his awareness. This development Piaget calls *object permanence*—the awareness that objects continue to exist even when they can no longer be seen. Object permanence is an important indicator of the development of children's object concept and spatial concepts.

Around two years of age, the child typically searches for objects that are hidden from his view. (Piaget 1952a, Wadsworth 1971). These searches are systematic. The child sees a desired object hidden in one spot. It is then moved and hidden in another spot without the child being able to see the object but able to see the movement. The child searches for the object in all possible places, first where it was initially hidden, then where it was moved.

The typical four-year-old can visually distinguish open from closed spaces (i.e., 1, 0). A little later, children demonstrate comprehension of topological relationships such as juxtaposition, separation, proximity, and enclosure. If a child is asked to copy several drawings ($\bigodot$, $\bigodot$, $\bigodot$•) where a dot is in different relationships to a closed figure, the child can place the dot properly in relation to the closed figure even though the artistry of the drawing may be lacking. Not for several more years does the typical child become able to distinguish (in his drawings, etc.) lined shapes from curved shapes ($\square$, $\bigcirc$), and the dimensions of length, height, and width ($\square$, $\square$). These properties are Euclidean properties and develop only after topological relationships are acquired.

The child who views space from a topological perspective rather than a Euclidean perspective seems to conceptualize space in a manner different from older children and adults. The child with only topological conceptions sees b, d, p, and q as all being the same. Topologically these shapes are identical and have the same distinctive features. Each is composed of a circle (o) and a line (l). A child without Euclidean conceptions of space may not make all the visual differentiations among letters necessary for reading and writing because of his current level of development with respect to spatial concepts and not for any reason having to do with vision. Thus, the child without Euclidean conceptions may not be able to "see" the differences between shapes that are topologically similar.

Shilkret and Friedland (1974) have suggested that some children with letter reversal, inversion, and rotation problems may be operating on a topological level rather than a Euclidean level. In recent studies (Dunn and Wadsworth 1974; Mar, de la Vega, and Wadsworth 1975) it was found that public school children as old as nine years, who were diagnosed as having reading reversal problems, were unable to make accurate representations (drawings) of simple Euclidean shapes.

AUDITORY DISCRIMINATION

Auditory discrimination is the ability to identify and accurately choose between sounds of different pitch, volume, and pattern. This includes the ability to distinguish one speech sound from another.

Theoretically, a child can learn to read without either vision or hearing. Reading involves giving meaning to written language, and meaning resides in cognitive structures. One does not need to associate written language with spoken language in order to read. Connections need to be made between cognitive structures and written language. Indeed, children who are deaf and mute learn to read, although with less efficiency than children with spoken language. Reading instruction in schools typically requires listening to the teacher. Thus, while auditory skills may not be involved directly in learning to read, the absence of such skills can profoundly affect the benefits of instruction.

The phonics approach to reading instruction assumes that auditory skills are necessary in learning to read. Phonics assumes a direct link between spoken language and written language. It suggests that reading skills cannot be acquired efficiently without solid auditory concepts and phonics skills. This book disagrees with this view and argues the psycholinguistic approach to reading. In part, the psycholinguistic view asserts that *phonics are learned by reading*, and not that reading is learned through phonics (Smith 1975).[17]

17. Smith (1975) asserts that meaning precedes the discrimination of sounds. "There is a special term for the many clusters of different sounds which do not make any difference to meaning in language and are therefore usually heard as the same. Each cluster is called a *phoneme*. A language could have thousands of different phonemes if all the variations in its sounds were employed to represent differences in meaning. . . . English is usually considered to have between forty and forty-five phonemes, depending on how the counting is done and whose dialect is being tabulated. . . .

The point is that listeners do not hear the infinite variety of language *sounds* that speakers produce, but organize all these sounds into a few categories (phonemes) depending on whether they make a difference in the language. We do not hear the sound the speaker produces; we hear the sound as we have categorized it. We hear what we think the speaker his said" (pp. 85–86).

Theoretical issues aside, auditory discrimination is an important supportive skill to the reading process. In the same way that children "learn to see" the differences between letter and word shapes, they "learn to see" the differences between sounds. Auditory discrimination is acquired. Most of what has been said about visual discrimination can also be said about auditory discrimination.

Children normally learn to discriminate among those sounds that are present in their particular auditory environment. The patterns of phonemes vary from language to language and from dialect to dialect within a given language. The Maine farmer and the southern truck driver have difficulty understanding each other not because they speak different languages (though it may seem like it), but because they have learned to produce and discriminate different phonemes. Similarly, the child raised on Black English may have difficulty comprehending the speech of a white middle-class teacher. Auditory discrimination develops to the extent the environment of the child requires it. Clearly, learning to discriminate auditorially is adaptive.

Kephart once told a story about going to a concert with a friend who had been a violinist for many years. At one point in the concert, the friend remarked that "the third violin in the second row is out of tune." Kephart was amazed and asked the violinist whether he could really pick out the third violin in the second row. His friend assured him that he could. This is an example of auditory discrimination developed to a very high degree. Undoubtedly this particular discrimination came about because it was useful (had adaptive value) to the violinist. The average person cannot make this particular auditory discrimination because he does not have to. The world does not ask most of us to "pick out the third violin in the second row." Indeed, many of us would have difficulty picking out the violins.

In reading instruction a child is frequently asked to look at a printed word and recall the associated pronunciation and meaning. Each child has learned to discriminate a set of language sounds (phonemes). If the phonemes the child has learned are the same as those the teacher uses, then auditory discrimination should not be a problem for that child. On the other hand, if a child tries to learn to read in an auditory environment that is substantially different from the auditory environment in which he learned to discriminate, there probably will be interference. The child may have difficulty understanding what the teacher says. The child who moves from Kansas to Boston may, in essence, encounter a new language in the classroom.

This can be true whenever the auditory environment of the child changes. The kindergarten child's transition from home and neighborhood to school can have the same result. This type of auditory confusion is particularly severe among minority-group children who have learned nonstandard English and encounter standard English in the classroom.

The child who has not developed the necessary auditory discriminations to function in a particular classroom may have difficulty benefiting from verbal instruction in all subject areas. The meaning of spoken language will be unclear at times. Yet teachers frequently assume that their students can adequately differentiate and comprehend their speech. This assumption should be questioned by all teachers.[18]

EYE CONTROL

The goal of reading is to rely on the visual system as little as possible. The inefficient reader or the child learning to read relies on the visual system considerably more than the efficient reader. Thus the proper functioning of the visual system is of more importance to these individuals.

When we read, we must move our eyes across a page from left to right. Both eyes must triangulate or converge on the same point, and convergence must be held for extended periods of time. Each eye has three pairs of small muscles that control the movement of the eye. Efficient control of eye muscles is necessary for proper movement and use of the eyes. These are but a few of the things the eyes must be able to do in reading.

The reader must be able to move both eyes in unison from left to right across the printed page. The eyes should not skip letters or elements and should stay on the same line. The eyes must also be capable of making diagonal movements (to see Z, X, etc.), vertical movements, and to move backward as well as forward. Erratic movement can result in loss of visual information and create general visual inefficiency.

The child must be able to triangulate both eyes as he sees *one* image. The eye muscles must focus both eyes on the same point. This must accompany movement across the page and be done for

18. Children with problems in auditory discrimination that are not physical can usually benefit from auditory discrimination training. Physical problems may be correctable. Children who are suspected of having auditory difficulties should have a thorough hearing test.

extended periods of time. If convergence breaks down or is not established, regardless of the reason, the viewer will see two images or one blurred image. This is commonly called double vision:

B̶I̶L̶L̶ C̶A̶N̶ R̶U̶N̶ F̶A̶S̶T̶

I once examined the eye control of a class of third graders, several of whom were reported by their teacher to have reading difficulties. The method of examination used was the Ocular Control subscale of The Purdue Perceptual Motor Survey developed by Roach and Kephart (1966).[19] Two of the children were found to have convergence problems, which affected all close vision tasks (such as reading and desk work). Convergence broke down when they were looking at anything closer than twenty-four inches from their eyes. When they looked at a book held at normal distances they experienced double vision. It was interesting that both children were aware that they were seeing double when they looked at things close to them. They also thought that seeing double was normal. They were quite surprised to find out that most people did not experience double vision.

The eye-control skills described are essential if reading is to be maximally efficient. A lack in any area can make reading progress (or progress in any academic area) difficult. Clearly some children are diagnosed as reading problems when their real problems are perceptual.

The perceptual or "mechanical" skills are acquired skills. They normally begin developing early in life and continue to develop throughout early childhood. The typical seven year old has developed these skills well enough not to have perception problems interfere with reading efforts. But some children have not developed these skills to a necessary level. Upon entering school, all children should be examined to ensure that they have all these skills; if some are missing or inadequate, inefficient learning patterns may result.

19. The Purdue Perceptual Motor Survey is an instrument for assessing five aspects of perceptual and motor development as they are related to learning by Kephart (1971a). The Ocular Control subscale can be used to examine eye movements and convergence. Additional visual tasks teachers can learn to administer are described in Simpson (1968).

Piagetian Theory

15

and Reading Instruction

There are few references to reading in any of Piaget's writings, and he has never researched children's learning to read. Nevertheless, Piaget has done an enormous amount of research and writing on learning and development. It is reasonable to suggest that the principles involved in learning to read would not vary drastically from the principles of learning and development in general. With some certainty, then, one can suggest a reading program consistent with Piagetian principles of development and learning.

1. Learning to read should be viewed as an attempt by the child to learn to predict and anticipate the rules of the written aspects of language. The *child* must *actively* try to figure out what letters and words are all about. As with all other learnings, the *activity* of the child is crucial. The child must organize the world of written symbols as he organized the world of spoken symbols. The organization must be *constructed by the child*. Learning to read should not be a passive process of incorporating an external structure of reading. The emphasis is on the child's active organization and construction—the incorporation through assimilation and accommodation of the written aspects of language into cognitive structures.

2. The content of the child's reading activity should be clearly meaningful to the child. That is, the child should have previously assimilated into structures the objects referred to by the written symbols in the materials he is learning to read.[1] It is essential that chil-

1. To say a child has assimilated into structures an object does not mean the child's concept of the object will be the same as an adult's concept. Concepts evolve. The important thing in learning to read is that the child have a concept of the object written and thus have "meaning" to attach to it, even if it is not yet a fully evolved concept from an adult perspective.

dren "discover" for themselves that written symbols represent things. This is most likely to occur when the child has structures relating to the symbols. It is least likely to occur when the symbols have no meaning to the child. The best source of words certain to be meaningful to the child is the child. The child's spoken vocabulary and spontaneous interest about words ("How do I write airplane?") are reliable sources of words for which the child has concepts. Premade books and written materials cannot ensure this meaningfulness.

3. The child's engagement in reading should be spontaneous. The child will spontaneously begin to predict word meaning when there is some reason for *him* to do so.[2] There should be something adaptive *to the child* in sorting out the reading process. If this is the case, motivation will be high and the child will actively set about trying to read.

4. Children learn to read on their own. The constructive process is an individual one. Each child constructs the reading process at his own rate. In learning to read, no two children can be expected to learn the same thing at the same time. Any type of group instruction in reading that orients the child toward acquiring particular learnings is inconsistent with this principle.[3] Any reading instruction should be completely individualized to account for individual differences.

A reading program consistent with Piagetian principles of learning would be structured (1) to permit the child to break the reading code, (2) to permit the child to deal only with words that are meaningful to him, (3) to permit the child to engage spontaneously the problems of reading, and (4) to be individualized in every sense of the word.

---

2. To say the child must learn to predict word meaning in reading *is not* an argument for teaching the child decoding strategies, as some educators are inclined to do. Just the opposite—the child knows how to break codes. Every child figures out the code for spoken language. With the development of prerequisite cognitive and perceptual skills and some motivation to learn to read, the child will set himself the task of breaking the reading code. Teaching decoding skills or strategies for reading can interfere with the child's inherent wisdom and persuade the child to attend to irrelevant and inefficient processes. Of course, some children ignore their instruction, and on their own learn rapidly enough not to be forced to abandon their own structuring of reading.

3. This does not preclude group reading activities. Children should be free to interact, ask one another questions, read to one another, exchange information, etc. The teacher can read stories to a group. These types of activities do not have to impose a particular learning on a child.

Adaptation

At this point I must stress once again that a child will learn to read if there is some *reason* to learn to read. According to Piaget, the child has an internal "need" to make sense out of his environment. Those events in the child's environment that are not readily assimilated are "problems" to be solved. They result in disequilibration. Events so viewed by the child activate the accommodation mechanism until assimilation is possible. The general direction of solving problems (assimilation to structures) is viewed as adaptive because it makes the child's actions on the environment more efficient. Thus, disequilibrium (a problem), *always* leads to active efforts to assimilate and accommodate. Disequilibrium is Piaget's primary explanatory concept for motivation.

At some point, for every child, written language begins to pose such a problem. The normal response will be spontaneous efforts to reach solutions. Once the assimilation mechanism is activated with respect to reading and the child sees some success (assimilation to structures), the mechanism will continue to be active. Reading is not a single

problem. At some point, something about written language activates the child's interest. Resolution of that particular "something" leads to other specific "problems," and this goes on until the skills of reading are mastered. The child's initial "problem" may be his name, a message on a birthday card, a comic-book story, or a car-repair manual.

Reinforcement and Reading

Most behaviorist psychologists assert that reinforcement is responsible for all learning. Reinforcement is thought to be most effective when it is "immediate," when it follows as closely as possible the behavior being reinforced. In teaching, reinforcement is typically conceptualized as something the teacher can manipulate, such as praise, attention, or material objects (e.g., stars, candy, tokens). According to this view, teacher-controlled rewards can facilitate learning. Reinforcement is seen as *necessary* for learning to occur.

From a Piagetian perspective, reinforcement from the teacher can be a hindrance in the learning process. For the child, learning to read is a form of problem solving, and the child is best left to his own intellectual devices to organize and make sense of written symbols. Anything that interferes with this is potentially counterproductive. If the teacher exclusively reinforces certain reading behaviors ("look carefully at every letter and word; sound every word out"), the young reader can come to believe that what the teacher suggests he attend to is more important that what his cognitive system suggests he attend to. A child may come to believe that reading is not something he has to figure out, but something that can be arrived at by paying attention to a set of rules. In such instances, these forms of reinforcement are inappropriate.

If a child seems to need external reinforcement to learn, something is probably wrong. Smith writes: "If reinforcement of some kind is required, then it should be concluded that whatever the child is expected to do does not make sense to him" (1975, p. 231). The child who needs reinforcement in reading does not comprehend what he is doing. This could be due to many factors including a lack of cognitive or perceptual prerequisites, reading material that is not meaningful to the child, and so forth.

All this does not mean that teachers *should not* praise children. Praise, recognition, attention, and love are things that all people need.

But reinforcement should not be used to *direct* the child's attempts to solve the reading problem; the child's own cognitive intuitions should direct his efforts. We all function best in an environment that is supportive. External reinforcers unquestionably control much of our behavior and have the potential for controlling learning-directed behaviors as well. Traditional educational methods are based on telling people how to do things and reinforcing those who succeed (e.g., with good grades).

Children acquire number-related concepts without external reinforcement. Attempts to teach these concepts to children through reinforcement techniques are futile. Children can memorize verbal rules, too, but the comprehension of concepts can come only when a child actively constructs the concepts. The Piagetian position is that learning is more effective when it arises out of the child's spontaneous interest and is directed by *inner* directives rather than outer directives.

Feedback and Reading

In traditional reinforcement theory, one form of reinforcement is called *feedback*, or *knowledge of results*. This is the notion that information about how well one is learning acts to reinforce that learning. In most instances, feedback is provided by written or verbal questions. The learner answers the questions and finds out which answers are correct, and which are incorrect. Information about the correctness or incorrectness of one's answers is the feedback. As with other types of reinforcement, feedback is thought to be most effective the closer in time it occurs to a response. Immediate feedback is thought to be more effective than delayed feedback. Feedback as it is described above has its source *outside* the learner.

Piaget (1970) asserts that learning provides its own feedback. The child tries to "figure out" what a set of words means, to predict their meaning. After making a prediction about word meaning, the process continues, and the child gets information from his predictions to see if they make any sense. If predictions do not make sense, the child normally is motivated to return to the words, take a closer "look" (get more contextual information or visual information) and re-predict word meaning. If predictions then make sense, the child is motivated to move on in the reading. This is a form of internal feedback that is inherent in the reading process. Smith (1975) says it this way:

> One notable characteristic of good readers is that they correct their own errors when such errors make nonsense of what they are reading. In other words, the feedback such a child requires can only come when he has read a few words more and found that his prediction about meaning is not supported. But such feedback is denied to him if he gets the "immediate" but totally inappropriate feedback that he has read a word wrong. Such feedback may direct the child into poor reading, forcing him to worry more about words than about meaning.
> . . . reading, like many other potentially meaningful school activities, can provide its own feedback. It is not necessary for the teacher or the rest of the class to say "You are wrong" when a child is reading for meaning; it is not even necessary for a child to read aloud for meaning to get feedback. Reading itself will supply feedback. To emphasize the point, activities that are meaningful provide their own feedback; it may not be necessary for the teacher to intervene at all. (p. 235)

Thus, meaningful reading and learning activities will provide their own systematic feedback. There is no need for teacher feedback.[4] This does not mean that there is no role for the teacher. Children have questions that need answers, and they need to be directed in seeking answers. Children need encouragement and support. Children need to have their reading monitored to make sure they are generally getting the "correct" meaning from their activity. But the burden for figuring out reading should rest on the child. The teacher's role is to support the child in his attempts to learn.

4. Children make mistakes, and making mistakes is part of learning not to make mistakes. For example, take the sentence "The boy threw the ball." A child may read it as "The boy threw the *bell*." It is a mistake, but it makes "sense" and in certain context may be a reasonable if incorrect meaning. If the same child reads the sentence "The boy hit the ball with the bat" as "The boy hit the *bell* with the bat" it may make less sense, and the child will probably revise the meaning he attaches to "ball." If the child encounters the first sentence again ("The boy threw the ball"), he is likely to read the word "ball" with the revised meaning. If the same child had initially been corrected on his reading of "ball," it would have encouraged him to look at words rather than attend to meaning.

Facilitating Learning to Read

Piagetians have largely ignored reading, and research on reading has tended to deal with isolated aspects of reading rather than the totality of instruction. Thus there is not a research base for reading instruction that leaves the practitioner free of extensive interpretation.

The purpose of this section is to set forth *one* approach to reading instruction that I feel is consistent with Piagetian principles of learning. The approach described here did not evolve out of an extensive search through all reading methods to find the most Piagetian method but stems from my familiarity with Piagetian concepts.

Sylvia Ashton-Warner (1963) describes an approach to reading instruction with young children that incorporates writing and spelling instruction with reading.[5] Her rhetoric is pleasantly free of educational and psychological jargon, which may lead some overtrained Ph.D.s to conclude that she is not talking about anything important. But, of course, it is not the complexity but the meaning of one's vocabulary that is important.

Ashton-Warner developed her techniques for teaching reading, writing, and spelling from seventeen years of working with Maori children in New Zealand.[6] These children needed a "bridge" from their culture to Western culture. Ashton-Warner's method for introducing reading to these children became that bridge. Her method is very simple and not really new. The "one word" approach she suggests is similar to Egyptian hieroglyphics and the approach Tolstoy used in his school.

Ashton-Warner uses no premade or manufactured reading materials. She begins when children are about kindergarten age. Each morning she sits down individually with each child in the multi-grade-level class. She has some large, durable paper cards and a dark crayon.

5. Ashton-Warner's methods can be classified as one of the *language-experience* approaches to reading. Language-experience approaches to reading are based on the assumption that learning to read must be based on the experience of the learner to be effective. Reading becomes an extension of the experiences the child already has had. DeMao (1976) states that the language-experience approach to reading is the method most consistent with Piagetian theory. My endorsement of Ashton-Warner's methods for teaching reading is not a general endorsement for all language-experience approaches and all their practices, though as a general statement, language-experience methods of instruction are viewed as more consistent with Piagetian concepts than other methods of instruction.

6. Maoris are natives of New Zealand and constitute a minority group in that country.

She asks what word or words the child would like her to write that day. The child gives her a word, which Ashton-Warner writes in big, bold letters. The card is given to the child. Children may talk about the words, trace them with a finger, or even, usually later on, copy them on paper. The child's word card for the day goes into his "deck" of such cards. Later in each day the teacher and the child go through the deck of cards for a few minutes. The child is asked to identify each word by sight. If the child recognizes the word, it remains in the deck. If the child does not recognize the word, it is removed from the child's deck as it is not a "one look" word. Only the words that the child can remember remain in the child's deck.

Over time, each child develops a set of words that he or she recognizes. Children's decks grow at different rates and with many different words. The children are encouraged to trace their words and write them. Eventually, when children have acquired enough words, the same procedure is carried out with "stories" of a few words. Thus children move from single words to many words and eventually into more formal sentences. Reading, writing, and spelling are all integrated.

Ashton-Warner refers to her approach as "organic reading." The emphasis is on using words that come from the individual child or the "key vocabulary." The key vocabulary is a set of emotion-laden or "power" words that Ashton-Warner says are common to any child, such as *mummy, daddy, kiss, frightened,* and *ghost*. The words children come to deal with in reading must be meaningful to the child. Ashton-Warner writes: "First words must mean something to a child. First words must have intense meaning for a child. They must be part of his being" (1963, p. 40).

Ashton-Warner (1963) insists that the words children learn should be, for each child, words charged with emotion. These words are learned quickly (one-look words), while children spend endless amounts of time learning words that are not emotional words. Emotional words are meaningful words. For example,

> Puki, who comes from a clever family, and whose mother and father fight bitterly and physically . . . after learning two words in six months burst into reading on Daddy, Mummy, Puki, fight, yell, hit, crack, frightened, broom. (p. 39)

Emotional words are meaningful words. Ashton-Warner's course of letting children select their own "reading material" virtually ensures that the words they learn will have meaning to them. This in turn ensures, as much as one can, that children will grasp the fundamental notion that written language means something.

That written language has meaning is an understanding that each individual must discover for himself. Teachers cannot take it for granted that all kindergarten, first-grade, and second-grade children have developed this understanding. The discovery that written language has meaning is not potentially possible unless the child has concepts of the referents for the written language he encounters. Can you imagine, as an adult, trying to learn to read and write a foreign language that uses written symbols entirely different from English (e.g., Chinese, Korean) with no idea what the "words" mean? One could learn to word-call: say the proper sounds for the proper symbols. But would you have learned to read?

Ashton-Warner does not use any manufactured reading materials in the first years of acquiring reading skills. The content of reading for each child comes from that child. Initially children deal just with their own words. Inevitably, they share their words, sentences, and stories with other children. Reading and reading-related matters thus are not carried out in isolation. There is continuous sharing and interaction of ideas and materials, as there is in any "open" educational setting. Says Ashton-Warner:

> It may sound hard, but it's the easiest way I have ever begun reading. There's no driving to it. I don't teach at all. There is no work to put up on the blackboard, no charts to make and no force to marshall the children into a teachable and attentive group. The teaching is done among themselves, mixed up with all the natural concomitants of relationship. (1963, p. 45)

Reading, writing, and spelling are all part of the same process for Ashton-Warner and her children. She has put these "subjects" back together where they belong. Five-year-olds begin by merely copying their own "key words."

> The creative writing of fives begins with their attempt to write their own key words, and since they have found out that these scrawley shapes mean something, they know what they are writing about more than I do.
> From here they join in with the stream of autobiographical writing that they do in the morning output period, and a

few days of this is enough to show any writer or teacher where style begins. Fives have a most distinctive style. And they write these sentences of the same pattern with its varied content so often that they learn automatically the repeated words and consolidate this style. With scarcely any teaching from me, which transfers the whole question of spelling, word study and composition into the vent of creativity. . . .

After a while, as their capacity increases, they write two sentences about themselves and their lives, then three, until six-year-olds are writing half a page and seven-year-olds a page or more a day. But I don't call it teaching; I call it creativity since it all comes from them and nothing from me, and because the spelling and composition are no longer separate subjects to be taught but emerge naturally as another medium.

The drama of these writings could never be captured in a bought book. It could never be achieved in the most faithfully prepared reading books. (pp. 46, 49)

The uniqueness and apparent lack of teacher control (really a lack of teacher domination) of Ashton-Warner's methods may suggest laxity and indulgence to some. If it does, the reader has missed the whole point. Ashton-Warner (the teacher) is in complete control of

what goes on in her classroom. With her warmth and understanding of children, there is still order within an open atmosphere. Children's work is carefully examined. While her methods are not conventional, her goals are very conventional: to develop emotionally healthy children who are skilled readers and writers.

Ashton-Warner's Methods and Piagetian Theory

I have tried to present enough of Ashton-Warner's method to suggest to the reader that there *are* reading methods that are practical and consistent with developmental concepts, but it would be a mistake to judge her methods on the outline presented here. This section attempts to clarify the similarities between Ashton-Warner's conceptions and those of Piaget.

1. Ashton-Warner's method ensures that the content (words) a child tries to learn is meaningful to the child. This is not the case with mass-produced basal readers. The teacher can only hope that such materials are in part meaningful to each child. Ashton-Warner's method maximizes the probability that children will grasp the crucial notion that written language represents things.
2. Ashton-Warner's method elicits the "spontaneous" interest of the child. The words that a child selects are his own at the moment. Motivation is generally enhanced. Motivation relies less on social pressures than traditional reading approaches ("Learn to read because I [the teacher or parent] say it is good for you"). The child is encouraged but not forced to get into reading.
3. Ashton-Warner's method is individualized. Each child works with materials that he or she has created. Each child advances at his or her own rate. There are no pressures on children for a standard level of performance in reading, writing, and spelling. Implicit in the method is the notion that children are at different levels of readiness and that not all children will be equally motivated and equally capable at the same time.
4. While not specifically a Piagetian consideration, Ashton-Warner's methods generally preclude any negative effect, as much as a method can. The child *cannot fail* as such,

and the method avoids negative reinforcement. On the contrary, the method lends itself to the child's development of positive attitudes about himself, about reading, and about learning.

From a Piagetian perspective, a most important aspect of Ashton-Warner's method is that, within a structured methodology, it permits each child to figure out what reading is all about. Each child "breaks the code" of reading and constructs structures for the rules of written language. There is little room for the child to attempt to internalize an external structure of reading, such as there is in most traditional methods. *Memorization* of reading rules is minimized. In effect, the child is not taught how to read, the *child learns* how to read.

Ashton-Warner introduces children to her method at an early age: five years. Piagetians consistently suggest that formal reading instruction typically begins too early and should not begin before the ages of seven to nine for most children (Furth 1970a). I agree with this where traditional teaching techniques are used, that is, if a reading method is used in which essentially the teacher *tells the child how to read* and relies on materials that are only meaningful by chance. Reading instruction of this type can be postponed until age eight or nine for most children.[7] Introduced too early, such methods can have serious debilitating effects on many children. In contrast, Ashton-Warner's method does not place any *performance* demands on children. Children move at their own rate, use only meaningful materials, and are encouraged to make sense out of what they are doing rather than incorporate an external structure of reading.

Children know how to make sense out of things. But they have difficulty making sense out of things when they are instructed, in effect, not to be concerned with making sense out of things. Children seven years of age and younger typically do not have all the necessary cognitive and perceptual prerequisites to benefit from most forms of traditional reading instruction. The advantage in Ashton-Warner's method is that children can operate within a program that recognizes where each child is. In essence, a child has initially to "know" a lot

7. The average eight- or nine-year-old will be better equipped than the average six- or seven-year-old to deal with formal instruction. Children are going to try to "figure out" what reading is all about even under formal instructional situations. The older child is more likely to succeed and learn to organize the reading process "in spite of instruction" than the younger child.

more to learn to read under traditional methods than under Ashton-Warner's method.

Children remain in Ashton-Warner's program for at least two years before they are ready to move into traditional readers. This means that most children do not get into more traditional reading materials until at least the age of seven. In my opinion one could use an approach to reading such as Ashton-Warner's in first and second grades and still have children advance into traditional reading materials by age eight or so.

The important point in reading instruction is not how well a child performs on standardized reading tests (usually tests of recall, not reading ability) at the end of grades 1, 2, and 3, but how well the child can read as a teen-ager and adult, and how he or she feels about reading and learning. Children who learn to read through a method such as Ashton-Warner's may not perform as well on standardized reading tests at the end of first and second grades as children who have been taught by traditional methods. This does not mean that the former group reads less well than traditionally taught children. It means they have learned different skills. Only the insecure educator or narrow-minded statistician would conclude that reading is no more than scores on standardized paper-and-pencil tests.

Additional Reading Practices

Ashton-Warner's method of reading instruction is consistent with Piagetian conceptions of how children learn. In general, the other language-experience approaches are also consistent with Piagetian theory. The remainder of this section deals with other practices that can fit into reading programs. None of these practices are as complete as Ashton-Warner's reading program, but they are consistent with Piagetian theory. They illustrate for the reader the range and types of activities that can legitimately be part of a school reading program.

Something Other Than Books

There are lots of things to read besides books; the world is full of written words. For young children (and adults), many of the more meaningful words are not found in books. A traveler in a foreign country with no knowledge of the language of that country is not going to try to read a book in that language. But he does try to read a lot of things while "navigating" on unfamiliar ground. He tries to figure out road signs, store signs, writing on packages, menus, and so forth. Generally, for the learner, there are more meaningful places to start reading than regular books.

A reasonable approach to reading, particularly with young children and with adolescents who are having difficulty with reading, is to engage them in learning to read signs and other written words found in the classroom or neighborhood. Words found on street signs, inside buildings, or on billboards are likely to be meaningful to children. Many school systems have instituted programs of this type. Sol Gordon at Syracuse University has developed a whole program for junior high nonreaders that uses street signs as the primary content for reading.

In the classroom, teachers can replace many spoken instructions and directions with "signs." Directions for the use of materials can be written out as signs and placed in learning centers. Lists of things to do and suggestions of activities can be put on signs. Much of the communication that is usually carried out through spoken words can be carried out by signs (see Lee and Allen 1963, Hall 1970).

Shore and Massimo (1966) described a program for rehabilitating delinquent adolescents that involved learning to read as part of the therapy. Nonreading delinquents were placed in jobs where the employer had agreed to take part in the therapy process. The adolescents were permitted to become comfortable in the job and overcome any feelings of threat from others. Typically, the adolescents had become completely alienated from the school system and saw themselves as failures. Once the adolescent became accustomed to his new job and to the people he had to work with, calculated reading demands were carefully introduced. A boy working in an auto repair shop was asked by one of his fellow workers to get "five quarts of twenty-weight high-detergent oil." A request of this type required some reading. The boy was faced with a crucial reading problem. He had to figure out which oil was the correct oil. Once he had found the oil, even if it required the help of others, he was typically highly motivated to remember how to identify that particular oil. Shore and Massimo state that the crucial point in this therapy is when the initial reading demands are made. If the adolescent's feeling of being threatened has been diminished sufficiently, he does not try to avoid the "reading problem" and tries to learn what is required. Simple reading tasks of this nature are introduced more frequently if there is success. A therapist oversees the program. At some point the adolescent typically comes to realize that he is doing some "reading" and is capable of learning to read; an important psychological barrier has been overcome. The adolescent's expectations of what he is capable of doing have changed.

An obvious course to pursue in reading instruction is to have children read things they are interested in. Children are much more inclined to try to "figure out" things when they have an interest in them. Interest generally indicates meaningful materials. I know one boy who experienced great reading difficulty throughout elementary school. He was almost completely a word-caller. At age sixteen he bought an old, dilapidated pickup truck that did not run. Lacking the skills to perform major automotive surgery, he purchased an auto-repair manual that covered trucks. It was a long struggle. Truck parts lay scattered all over his parents' garage for the better part of six months. Eventually the truck was put back together and ran, very roughly at first. The youth had spent innumerable hours looking at his manual and trying to figure out how to do things. He learned to read the manual. Indeed, *everything* useful the boy knew about reading thereafter had been acquired in his garage with the auto-repair manual. I am absolutely convinced that he first discovered that written words have meaning during his efforts to figure out how to repair his truck. Today he reads well and even enjoys reading.

In this case, motivation was a primary factor. Strong interest in what he was doing motivated the boy to overcome years of bad reading instruction, failing grades, and a poor self-concept. This was an extreme case, but many adolescents like this one can be found in any high school. Interest is a great motivator at any age. If one is going to teach reading, an appeal to the individual student's interest is only reasonable. The necessary content for reading is words and sentences. One can learn to read stories about race cars as well as standard reading materials. Heightened motivation to learn to read is more important than the content of the reading material.

Eleanor Duckworth (1973) describes an approach to spelling developed by three first-grade teachers in a school in Montreal, where French is spoken. While the emphasis is on spelling and writing, the carryover to reading is obvious. The approach is slightly more appropriate to French than to English, but aspects of this approach could certainly be adapted to English.

The reading program starts with writing—not handwriting, but writing to say something. A child suggests a word he wants to be able to write. Then the class together breaks it up into component sounds. Cousin, for example (I shall use the French version of the word) is broken down into Koozin. The teacher then presents all possible ways of spelling each of the sounds: c or k; ou or oo; s or z; EIN, AIN, or IN. The children procede to produce all possible ways of spelling the word. "Yes, that's one way: Any more?" The more ways they get the better. They write them on the board, and if a child has a way that is not yet on the board, he adds it to what is there. When all possible ways have been produced, the teacher tells them which is the way that is conventionally used.

Note that instead of feeling stupid for creating an unconventional spelling, the children feel clever. And they know that whoever may be dumb, in making spelling such an arbitrary exercise, it's not they! They also know, just as well as any other child, that there is only one correct way to write any given word, and this way is underlined in their notebooks, among all the possible ways. Moreover, as time goes on they develop greater and greater ability to guess, for themselves, which is likely to be the conventional way.

At the same time, the emphasis in general is on their saying what they have to say through writing. By the time they have built up a collection of how to write all the sounds, they can write anything adequately enough for someone to be able to read what they have said. The spelling may be unusual but is always readable, and the writing is accepted for what it says. . . . The first requirement of spelling is that writing be readable afterward, and the writing of these children always is. Then, to make it easier for readers, a single conventional spelling is learned. . . . The point is that these children really learn to spell, withal. They learn to spell not by avoiding wrong spellings in a panic, but by actively seeking out every possible wrong spelling! When the children start reading, they notice the spelling of new words that they read. Since they realize that any number of other spellings might have done the communications job just as well, they sit up and take notice. "Gee, is that how you spell that?" . . . They are, in budding form, aware . . . that the words themselves aren't the substance; they are one possible way of trying to express the substance, and they needn't be taken at face value. (pp. 151–53)

This approach to spelling and writing helps children develop an understanding of the irregularities in written language. It also helps establish the understanding that written symbols are arbitrary. These qualities make the program described by Duckworth an excellent activity for children prior to formal reading instruction.

Another way to conceptualize the issue of motivation for reading is to think of ways to structure situations so that learning to read has *real* adaptive value. Classroom situations can be structured in which reading and writing are the only acceptable means of communication. This might be carried out in any number of ways. An hour or half hour a day could be established as "no talking" time in a class. The students and the teacher would communicate only through reading and writing during this time. Or certain types of activities could be requested only through writing. The point is to establish genuine value to reading and writing. Suggestions such as these, carried out in a positive way, can generate a situation where reading and writing are adaptive. Of course, this suggestion would not be viable unless the children had some reading and writing skills.

A last idea is to have children voluntarily produce their own reading materials in as many different types of situations as possible. Writing class "newspapers," short plays, and letters to sick classmates are some examples. All forms of writing help make written language meaningful to the individual child.[8] For six-year-olds, the teacher or an older student may have to do the initial writing, but as Ashton-Warner points out, the words that flow from children are more meaningful to them than ready-made words.

8. One valuable practice is tracing. Ashton-Warner encourages children to trace with their fingers the large words she has written on their cards. Many five- and six-year-olds are going to have difficulty forming letters, which requires fine motor control, or kinesthetic awareness; knowledge about what the muscles are doing. This can be effectively developed through tracing.

The Development and Learning

16

of Mathematics and Science Concepts

I hear, and I forget
I see, and I remember
I do, and I understand

Chinese Proverb

From a Piagetian point of view, most traditional mathematics and science instruction is inappropriate. As with all knowledge, childrens' mathematical and science knowledge is built up from their actions on objects. Methods that limit the child to learning from representations of knowledge rather than from the sources of knowledge limit the nature of concepts children acquire.

The Development and Learning of Mathematical Concepts

As described in chapter 9, the structures underlying mathematical reasoning are similar to the structures of logic. Piaget (1969a) writes:

> . . . mathematics constitutes a direct extension of logic itself, so much so that it is actually impossible to draw a firm line of demarcation between the two fields . . . so that it is difficult to conceive how students who are well endowed when it comes to the elaboration and utilization of the spontaneous logico-mathematical structures of intelligence can find themselves handicapped in the comprehension of a branch of teaching [mathematics] that bears exclusively upon what is derived from such structures. (p. 44)

Piaget is saying that the development of the logic and reasoning of mathematics is indistinguishable from the development of intelligence or logical reasoning in general. This suggests that as cognitive development proceeds, so too does the ability to develop mathematical concepts. But such is not always the case. Many children do not develop adequate mathematical concepts.

Dienes (1971) writes:

> . . . the majority of children never succeed in understanding the *real meaning* of mathematical concepts. At best they become deft technicians in the art of manipulating complicated sets of symbols, at worst they are baffled by the impossible situations into which the present mathematical requirements in schools tend to place them. (p. 1; italics added)

If Piaget is correct, the failure of students to develop comprehension of mathematics does not imply any lack of intelligence or ability to learn the concepts but results from the type of instruction to which children are exposed in schools. Children clearly have the ability to comprehend mathematics, but many of them do not do so.

Mathematics instruction even in the early elementary grades typically takes the form of oral and written (symbolic) presentations of concepts and procedures for computation of answers to problems. They are not based on "active" methods that permit the child to build mathematical concepts in *the only way he can acquire them*. Piaget (1973) writes:

> It is here [in teaching mathematics] that teachers encounter the most difficulty, and where in spite of all the qualities of their teaching, the nonactive methods that they are habitually compelled to use result in difficulties that are generally well known. It is notorious that in classes that are normal in other respects only a fraction of pupils absorb mathematics, and this fraction does not necessarily encompass all the more gifted in other branches. Sometimes the comprehension of elementary mathematics comes to be considered as a sign of special aptitude. The presence or absence of this mathematical "gift" is then considered to explain success and failure, whereas it could be asked whether they are not perhaps attributable to the classical method of teaching itself. Mathematics is nothing but logic, extending general logic in the most natural way, and constituting the logic of all the

more evolved forms of scientific thought. A failure in mathematics thus would signify a lack in the very mechanisms of the development of the intellect. Before making such a serious judgement on the probable majority of students and on the large majority of former students in our schools . . . it must be asked if the responsibility does not lie in the methodology [of teaching]. (pp. 95–96)

One can observe and examine how children develop mathematical concepts spontaneously. Piaget (1973) writes:

A series of ascertainments important to teaching can be made by studying psychologically the development of the spontaneous mathematical intelligence of the young child and adolescent. In the first place, when the problems are posed without the child's perceiving that it is a question of mathematics . . . they are solved by the students with their general intelligence and not by any special individual aptitudes. In particular, students are frequently found who, though mediocre in lessons of arithmetic, prove to have a comprehensive or even inventive spirit when the problems are posed in relation to any activity that interests [has meaning to] them. They remain passive and often even blocked in the school situation that consists of resolving problems in the abstract (that is, without relation to any actual need). About all, they remain convinced of their inadequacy and give up beforehand, inwardly considering themselves defeated. . . . Every normal student is capable of good mathematical reasoning if attention is directed to activities of his interest. . . . In most *mathematical* lessons the whole difference lies in the fact that the student is asked to accept from outside an already entirely organized intellectual discipline which he may or may not understand. (pp. 97–99)

Traditional teaching practices impose the formal, external structure of mathematics on children rather than permitting children to build up the meaning of mathematics out of their activity. In addition, mathematics instruction, from the beginning, typically takes place in the abstract. Children are introduced to *signs* (numbers) at the outset and encouraged to deal with abstractions *they have not abstracted*. School instruction at the preschool and early elementary years rarely permits the active construction of mathematical concepts (logical-mathematical knowledge) from actions on objects. Instruction centers on the manipulation of abstract numbers and is frequently empty of meaning *to the child.*

It is common practice in the early grades to give young children "worksheets" like those that require matching pictures of groups of objects to numbers. Even these types of activities, which may look to some like "concrete" experiences, are essentially abstract. Matching pictures and numbers is matching symbols and signs, both of which are abstract forms of representation. Such activities in the absence of comprehension of number and/or before children comprehend the use of symbols or signs is likely to be completely meaningless to the child. The meaning and comprehension of mathematical signs and symbols cannot be built up from the manipulation of signs and symbols.

The negative effects of a form of instruction that is largely abstract are not just in the learning of mathematics, but occur in *all* content areas. But the effects may be harder for the child to overcome in mathematics than in other areas. True comprehension of mathematics may be permanently blocked, as it frequently seems to be in children. Children can become persuaded (as their teachers and parents frequently have been) that mathematics is nothing more or less than the manipulation of signs (computation). Since many parents and teachers do not themselves understand mathematics, it is no wonder that true comprehension is not a goal that children are usually seen as capable of achieving.

All Piaget's work suggests that the "meaning" of mathematical concepts should be acquired before the child tries to deal with the signs used to represent those concepts. Piaget (1973) writes:

> . . . one of the basic causes of passivity in children . . . is due to the insufficient dissociation that is maintained between questions of logic and numerical or metrical questions. In a problem of velocities, for example, the student must simultaneously manage reasoning concerning the distances covered and lengths utilized, and carry out a computation with numbers that express these quantities. While the logical structure meaning of the problem is not solidly assured, the numerical considerations remain without meaning, and on the contrary, they obscure the system of relationships between each element. Since the problem rests precisely on these numbers, the child often tries all sorts of computations by gropingly applying various procedures that he knows,

which has the effect of blocking his reasoning powers. . . . When . . . the two types of factors are dissociated, one can advance more surely. . . . Freed from the necessity of computation, the child enjoys building actively all the logical relationships in play and arrives thus at the elaboration of procedural operations that are flexible and precise, often even subtle. Once these mechanisms are accomplished, it becomes possible to introduce the numerical data [signs] which take on a totally new significance from what they would have had if presented at the beginning. It seems that a lot of time is lost in this way, but in the end much is gained, and, above all, an enrichment of personal activity is achieved. (pp. 99–101)

And Piaget again:

. . . mathematics is taught as if it were only a question of truths that are accessible exclusively through an abstract language [symbols], and even of that special language which consists of working symbols. Mathematics is, first of all and most importantly, actions exercised on things, and the operations themselves are more actions. . . . Without a doubt it is necessary to reach abstraction, and this is even natural in all areas *during the mental development of adolescence,* but abstraction is only a sort of trickery and deflection of the mind if it doesn't constitute the crowning stage of a series of previously uninterrupted concrete actions. The true cause of failures in formal education is therefore essentially the fact that one begins with language (accompanied by drawings, fictional or narrated actions, etc.) instead of *beginning* with real and material action. (pp. 103–4; italics added)

According to Piaget, the general principles that apply to cognitive development in general apply to the development of mathematical concepts as well. Before children can comprehend the *representation* of mathematical operations, they must comprehend the operations themselves. To put it another way, before children can deal meaningfully with numbers and computation, they must comprehend what the numbers and computations mean. Otherwise, children are reduced to memorizing what to them is a meaningless content. The comprehension and meaning of operations, as has been stressed repeatedly, is a result of the individual child's *construction* of knowledge. This knowledge, in this case logical-mathematical knowledge, is abstracted by the child from the child's actions on objects. According to Piagetian principles, there is *no other way* that comprehension and meaning can be derived. The child must construct it out of his experiences.

Children develop the concepts of length and the notion of constant units of measurement by acting on objects. The understanding of conservation of length, that the length of an object does not change when the object is moved, is only established after repeated active experience with lengths, displacements of objects, and other developmentally prerequisite knowledge (like conservation of number) are developed. There are no shortcuts around the need for active experience. Any apparent understanding that arises without such experience is probably incomplete as well as deceptive and does not reflect genuine knowledge.

Representation of mathematical concepts and operations, like the use of written numbers and written computation, can take place meaningfully only after children have come to understand what *signs* are. As with letters and words, numbers are abstract, arbitrary signs. The child must comprehend this before the use of numbers can be meaningful. The child who counts to a hundred, who carries out physical one-to-one correspondence, and who can tell you that nine is more than eight may or may not comprehend seriation and the number concepts that appear to be present.[1] It is incumbent upon kindergarten, first-grade, and second-grade teachers (and teachers at higher grade levels) to make sure that children understand signs *before* they are introduced to them in mathematical instruction. By no means is it reasonable to assume that first- or second-grade children have developed a comprehension of arbitrary signifiers such as numbers and letters.

Problems in learning to read and learning mathematics are similar in that both require the comprehension of arbitrary signs. The learning of mathematics presents some special difficulties. If children initially learn to read using representations of words that are meaningful to them, the probability that they will come to comprehend that signs are representations of real things is relatively high. With

1. Counting can be a memorized verbal sequence. Like a song, it can be empty of meaning, though verbally accurate. The child who can only solve $8 + 2$ by counting from zero to eight and then two more to ten, displays a dependence on the memorized verbal sequence and indicates a lack of comprehension of numbers.

number, although the structures of mathematics and the structures of logical thought *are the same structures*, the meaning must be brought into the conscious mind from their existence as structures of actions or operations. Piaget (1969a) writes:

> . . . if what we have . . . posited as to the relationship of this form of knowledge mathematics with the fundamental operational structures of thought is true, then . . . it is related entirely, not to mathematics as such, but to the way in which mathematics is taught. In fact, the operational structures of the intelligence, although they are of a logico-mathematical nature, are not present in children's or adults' minds as conscious structures: they are structures of actions or operations, which certainly direct the child's reasoning but do not constitute an object of reflection on its part (just as one can sing a tune without being obliged to construct a theory of singing and even without being able to read music). The teaching of mathematics, on the other hand, specifically requires the student to reflect consciously on these structures, though it does so by means of a technical language comprising a very particular form of symbolism, and demanding a greater or lesser degree of abstraction. (pp. 44–45)

Thus, according to Piaget's formulation, most people develop the structures required for mathematical thought because they are the same structures necessary for thought in general. The problem would seem to lie largely with teaching methods that rely on the use of the language of mathematics, the symbolism that confuses and makes difficult the application of thought. In a sense, the child's comprehension of signs (numbers) as arbitrary signifiers and the comprehension of what is signified must be more complete in the "reading" of mathematics than in the reading of ones own spoken language.

While the general structures of mathematics are abstract, these same structures come to be represented in the mind of the child in the form of concrete manipulation. That is, the mathematical (and logical) structures that evolve are a product of the child's "actions" on objects. The child manipulates, explores, and comes to know objects and the relationships between objects, some of which we call mathematical. The mode of development of mathematical structures is the child's "activity."

The importance of concrete "activity" by the child in developing abstract (mathematical) thinking may sound like a contradiction, but it is not. This point seems to be at the crux of the issue and is frequently misunderstood. Piaget (1969a) clarifies:

> The mathematician who is unaccustomed to psychology . . . may suspect any physical exercise "activity" of being an obstacle to abstractions, whereas the psychologist is used to making a very careful distinction between abstraction based on objects (the source of experiment in the physical field and foreign to mathematics) and abstraction based on actions, the source of mathematical deductions and abstraction. We must avoid believing, in fact, that a sound training in abstraction and deduction presupposes a premature use of technical language and technical symbolism alone, since mathematical abstraction is of an operational nature and develops genetically through a series of unbroken stages that have their first origin in very concrete operations. . . . Nor must we confuse the concrete either with physical experiment, which derives its knowledge from objects and not from the actions of the child itself, or with intuitive presentations . . . since these operations are derived from actions, not from perceptual or visually recalled configurations. (p. 47)

How to Teach Mathematics to Children

Piaget provides some principles of how children develop and acquire mathematical concepts. He does not state specifically how instruction should proceed, although his theory makes some clear suggestions for mathematical instruction. First, mathematical concepts can be constructed by the child *only* out of his spontaneous actions on objects. Second, the child can comprehend the representation of mathematical processes only *after* he comprehends the use of signs. Third, the child should have comprehension of mathematical concepts *before* he is encouraged to deal with mathematical concepts symbolically (i.e., use numbers).

Lest there be some misinterpretation, Piaget would not argue for letting children learn "whatever they want." He would agree that children should eventually learn the symbols of mathematics. He would agree that children should learn computation and learn to solve mathematical problems. In addition to these conventional

TABLE 4

Average Ages When Some Mathematical Concepts Are Developing[a]

Concept	Late Preoperational Period (4–7) ages	Concrete Operational Period (7–9) ages	(9–11) ages	Period of Formal Operations (11–15) age
Topological space	x			
Classification	x x			
Seriation	x x			
Number conservation	x x			
Length conservation	x x			
Area conservation	x x			
Closure	x x			
Addition of classes	x x	x		
Multiplication of numbers	x x	x		
Euclidean space	x x	x		
Multiple classification	x x	x x		
Identity	x x	x x		
Commutativity	x x	x x		
Associativity	x x	x x	x	
Distributivity	x x	x x	x x	
Space	x x	x x	x x	x x
Time	x x	x x	x x	x x
Movement, velocity	x x	x x	x x	x x
Volume	x x	x x	x x	x x
Measurement	x x	x x	x x	x x
Functions	x x	x x	x x	x x
Proportion	x x	x x	x x	x x
Deduction/induction				x x
Formal logic				x x
Probability				x x
Proofs				x x

[a] The initial steps in the construction of many of these concepts can be traced back to the sensorimotor period.

objectives, Piaget argues in favor of children coming to *comprehend* the principles of mathematics.

If one agrees with the view that during the elementary school years mathematical concepts can be constructed only out of the child's actions on objects, then one need only look at the curriculum and materials used in teaching mathematics at most elementary schools to see how inappropriate instruction usually is. Most school systems, beginning in the first grade, use a workbook series of some kind, such as *Holt School Mathematics* (1974). These workbooks typically contain tear-out sheets that children usually work on in a sequential manner. The content of the Holt first grade workbook is composed entirely of pictures (symbols) and numbers (signs). The workbook is composed entirely of abstract materials, ranging from simple matching tasks to double-digit addition and subtraction problems. The Holt program can be obtained with "multimedia" components: cassettes, sound filmstrips, transparencies, and blocks and boxes. All these supplementary materials are again abstract materials except for the blocks and boxes, which are suggested to be for "providing a concrete starting point as well as manipulative examples and illustrations for number concepts and algorithm development" (p. viii).

While the Holt series and similar series refer to concrete materials that one can buy, the most important item is, of course, the workbooks. In many schools, the elementary school child's mathematics activity takes place 99 percent of the time in his workbook, completing worksheets. What experience there is with concrete materials is usually limited to the child's watching the teacher demonstrate something (with the blocks or boxes) to the class. Some experience unrelated to the worksheets may be occasionally permitted for those students who finish their worksheets early.

In such classrooms the primary "activity" of the child is pushing a pencil or crayon over a page! One wonders how children are expected to construct concepts under such conditions. How limited their concepts must be![2] The overwhelming emphasis on working with numbers can lead the child to believe that mathematics is learning to manipulate numbers. Where is the child's comprehension

---

2. It is probable that when children in such classrooms do construct mathematical knowledge, it is based on experience outside school or on school activities not related to mathematics instruction.

of mathematics expected to come from? Children without formal operations cannot learn concepts from books or from teachers' demonstrations or lectures. Children must be given opportunities to construct mathematical concepts. At the elementary school level, the construction of concepts is *more important* than manipulation of numbers. An ideal elementary school program is one that follows a format that begins with concrete activities and proceeds eventually to representation of and symbolization of the actively acquired concept. Activities such as the Holt School Mathematics program emphasize and encourage children's working with representations (abstractions). The most important step, construction of the concepts through experience, is passed over lightly and viewed as a "supplement" to what some apparently consider "real mathematics."

Until American educators come to realize the *necessity* of active learning, the mathematics instruction in schools, and what children learn, will remain as dismal as it has been to date. The attempt to implement the "new math" in the United States during the late 1950s and '60s was an effort to get children to learn an important set of mathematical concepts that were neglected under the "old math." The failure of the "new math" to succeed in the United States on any large scale has probably been due to the fact that while the content of mathematics instruction changed somewhat, the teaching methods did not. In practice, instruction usually has been directed at teaching young children sophisticated concepts (and some that they were incapable of learning without formal operations, like induction and deduction) through the use of signs and symbols. Paper, pencils, and written and spoken words and numbers remained the media of instruction. From a Piagetian point of view, the "new math" did not succeed because its implementation in classrooms was no more in keeping with how children develop and learn mathematical concepts than was the old math! Without active methods that permit the child to construct mathematical concepts, a change in content can have little effect. This essential point was overlooked.

In addition, the "new math" was generally not understood by teachers and parents. Teachers frequently were trying to teach concepts that they themselves did not understand. Parents, equally in the dark, were usually at a loss about how to help their children. The tendency to invoke memorization in place of comprehension was powerful.

Materials for Learning Mathematics Through Active Methods

Nuffield Mathematics Project

The Nuffield Mathematics Project is a complete and well-established mathematics program designed for use with children from the ages of 5 to 13 years. Originated in England, the program is outlined in a series of small books. These books describe structured activities designed to foster the development of mathematical reasoning in a manner based on and consistent with Piagetian and developmental concepts. The child moves from concrete experience to abstractions. Skills in computation, etc., are not neglected but are put in proper perspective with respect to acquisition of concepts. This is probably the most complete "active" program available at this time. Nuffield materials are available from John Wiley and Sons, Inc., 605 Third Avenue, New York, New York 10016.

How Children Learn Mathematics: Teaching Implications of Piaget's Research

The second edition of the book by Richard Copeland (1974a) is a comprehensive presentation of Piagetian research as it relates to mathematics instruction. It is not a teachers' manual but an explanation of how and when, in terms of conceptual development, mathematical concepts are constructed. Copeland also has a brief companion book, *Diagnostic and Learning Activities in Mathematics for Children*, which describes how children's level of reasoning with respect to mathematical concepts can be diagnosed and makes suggestions regarding appropriate teaching considerations. *How Children Learn Mathematics* is a must for all readers interested in an in-depth and complete presentation of Piaget's research and concepts as they relate to the development of mathematical knowledge.

The Methods of Zoltan Dienes

Zoltan Dienes is a mathematician who has spent most of his time since receiving his doctorate from the University of London in 1939 investigating children's learning of mathematics. Currently Professor of Education at Brandon University, he has evolved a comprehensive rationale for mathematics instruction that is consistent with Piaget's theory and the principles of child development. Because Piaget has on many occasions indicated his basic agreement with Dienes' methods (Piaget 1973, 1969a) and Dienes' efforts are consistent with the intent of this book, a brief presentation of Dienes' method and system for teaching children mathematics is included here as another example of mathematics instruction that is consistent with Piagetian theory. The reader, of course, is encouraged to read Dienes' original writings (see Bibliography) and in particular, *Building Up Mathematics*.

Dienes has noted the shortcomings of traditional mathematics teaching in a manner similar to that of Piaget. Mathematics, according to Dienes (1971), is the "actual structural relationships between concepts with numbers (pure mathematics), together with their applications to problems arising in the real world (applied mathematics)" (p. 18). Regarding instruction, Dienes and Golding (1973) write:

> The old point of view is to regard mathematics as a set of mechanical processes to be learned. The new one is to regard these processes as parts of an interlocking set of more and more complex structures: children are led to discover what these structures are, what they are made of and how they relate to each other, by being put in situations which *physically* embody these structures. The initiation of this kind of learning demands a complete shift of emphasis on the part of the teacher. The "answer" will now have only a secondary importance, ability to find one's way in the more and more complex situations will become emphasized, rather than the static end-point of the "answer" . . . the children's learning activity, singly or in groups, will take precedence over "teaching" by the teacher, standing in front of the class. Discussion will give way to authoritative statements, involving respect on the part of the teacher for the child's thought as a growing dynamism. (p. 10)

Dienes (1971) says that there are three broad stages in the formation of any mathematical concept, each stage involving a different type of learning. The first stage in concept formation he describes is essentially undirected "play," or acting on objects.

> To the preliminary or play stage corresponds a rather undirected activity, seemingly purposeless—the kind of activity that is performed and enjoyed for its own sake. It is this

kind of behavior that is usually described as play. In order to make play possible, freedom to experiment is necessary. This stage of concept learning should therefore be as free as possible, with the ingredients of the concept one is trying to teach available as play material. . . . The second stage is more directed and purposeful but is characterized by lack of any clear realization of what is being sought. At this stage a certain degree of structured activity is desirable. How this is developed will depend on the structure of the concept as well as the subject's particular way of thinking. Until more is known about these factors the safest procedure is the provision of a great number of experiences, of varying structure but all leading to the concept. . . . The third stage must provide adequate practice for the *fixing* and *application* of the concepts that have been formed. (p. 26)

More recently, Dienes (1971) has further refined his stages of development of mathematical concepts to six specific stages that can be more readily interpreted with respect to instruction.

According to Dienes, in a proper educational environment, the development of each mathematical concept moves from the initial "free play" stage where children act on objects that the teacher has placed in the environment. These objects contain mathematical features relevant to a concept. As the child comes to know the materials and their properties, he begins to see regularities and starts to make predictions about the objects and his actions on them. Eventually, after experiencing a variety of materials, the child begins to detect communalities or similarities between different "games" or actions on different objects (e.g., blocks can be ordered by size, coins can be ordered by size, stones can be ordered by size; adding 2 blocks to 5 blocks produces the same result as adding 2 stones to 5 stones). The child begins to construct the abstract notion that mathematical operations can be applied to any materials. Once the abstractions (concepts) are built from concrete experience, the child is ready to begin to represent the abstraction graphically, and shortly thereafter, in terms of signs (numbers and mathematical symbols). With the use of signs to represent the constructed mathematical operations, the child has developed part of a formal system.

Dienes' approach to mathematics instruction is a *structured* method based on the actions of the child on concrete objects. It leads gradually to the use of conventional numbers *after* comprehension of concepts has been built up. What is presented here is a very restricted overview of the Dienes methodology. Other authors well worth investigating are Kenneth Lovell (1972, 1971b, 1961), Celia Lavatelli (1970), and Molly Brearley (1970).

It is clear that Piaget and those referenced here do not know *all* there is to know about teaching mathematics. Much remains to be learned. But an overall view of how best to learn mathematics is clear. Traditional instruction that begins with numbers *is the wrong approach*. Numbers are abstract signs and have no meaning. Mathematical concepts can be built up only from the child's actions on objects. Active learning should be the *major* component of mathematics instruction in the initial stages and until children develop formal operations. To permit children to play mathematical games or work with Cuisinaire rods after they finish their worksheets is the wrong idea. Active learning should not be a supplement to work with symbols; work with symbols should be an outgrowth of active learning.

This chapter has not related in great detail any specifics about how to teach mathematics. That is too large a project for a few pages. The message here is basically that children learn mathematical concepts in the same way that they develop thinking in general, *through actions on objects.* Instructional methods that emphasize work with numbers before mathematical concepts are built up from experience are not consistent with what is known about children's development and learning.

The reader who is persuaded or enticed by this notion will have to read further. A problem for the reader, if he/she is like most Americans (and the author), is that he will have to fight his own poor comprehension of mathematics in the process of trying to comprehend how children can ideally learn mathematics. In addition to reading, teachers and school personnel who are interested in instituting active approaches to learning mathematics in schools are advised to contact professionals competent to train teachers in the use of active methods. Teachers should be *retaught* mathematics by the active method in workshops, summer courses, at a university or college, and the like. Care should be taken to ensure that the instruction is consistent with the ideas suggested here. This need not take a long time, but teachers will not be able to comprehend the use of active methods in teaching mathematics unless they themselves have learned that way—either formally or on their own.

Spontaneous Interests and "Messing About" in Science

Childrens' learning of science concepts is developed from their actions on "concrete" objects in the same way that mathematical concepts are built up and thinking in general develops. Comprehension of scientific knowledge and principles cannot be derived solely from reading about science and listening to lectures. The major criticism of most conventional science instruction from a Piagetian point of view is that it takes place largely through books and lectures instead of being based on the actions of the child. Teaching methods that deal primarily with representations of knowledge rather than permitting children to construct knowledge are ineffective.

Four ways of assessing children's readiness to learn have been discussed: (1) the spontaneous interests of the child, (2) the disequilibrium concept, (3) surprise, and (4) the borderline concept. Indeed, they are really four different aspects of the same phenomenon. Each of the four conceptions depends on the activity of the child for disequilibrium and, subsequently, equilibration to take place.

Using Spontaneous Interests

The spontaneous interests of the child should be capitalized on whenever possible. They are direct expressions of disequilibrium and reflect high motivation to deal with the cognitive questions relevant to the disequilibrating experience. These spontaneous interests generally reflect the child's current competencies. The child who selects sandbox pouring as an activity, and sticks with it, is saying in effect, "I can do this, it's fun, I'm fascinated by pouring sand." This is active learning in its most fundamental sense—active assimilation of the event. Spontaneous experimentation is very meaningful to the child, for he is tampering with his equilibrium.

At times, of course, children begin activities and give them up quickly. This can indicate that the child is not "ready" to assimilate a particular activity even though it may have aroused his interest. Thus, even abandonment of activities can have great significance. Children may want to "mess around," explore, try out a variety of things. What may appear to be a waste of time from an adult perspective is a form of active exploration and a response to spontaneous interests that serves a very important function in learning and development. It is an aspect of learning that education has generally neglected and that needs to be effectively incorporated into school instruction. Hawkins (1965) writes:

> There is a time, much greater in amount than commonly allowed, which could be devoted to free and unguided exploratory work (call it play if you wish; I call it work). Children are given materials and equipment—*things*—and are allowed to construct, test, probe, and experiment without superimposed questions or instructions. I call this . . . "Messing About," honoring the philosophy of the Water Rat, who absentmindedly ran his boat into the bank, picked himself up, and went on without interrupting the joyous train of thought. . . . (p. 6)[3]

As a student in a three-room schoolhouse during grades five through seven, I experienced exactly this essence of "messing about." We had a class composed of about twenty students. Our regular time for science was an hour or two twice a week. It was a relaxed school, and time periods were very flexible. Our science teacher, a retired biologist, was a marvelous person.

In the basement of the school building was a large rectangular room with a single lightbulb hanging from the ceiling. The walls of the room were covered with rough shelves. Our teacher had loaded the shelves with all sorts of "junk." There were old electric motors, radios, stuffed birds, old tools, boxes of shells, rocks, soil samples, sticks, leaf collections, nuts and bolts, wire, scrap lumber, bottles, jars, etc. Everything imaginable seemed to be in that room. Sometimes we went outside for a "class" and investigated the surrounding countryside, but during most of the winter and on rainy days we spent our time in the science room. And time here was primarily

---

3. It is interesting to note the similarity in the ways Dienes (1971) conceptualizes the stages of learning mathematical concepts and the way Hawkins (1965) conceptualizes the stages involved in learning science concepts. Hawkins' first stage, which he calls "messing about" is essentially the same as Dienes' first stage. Both men reflect the need for *structure* in their advanced stages.

spent "messing about" with the stuff in the room or with something someone brought from home to add to the clutter.

Each of us became interested in something. We would spend weeks working at whatever interested us, dragging our projects back to our classroom so that we could work on them in our spare time. I remember two boys who took a small electric motor apart. They did not have much trouble taking it apart but had considerable difficulty putting it back together again. Eventually, with occasional help from the teacher, the motor was reassembled, plugged in, and actually ran. Such a culmination to a project called for a class assembly, during which the budding electricians and the teacher talked about the electric motor. Occasions such as this were frequent, and I think we learned a lot.

Occasionally, we sat around and listened to our science teacher describe something and then ask us questions. We were motivated and encouraged to do a lot of reading. Students were always talking to one another and examining what everyone else was doing. There did not seem to be any structured science program, although I am sure our teacher knew what was going on all the time and did take opportunities to make sure we focused on certain things. The fifth, sixth, seventh, and eight graders worked together and learned together. It was assumed that if we were active and intensely interested in what we were doing, we were learning efficiently. I suspect our intensity and activity produced more "learning" than we would have gotten from required reading, listening to lectures, or even doing pre-planned "experiments."

Hawkins (1965) points out that "messing about" is the way that children learn *before* coming to school and suggests that this form of learning be continued:

> To continue the cultivation of earlier ways of learning therefore; to find *in school* the good beginnings, the liberating involvements that will make the kindergarten seem like a garden to a child and not a dry and frightening desert, this is a need that requires much emphasis on the style of work I have called . . . "Messing About." Nor does the garden in this sense end with a child's first school year, or his tenth, as though one could then put away childish things. . . . Good schools begin with what children have *in fact* mastered, probe next to see what *in fact* they are learning, continue with what *in fact* sustains their involvement. (p. 7)

Hawkins states that pure "messing about" is the most overlooked phase of good science teaching. The other two phases are when the teacher provides opportunities to explore from a selection of topics and when students and teacher discuss, argue, and present views. Pure "messing about" permits the child to explore spontaneous interests. Teacher-controlled "messing about," offering children a variety of related things to try out, helps ensure that the *content* children come to know is not unique to each child; it helps provide a common basis for "thinking." Class discussions serve to bring alive questions that might not arise as each child works on his own. These discussions also help stimulate abstract thinking.

From a Piagetian point of view, the types of experiences that Hawkins describes make sense. What Hawkins calls "messing about" Piaget would describe as letting children pursue with concrete experience their spontaneous interests with its potential for disequilibrium and surprise.

Piaget has frequently used the analogy of the scientist when describing the young child's intellectual development. The child is constantly exploring the environment, making hypotheses, and checking hypotheses. Such development of thinking and reasoning is encouraged best by freedom to evolve and test hypotheses. Indeed, "messing about" might well be called "hypotheses formation and testing."

Learning about

17

Society and History

Education has traditionally divided the school's instruction into distinct content areas. Thus, a typical curriculum consists of classes in mathematics, science, English, social studies, history, and a few other "special" subjects. This division, of course, is for the convenience of educators, not the convenience of children. Children's spontaneous development of knowledge and reasoning is not segregated into content areas. Piaget depicts knowledge "as a molar entity, synonymous with conceptual wholes" (Presseisen 1973, p. 9). In the mind and perception of the child, and in the development of knowledge, there are no academic disciplines.

Knowledge, according to Piaget, is rooted in one logic that is basic to all knowledge. No special set of mental operations, logic, or form of reasoning exists for "science" or "English" or "mathematics" or "social studies." The child (and the adult) has one logical system. Thus, Piaget's works suggest that the traditional divisions between subject areas are *not necessary* for the development and acquisition of knowledge in young children.[1]

At the elementary school level, *at least* until grades four or five (prior to the development of formal operations), there is no reason to compartmentalize knowledge. Young children's mental development does not reflect such categories of traditional academic areas, and it is unclear how such categorization can help children acquire

1. The division of knowledge into separate areas is probably more justifiable at the college and high school levels, after formal operations are developed. Even so, some of the criticisms offered here still apply. Of course, teachers of young children will continue to think in terms of separate content areas. The point is that children do not divide knowledge this way, and the value of imposing adult classifications should be considered.

180

knowledge. Indeed, categories such as these encourage children to believe that certain behaviors and types of thinking are appropriate in one area of study and not in another. One can learn that in studying science, one must reason "scientifically" but that this type of reasoning is not necessary in social studies; one should pay attention to spelling, grammar, and punctuation while doing English but not when writing a science paper. Such attitudes affect students' motivation and behavior. Rather than speculate on the nature of a particular discipline, Piaget suggests that a question to ask is: "How does the child develop concepts of social studies (or history, mathematics, science, English)?"

Acquiring Social and Historical Knowledge

Children acquire knowledge about their social environment in the same way they acquire knowledge about their physical environment. Indeed, the social environment is part of the physical environment. The primary mode of learning and acquiring "meaning" is through action. The child learns by acting on the objects and events to be known. Experience is assimilated into cognitive structures. Structures are transformed through accommodation to fit external realities.

Although the process of acquiring physical and social knowledge is the same, Bearison (1975) suggests that "the experience of physical events has a greater consistency of recurrent patterns than social experience" (p. 7). Social experiences are less consistent over repeated occasions than experiences with physical objects. Actions on physical objects reveal their meaning in a more regular manner than action on social objects. Thus the nature of rock, or water, or sand is stable over time. Children's discussions about right and wrong (social knowledge) are less stable over time, their features at a given time being influenced by many factors. Reinforcement for physical knowledge comes from the objects themselves. Reinforcement from social "objects" (i.e., other children, adults) is more variable. In this sense the organization and construction of social knowledge is more difficult for the child than the organization and construction of physical knowledge. Thus, as was previously suggested (see pp. 52–56), the "correctness" of social knowledge should be reinforced by the teacher, whereas physical knowledge should not be reinforced.

What kind of social-knowledge learnings are appropriate for children at different levels of development? Corresponding to the four major levels of development of Piaget, four general levels can be used to conceptualize appropriate social studies activities for the school-age child (Presseisen 1973).

At the first level the cognitive operation is that of preoperative thought. The average five- to seven-year-old child is self-centered in his social experience (Presseisen 1973). The world is viewed through the child's personal experience. The child is egocentric in thought and unable to view events from the perspectives of others. Perception dominates reasoning and the child tends to believe what he sees, not what he thinks. It is within this framework that social knowledge (and all forms of knowledge) evolves during these years.

At the second level the average eight- to eleven-year-old "will become aware that others have views both different from and similar to his own, and he will become cognizant of the influence of group orientations on his own views" (Presseisen 1973, pp. 14–15). The concrete operational child becomes capable of applying reasoning to concrete experience; reasoning gradually comes to dominate perception. The source of knowledge and meaning is still concrete experience; the child at this level is still not capable of constructing knowledge from abstract materials.

At the third level the average twelve- to fourteen-year-old child developing formal operations sees that the world and social relations are more complex than he previously believed (Presseisen 1973). Significant is the capability at this age to *begin to* formulate new knowledge based on symbolic representations (e.g., writings, lectures).

At the fourth level the average fifteen- to eighteen-year-old with formal operations brings the powers of hypothetical thought and prediction to his reasoning and knowledge. The child becomes as capable as fully developed adults of reasoning about social relations and social conditions and *capable* of constructing all possible theories for examining information about social relations and history. At this level of development, deductive and inductive reasoning become operational, and students can evaluate symbolic evidence in a logical manner.

General Implications for Teaching

First, new knowledge is always built on and transformed from existing knowledge. New experiences, if they are going to be assimilated effectively, must "fit in" with the child's prior experiences and level of conceptual development. A teacher needs to be aware of the child's current state of knowledge to be able to predict what the child may or may not be able to learn. Presseisen and D'Amico (1975) write that "there is no real social learning unless the child can integrate experiences of the classroom into his own social reality" (p. 166). The construction of knowledge is an individual affair. This argues in favor of individualized programs of instruction. Whether or not instruction is "individualized," learning is!

Second, the traditional modes of social studies and history instruction through reading and listening to lectures are inappropriate for preoperational children if they are thought of as *sources* of knowledge and meaning. Reading and lectures can be appropriate for concrete operational children to the extent that they provide the child with language experience about those things he already knows from concrete experience. Obviously, spontaneous interest in reading and language usage should be encouraged. But readings and lectures at these age levels need to be selective and viewed as a supplement to experience.

McLaughlin (1963) suggests that the concrete operational child is capable of dealing only with variables of one type at a time (Hallam 1969, p. 4). With this in mind, readings for these children and for children just developing formal operations should restrict the number of variables (e.g., the number of names, cities, counties) to no more than four. In this way, the *number* of variables that a child needs to keep "in mind" to comprehend a written passage does not interfere with comprehension. Hallam (1969) suggests that if a story uses similar names, such as "Hamilcar," "Hannibal," and "Hasdrabal," the numbers of variables should be reduced to less than four to avoid confusion.

Reading and listening to lectures on history and social studies begin to be meaningful during the development of formal operations. It is not reasonable to expect the preoperational or concrete operational child to construct knowledge from what he reads. What appears to be comprehension is typically either (1) rote memorization and retention of written materials that suggests comprehension, or (2) true comprehension based on active experience that occurred prior to the reading.

This does not mean that younger children should not read and listen to talks about history, social studies, or any other content. Reading and listening and talking are essential for the development of language and communication skills. What this does mean is that preoperational and concrete operational children should not be expected to acquire knowledge and meaning through reading and listening to others.

Experience—active learning—remains crucial. Students with formal operations can combine the knowledge they have into new knowledge, given their capabilities for thought. But the knowledge they have can always be traced back to experience. Younger children can comprehend only those readings and talks that closely relate to knowledge they have constructed through active learning.

A third implication for teachers is this. A person cannot acquire truly meaningful knowledge of a new content area through reading and listening to others. Even the development of new knowledge for those with formal operations is always constrained by experience.

For example, I am interested in Eskimos and their culture. I have no direct experience with Eskimos. I recently finished reading a book, *The Netsilik Eskimo*, by Asen Balikci. From this book I acquired considerable verbal information. I can recall and relate that to build an igloo the Netsilik Eskimo uses a long snow probe to test the quality of snow at and below the surface to determine the appropriateness of the snow for building a snow house. Only snow of the correct thickness and density can be used. I can partially comprehend the idea that snow needs certain characteristics to be useful because I learned as a child that snowballs can be made from wet snow but not from dry snow. But I cannot *know* the type of snow needed for a snow house *only* from what I have read.

A fourth point for teachers to consider is motivation. Teachers of history and social studies might ask themselves, "Why *should* a child learn what I am asking him/her to learn?" Motivation is clearest when learnings have adaptive value to the child and when such learning capitalizes on the spontaneous interests of the child. Most children probably *cannot* view history or social studies classes as having genuine adaptive value to them before formal operations are developed. For younger children, motivation to learn history usually arises out of some spontaneous interest in the content or from social reinforcement (e.g., grades, parental and teacher encouragement). The potential hazards of social reinforcement have been described earlier (see pp. 49–52). According to Piagetian concepts, the history the child experiences is more likely to become a part of his knowledge structure if the child's involvement is spontaneous than if the child's involvement is motivated by social concerns.

Within reason, therefore, children should be encouraged to pursue their own spontaneous interests with respect to history and social studies. The question that invariably arises from this is, "Don't children who are not exposed to a set curriculum miss a lot?" The answer is that the child probably takes away from the traditional curriculum very little knowledge and meaning. The child who is permitted to pursue his own interests, to learn actively as well as to read and listen to others, will not be exposed to a particular range of content during a given time span but will come to know and comprehend the content with which he interacts more thoroughly. The latter approach also deemphasizes the acquisition of verbal information for the sake of obtaining social reinforcers (e.g., good grades).

Many progressive schools demonstrate considerable success in getting children to learn history through spontaneous interests. One such school is the Common School in Amherst, Massachusetts. Last year twenty-five pupils, seven to eleven year olds, spent a large portion of the school term working on activities related to quilt making. This was a spontaneous group project that evolved out of the interests of the group and was not initially a planned activity. The interest in quilt making and colonial quilts arose while the class was working on a math investigation of geometric patterns. Some members of the class noted the geometric patterns found in old quilts. Concurrently, the class had been working on colonial crafts such as candlemaking and weaving. The teacher's goal in encouraging these activities was to have the children "experience" some of what people did two hundred years ago.

Interest continued in colonial quilts and quilt making. The class took several trips to see quilt shows. The group decided to make a patchwork quilt with each member of the class contributing at least one square. Over a period of time, the students did a lot of independent reading and research on quilts and quilt making, trying to decide how their own efforts should be spent. Individual investigations led in and out of different aspects of colonial life and modern-day life in contrast.

Toward the end of the school year, discussions in the group arose about whether the children really wanted to have a quilt or whether each child would keep his own square. Eventually it was decided to make the quilt. The class spent two afternoons planning how the squares would best go together. The finished quilt, thirty-five patches in all, now hangs in the Common School, a lovely product of active learning.[2]

Clearly, this group of children learned a lot, and their comprehension of what they learned was considerable. In addition to replicating colonial methods of quilt making, they made a backing for the quilt which they dyed with natural dyes, and they carded all the wool they used from raw wool. Thus these children encountered and investigated many aspects of knowledge tangential and removed from quilt making. Contents in areas that we commonly call social studies, history, science, and mathematics became involved in the best interdisciplinary sense.

Under responsive educational circumstances such as these, children can follow their spontaneous interests as they develop and maximize the meaningfulness of what they do. This is more difficult in a rigidly fixed curriculum that assumes that all elementary school children benefit from being exposed to lectures and readings on a timetable. The key to comprehension, according to Piaget, is disequilibrium. Teaching methods that encourage children to pursue their spontaneous interest are more likely to result in disequilibrium and to maximize subsequent comprehension of their experience than traditional methods.

Social Learning Experiences for Preoperational Children

For most children five to seven years of age, social learning experiences in school should emphasize *direct* contact with the physical aspects of objects and events that offer the potential for social knowledge. This can include numerous types of field trips to local or nearby activities:

2. While the quilt was made using methods of colonial times, no attempt was made to duplicate a colonial quilt. Each child invented and decided on the pattern he or she wanted. Thus, some children developed patterns that incorporated rocket ships or baseball logos.

1. Government officials' offices: police, jail, courts, fire station, mayor's office, tree warden
2. Local industry and business: newspaper, restaurants, gas stations, factories, stores, banks
3. Local farms and orchards
4. Sanitary departments: dumps and recycling centers

Ideally, children should have the opportunity to *see*, and to whatever extent possible, *touch* the activities the above people engage in. Verbal description of things should be as "concrete" as possible; it should pertain as directly as possible to what children can see and touch.

Back in the classroom, children can be encouraged to talk about what they saw. Regular opportunities should be provided for students to *imitate* aspects of what they have experienced (e.g., pretend they are firemen going to a fire). Imitation is one method by which children accommodate to experience. Appropriate imitation at this level of development may take the form of class drama or "plays," drawings, or any form of representation, including spontaneous writing. Since language is one form of social learning, correct language usage *should be* reinforced. It is important for children to become familiar with the correct language used to represent the objects of knowledge they know. The appropriate use of language to represent knowledge should be encouraged.

At the preoperational level, the goals of social learning should be to become familiar with social objects and events through experience and to develop imagery and language. Children at this age can learn to recognize and describe, in their own way, their encounters. Of necessity, these descriptions will be egocentric. Preoperational children should not be expected to grasp the subtle significances of social knowledge.

Social Learning Experiences for Older Children

At the concrete operational level (ages 7–11), the emphasis should still be largely on direct contact with the physical aspects of objects and events. At this stage, children can be encouraged to pursue reading material of interest to them that can supplement their experiences and enrich the language associations for the knowledge they have developed and are developing. Similarly, children can be encouraged to write about and describe their experiences. Concrete operational children are increasingly guided by their *thoughts* about concrete events rather than by what they see. They are becoming increasingly able to benefit from discussions with peers and adults. Such interactions should be encouraged by the structure of the class situation.

"Current events" can be introduced. These studies should be restricted to local events with which students may have some contact and of which they may have some comprehension. The study of physically distant events (state, national, and world) remains more or less *like* abstractions and hypothetical events to children at this period. Similarly, historical events such as the American Revolution are essentially abstractions, which concrete operational children cannot fully comprehend. Concrete experiences, like the experience with the colonial crafts described earlier, can help to give meaning to the past for children. Reading and talks can be better appreciated if some concrete experiences serve as a frame of reference for the children. All the experiences described as appropriate for preoperational children retain their value at this level.

During the years twelve to fourteen, most children are beginning to develop formal operations. Students *begin* to be able to comprehend what the adult world sees as the real significance of social relations, history, social sciences, and so forth. Students *begin* to create theories (and understand what theories are), contemplate the past and future, make logical predictions, and understand cause and effect and the hypothetical. Readings and lectures *begin* to be activities that children can use to construct knowledge. It should not be expected that comprehension at this level will be completely sophisticated. Not until the development of advanced formal operations (ages 15–18) can students *begin* to comprehend the "real" significance of such abstract and remote areas of study as state history, American history, and world history, and current events. Until this stage, these topics are available to the child only in the abstract—through symbolic experience—and must remain on the level of fairy tales and stories as far as comprehension is concerned.

With formal operations well-developed, the student is capable of reading about and listening to talks on history and comprehending the significance of history. The one area of comprehension that remains elusive at this point in development is an appreciation of the distinction between what is logical and what is "realistic." The adolescent is capable of thinking logically, but remains "egocentric" in that he typically does not realize that the events of the world— past, present, and future—are not always ordered logically. That life is a consequence of factors other than logic is an understanding that does not come about until the "real world" is sufficiently experienced to construct this comprehension. Thus the adolescent with formal operations may be viewed as demonstrating "false idealism." This is a "normal" aspect of the development of formal operations. Further accommodation to the "real" world may or may not result in an idealism that takes into account reality (Wadsworth 1971). It is probable that the most sophisticated appreciation of history (and other humanistic contents) requires this reality orientation.

The construction of social knowledge and historical knowledge has its roots in concrete experience. Knowledge never quite escapes the constraints of experience. Even at the most advanced level of formal operations, experience remains crucial to knowledge. Until I experience what an Eskimo experiences, I shall not truly know his life and understand his history.

Cognitive Development

18

and Learning Problems

Piaget has focused his work on how children acquire knowledge. His theory is largely one of "normal" development and does not directly address individual differences in development and learning. Yet, educational implications regarding individual differences in cognitive development and learning are implicit in Piaget's work. For example, while there is a predictable course to the sequence in which logical and reasoning capabilities emerge according to Piaget, the *rate* at which these abilities emerge varies from individual to individual. These variations can be dramatic and can have important implications for childrens' learning and performance.

Most of this book deals with "normal" development and its implications for education. But attention needs to be directed as well to those children who have cognitive-developmental differences that make it difficult for them to keep up with their peers. This chapter deals only with some varieties of learning problems that can be seen in developmental terms. Other factors that can affect learning, such as teacher expectations, repeated failure, and brain damage, are not covered. Any comprehensive treatment of learning problems would take several volumes.

The section called "Symptons and Causes of Learning Problems" includes some of my beliefs about how learning problems should be conceptualized. The reader is cautioned that there are other ways of conceptualizing these difficulties. The end of the chapter contains two brief sections: "Diagnosis of Learning Problems" and "Some Principles for Working with Children with Learning Problems." Like the rest of the chapter, these sections are very conceptual and speculative and are not elaborately detailed. Reading these sections does not qualify one to diagnose and remediate learning problems. What is hoped is that the chapter will help the reader better understand conceptually the variety and complexity of learning problems and more effectively provide educational programs for children whose special needs have been identified.

The Nature of the Problem

Not all children who are regarded as "slow learners" are that way because of heredity or a genetic lack of potential. Intellectual development is a function of the *interaction* of maturational and environmental (experiential) factors. Neither maturation nor experience alone can ensure normal development and learning, although both are necessary for development and learning. Piaget's theory of cognitive development presents a picture of what intellectual development is like in normal children. Children, given an adequate environment and adequate heredity, move through a series of stages and substages. The sequence of passing through the stages of development is "fixed." *Rates of development* can vary considerably from individual child to individual child and from culture to culture.[1]

Many terms have been used to label children with learning problems: *mentally retarded, brain damaged, minimally brain damaged, dyslexic, perceptually handicapped, developmentally disabled,* and the currently popular *learning disabled.* Grzynkowicz (1971) lists thirty-eight ways to describe children with learning problems. These terms have frequently been used indiscriminately to classify children and to imply certain things about why children do not learn. Such labels usually communicate nothing specific about children's difficulties. Probably the most destructive aspects of the labeling process are that most of the terms sound *fatalistic*; communicate nothing about the child's strengths; and once applied to the child, often signal the end of his or her academic hopes. It is never long before the labeled child loses hope. In addition, the practice of mass labeling has frequently

1. Children in different cultures have different experiences. As a consequence of different experiential backgrounds, there is some variability between cultures as to the ages at which children acquire particular Piagetian concepts (see Bruner, Olver, and Greenfield 1966). In a general sense, the variability in development is greater within cultures than between cultures.

led to a uniformity of educational "remediation." Because children's learning problems are viewed as similar, teachers tend to treat all children with a particular problem (e.g., reading) the same way. Thus, children with visual problems in reading and children with auditory problems in reading frequently receive the same remedial-reading instruction.

If one wishes to figure out *why* children have learning and performance difficulties, one has to look very carefully at how children function overall. This evaluation should include a developmental assessment of cognitive processes of the type suggested by Piagetian theory, which can be used to determine a child's level of conceptual development.

Factors Influencing Development, Learning, and Performance

What follows are some of the developmental factors that can affect development, learning, and performance. It should be kept in mind that while these factors are described individually, children can have problems associated with several factors at the same time.

Rate of Cognitive Development

Some children develop cognitively more slowly than the average. On the other hand, some children proceed through Piagetian stages of development at a rate more rapid than the average. Rate of development, or age of acquisition of a particular developmental concept, can be looked at in the sense of a normal curve (see figure 7).

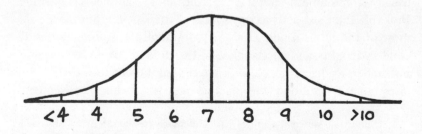

FIGURE 7
Ages at Which Children Enter the Concrete Operational Stage

The average child enters the concrete operational stage around the age of seven, although he or she does not become concrete operational with respect to all types of contents or problems at the same time.[2] A smaller percentage of children enter this stage at age six, and a very small percentage at age five. Some children, however, enter the concrete operational stage at age nine, and a small percentage at age ten or even later. These children are typically developing cognitively at a slower rate than the average child. For them, the educational implications are straightforward: they may not be able to comprehend materials that are developmentally appropriate for the average child of the same age. The average seven- or eight-year-old has mastered classification and seriation and should be "ready" to learn about numbers. The same-age child with a slow rate of cognitive development (who has not mastered classification or inclusion) does not have the prerequisite cognitive capabilities to begin to comprehend number concepts.

Some readers at this point may say, "But a slow rate of development does not tell anything specific about the child's difficulty!" That is absolutely correct. Slow rate of development is a broad conceptual term. Once its meaning is grasped, it is necessary to talk about what can affect rate of development.

Maturation

One factor that Piaget repeatedly asserts as affecting cognitive development is *maturation*, the unfolding of mental "possibilities" related to the physical aspects of the nervous system. Piaget uses the term maturation primarily to refer to the growth and development of tissue of the nervous system including the brain. This growth usually continues through age fifteen or sixteen (Piaget 1971b). Maturation of the nervous system, according to Piaget, places constraints on cognitive development as well as opening up possibilities for new development. Unless the nervous system has developed to the point where acquisition of formal operations is possible, formal operations cannot develop! Regarding maturation, Piaget writes:

2. Development is characterized by what Turiel (1969) calls "stage mixture." Thus, while children are described as being in a particular stage, they can be expected to evidence thinking of lower and/or higher stages some of the time. Piaget employs the term "decalage" to describe the child's conceptualizing some issues at higher levels than others. This is thought to occur primarily because children have more experience with some concepts than others.

> . . . heredity and maturation open up new possibilities in the human child . . . which still have to be actualized by collaboration with the environment. These possibilities, for all they are opened up in stages, are nonetheless essentially functional (having no preformed structures) is that they represent a progressive power of coordination. . . .
>
> Such maturation does not . . . depend solely on the genome [set of genes]. But it does depend on that among other things (with the intervention of exercise factors, etc.), and, in general terms, it is admitted today that every phenotypic growth [physical makeup of the individual] . . . is the product of close interactions between the genome and the environment. (1971b, pp. 21–22)

Thus maturation, construed in the past as relying entirely on genetic factors, is seen by Piaget (and modern biologists) as also influenced by such experiential factors as nutrition and the child's activity (exercise). A slower-than-average rate of maturation is reflected in a child's rate of cognitive development.

Experience

The second major factor necessary for development is active *experience*. Without actions on objects, children may not develop physical knowledge and logical-mathematical knowledge. A child must act on the environment for development to proceed. Maturation can open up the possibilities for development of preoperational thought, but without the active engagement of the environment, these possibilities will not be realized, and cognitive development will not proceed.

Children who do not actively engage the environment are likely to suffer this fate. Hunt (1961) describes the effects of experience and lack of experience on intellectual development. Children living in physically barren environments (e.g., those in institutions, crib-confined infants), where the possibilities for actions on objects are limited, are less likely than children living in normal environments to develop conceptually at an average rate. Children living in otherwise normal environments may not be motivated to "act on objects" because of factors competing for their time (e.g., television, excessive parent attention, isolation, hunger, physical injury).

Social experience also affects development. Language, moral concepts, values, and the like are all products of social experience. The child deprived of such experience will suffer restricted development of social concepts.

Figure 8 presents a hypothetical case. The apex of the triangle, A, is a concept for which B_1 and B_2 are prerequisites. C_1, C_2, C_3, and C_4 are prerequisites to B_1 and B_2, and so on down to the base of the triangle. Child 1 has all the cognitive prerequisites to master concept A. All Child 1 needs to learn A is some motivation and the opportunity to learn, and learning will proceed rapidly. Child 2 has *none* of the prerequisites for acquiring concept A (i.e., B_1 and B_2 have not been acquired). Thus it is theoretically impossible for Child 2 to learn A. Appropriate learnings for Child 2, who appears to be a slow learner, are D_1, D_3, and D_5. But not A. If Child 2 is called on to learn the same concepts as children who have the prerequisites for such instruction (e.g., Child 1), Child 2 will always appear handicapped and slow. But if the child has a slow rate of development, then the child *is not* a slow learner; the *instruction is inappropriate* for this child. The child is being asked to learn some things he or she cannot reasonably learn. For example, a child who cannot order and classify will not be able to comprehend initial arithmetic and number learnings.

It is important to recognize that *we are all slow learners* at tasks for which we do not have prerequisites. For example, if college students

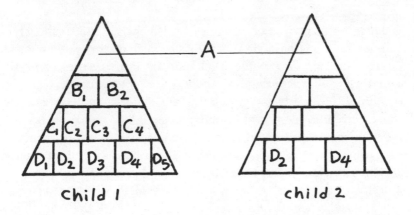

child 1   child 2

FIGURE 8

and older adults were asked to master some advanced aspect of nuclear physics, most of them would seem to be slow learners.

Summary

While the course of cognitive development is viewed as essentially the same for all children, the rate at which children develop is variable. Some children develop more slowly or more rapidly than others. Children who develop more slowly than the average child will typically have difficulty learning and performing on a level with children who have average or above-average rates of development. It is unreasonable to expect children with different rates of development to learn and perform in similar ways.

> Rate of cognitive development is controlled by two factors: maturation and experience. Growth and development of brain tissue (maturation) continues through adolescence, setting the limits that development can reach at a particular point in time, though not ensuring that development occurs. The "possibilities" created by maturation can be attained only through active experience. Knowledge is a construction and cannot evolve without experience. It is unreasonable to expect anyone to master learnings for which they do not have the prerequisites.

Sensory and Motor Development[3]

There are many sensory avenues by which the child can gather information from the environment: visual and auditory systems, taste, smell (olfactory sense), touch (haptic or tactile sense), and the kinesthetic and proprioceptive senses.

During the first two years of life the motor-kinesthetic and the other perceptual processes (vision and audition) begin to become differentiated, organized, and coordinated. While educators frequently give some attention to visual and auditory development in kindergarten or first grade, very little attention has been given to the motor-kinesthetic aspects of development, particularly as they relate to learning and school performance. Readers are aware that the child's

3. The importance of the development of the visual and auditory systems is covered in chapter 14.

first learnings are motor and sensory and that the child must be active on a motor level to develop knowledge. But the significance of motor development has rarely been considered seriously in education.

Motor development as it relates to learning and performance can be divided into two mutually dependent aspects, *proprioception* and *kinesthesis*. Proprioception is the internal awareness of the position of the body in space. It also involves awareness of what positions the body has been in and will be in (Furth and Wachs 1974). Kinesthesis is the internal sense that yields knowledge of movements of muscles of the body and the positions of the joints. Unlike other forms of sensory stimulation, kinesthesis and proprioception are movement-produced, internally produced, and continuous forms of sensory stimulation. Every movement of the muscles produces kinesthetic and proprioceptive information.

Control of all nonautomatic movement is best maintained through kinesthesis. Kinesthetic "feedback" (movement-produced stimuli) from the muscles is present during and directly after every movement. It is the *only continuous form* of information the individual receives about his movements. Vision provides information about movement, but only if the eyes are directed so the movement can be seen. This is not always possible (e.g., one cannot see while tying something behind one's back, or in the dark). Hearing is of little help in controlling movement. Many movements do not produce any sounds, and when they do, the sound produced is not continuous throughout the movement; sound usually occurs only at the end of movements.

Kinesthetic Awareness

Most behavior is motor behavior. There is little one can do that does not use some muscles of the body. Most school activities require the direct use of voluntary muscles. Reading requires the use of eye muscles. Writing requires the use primarily of finger and hand muscles. Talking requires throat and mouth muscles. Muscular control of posture is a part of virtually every activity.

All muscles and voluntary movements are most *efficiently* controlled through kinesthetic awareness. If you close your eyes and raise your right hand over your head while your eyes are closed, how do you know your right hand is raised and how do you know it is over your head? You can "feel" the movement. That "feeling" is kinesthetic awareness, an awareness of where one body part is in relation to another and what the parts are doing.[4] You can close your eyes and "feel" their position as they move around. You can move them to a selected position and predict the direction in which they will be looking when you open your eyes. Control of eye-muscle movement is kinesthetic. Visual activities are most efficiently carried out with kinesthetic control of the eye muscles.

Try writing your name while your eyes are closed and writing it again while your eyes are open, then compare the two samples. If you are like most people, you will find little difference between writing your name with your eyes closed and with your eyes open. When you write with your eyes closed, the writing may be a little larger and a little less regular than when you write with your eyes open. How can most people write so well with their eyes closed? Because they can "feel" the letter formation. Normally, writing is primarily a kinesthetic activity, not a visual activity. In efficient handwriting, vision is used primarily to monitor handwriting, not to control it.

Adequate control of movement (kinesthesis) is usually taken for granted. Schools generally assume that all children have adequate control of their movements when they enter kindergarten; if they do not, it is their responsibility. Actually, many children have poor kinesthetic awareness upon entering school, and some have none at all! These children have considerable difficulty controlling their movements, which results in many school performance difficulties.

The child (or adult) with limited kinesthetic awareness moves and uses muscles inefficiently and must rely on vision to control movement. The child may find the simple task of walking very difficult. He may have constantly to look at his feet while walking in order to control his movement. Handwriting becomes an arduous task of forming each letter very slowly, using vision to control the shape of each letter. Children with inadequate kinesthetic awareness are invariably erratic in movement.

Control of movement is a central problem of living and *should be* of concern to educators. Nothing is more fundamental to efficient personal existence than movement. Most people develop kinesthetic awareness to some average level that permits them to move reasonably effectively. Some persons (e.g., blind people) develop kinesthetic awareness to a very high level because it is adaptive for them to do so.

4. "Feeling" where the arm is in space is proprioceptive awareness.

Competition divers, pole vaulters, and ballet dancers develop an advanced awareness of what their bodies are doing, though this may be a "splinter skill," limited to the area in which they train.[5]

Kinesthetic awareness is one component of the "body image" and is something that develops (see Wapner and Werner 1965). The child is not born with kinesthetic awareness, and it is not automatically acquired with physical maturation. Kinesthesis begins developing at birth (probably before birth); as the child moves his limbs and body in the environment, there is normally a gradual differentiation of the muscles involved in a particular movement from those not involved in the movement. This differentiation can be seen as a motoric figure-ground relationship in which the muscles in a movement (figure) come to be contrasted against the muscles of the body not in movement (ground), (Grzynkowicz and Kephart 1975). This development is not automatic; it depends on the activity of the child. The development of kinesthesis tends to emerge in what seems to be an automatic way because kinesthetic awareness is the most efficient means for controlling movement. In this sense, the development of kinesthetic awareness is adaptive.

By the end of the first three or four years of life, children typically have developed sufficient kinesthetic awareness to move through space (walk, run, jump) without constant supervision. Kinesthetic awareness continues to develop, but skills such as fine motor control (e.g., handwriting) are not usually well established until later in childhood.

Some children do not develop adequate kinesthetic awareness. Clinically, it is not always clear why this is true for a particular child. Several factors can theoretically account for a child's not developing kinesthetic awareness. One cause of a kinesthetic deficit may be a gross lack of motor activity during a time when kinesthetic awareness normally develops. For example, a young child may be immobilized because of a cast on a broken leg. Such immobilization can preclude the activity essential to the development of kinesthetic awareness and control of movement. During such confinement the

5. A generalizeable skill is more useful than a splinter skill. Splinter skills can be acquired with respect to all tasks and are extremely deceptive because they may be inferred to suggest that a child has a generalizeable skill when he does not. Whether a skill is a generalizeable skill or a splinter skill can be diagnosed only by having the child use a particular skill in a number of different activities. If it is effective in only one setting, it is a splinter skill.

young child may become accustomed to relying on visual control of movement and never try to get back to kinesthetic control.

In some cases a young child may establish visual control over movement very early and never "tune in" to kinesthetic information. Such a child might get along reasonably well during the first few years of life with visual control of movement. By the time the child gets to school, however, the child will have demands made on him that require more efficient movement than he can manage with only visual control. Writing words, for example, takes more time if control of letter formation is visual rather than kinesthetic. Letter formation is invariably distorted unless inordinate time and attention is given to the process.

Children without adequate kinesthetic control are frequently "clumsy" children. Development of adequate kinesthetic and proprioceptive skills should be a *primary objective* of early childhood programs through the early grades and should be a concern of education at all levels. The more highly developed these skills are, the more efficient the movements of the individual can be.

Kephart (1971) believes that adequate kinesthetic development is essential to adequate perceptual and cognitive development. The issue of the relationship between the motor aspects of development and later cognitive development is not perfectly clear. From Piaget we know that the child's first learnings are motor and sensory and that all subsequent development builds on this base. Development is always seen as a reorganization of prior developments. This points clearly to a functional relationship between early development (motor) and later development (perceptual and cognitive). Whether kinesthetic and proprioceptive development, related as they are to motor development, can be concluded to be *necessary* for later cognitive development is a point of disagreement in the field of education.

The author's feeling is that kinesthetic and proprioceptive skills facilitate motor activity and active exploration of objects and events (in the manner that Piaget describes as necessary). The child can be more efficiently "active" with adequate kinesthetic awareness than without it. The ease with which one can be motorically active can be facilitated by the degree to which kinesthetic awareness is developed. As a lack of vision or a lack of hearing retards cognitive development, inefficient movement control probably inhibits development. In this sense, kinesthetic awareness is not strictly "necessary" for cognitive development, but it facilitates the acquisition of developmental skills and knowledge. Professionals may argue over the ultimate relationship between motor and cognitive learning, but there can be little debate over the importance of kinesthetic and proprioceptive skills in control of movement and school performance.

Teachers sensitized to the importance of movement control are in a position to identify children in need of assessments of their motor and movement efficiency. Inefficiencies in kinesthetic awareness do not appear to be self-correcting, but children who have inadequate kinesthetic awareness *can* be helped. Barring physiological inter-ferences, children who lack adequate kinesthetic awareness can be taught to differentiate muscles required for movements from those not required for movements.

I am familiar with one program that has had success in teaching kinesthetic awareness to children. This program was developed by Newell Kephart at the Glen Haven Achievement Center in Fort Collins, Colorado (see Grzynkowicz and Kephart 1975). The starting point is usually establishment of relaxation. The child must first be able to relax all the muscles of the body and recognize the state of relaxation. If relaxation training is called for, it proceeds generally along the lines described by Jacobsen (1938). Relaxation can be eval-uated by having the child assume a position that requires no use of muscles. The examiner can then "feel" the different body muscle groups to determine whether any tension exists. If tension exists in a resting position, then complete relaxation is not attained. After re-laxation has been attained, training in differentiating or recognizing kinesthetic signals from the muscles begins. Training usually begins with the muscle groups farthest from the center of the body working inward. Thus, training begins typically with the toes, then the feet, then the thighs; the fingers, then the hands, then the arms, shoulders, neck and stomach. Training proceeds inward gradually. The general form of training is to blindfold the child (to eliminate visual control of movement) and to establish relaxation. The therapist may begin by slowly manipulating *a toe* up and down with the therapist control-ling the movement. The child is asked to try to "feel" the movement. All other movements are discouraged. If other movements are ini-tiated by the child, the child is returned to relaxation and training begins again. When the child becomes capable of feeling the move-ment the therapist is making, the child is asked to try to make the same movement (move one toe up and down) himself. Relaxation of all unnecessary muscles is maintained.

Once control of one toe is established, work begins on other toes, always from a state of relaxation. Once control of toes on one foot is established, work begins on the other foot. The progression of training continues as described. In some cases, children have kinesthetic awareness in most muscle groups but lack it for a particular group. In these cases, training may be necessary only for the muscle group(s) that lacks it. In the Kephart program, complete training may take two years or longer before kinesthetic awareness is well established. A parent or other individual is taught to carry out the training. Training usually takes place during two daily sessions of ten to fifteen minutes. Training in kinesthetic awareness may lead to training in other necessary motor skills, such as balance, differentiation, laterality, directionality (see Kephart 1971).

Relaxation

Physical relaxation is an important aspect of efficient control of movement. For every movement, certain muscle groups are activated, but other muscle groups are not necessary. When a child is walking, there is a need for activation of the leg muscles for support and movement. There is little need for activation of the other muscles in the body. If a child is sitting at a table writing, the muscles needed are primarily those of the fingers, hands, arms, and shoulders, with some need for other postural muscles. Those muscles that are not necessary for writing should be relaxed to permit differentiation of the needed muscles and controlled movement. Some children (and adults) activate more muscle groups than necessary in executing movements. Some children activate nearly every muscle in the body during movement and are never relaxed. Activation of unnecessary muscle groups can have several consequences for motor performance and movement.

1. Differentiation between muscle movements *cannot* occur easily if there is a generally high level of muscle activation in the body. If unnecessary muscles are constantly activated, it becomes difficult to "feel" movement because there is little if any figure-ground contrast between the muscle groups. Frequently children with little kinesthetic awarness cannot "relax" and show signs of hyperactivity. In these cases, relaxation skills must be acquired before kinesthetic awareness is possible.

2. The child who regularly activates more muscle groups than necessary becomes fatigued quickly. Such a child may find copying a paragraph off the blackboard an exhausting experience because he literally puts his whole body into it!

3. Physical tension can lead to emotional distress. An eight-year-old boy was brought to a clinic because of reading problems. The boy, an "early" reader, was reading by age three and was encouraged, if not pushed, by his parents to read. At the clinic, within one minute of starting to read the boy was crying painfully. This was his usual reaction when required to read. The therapist noticed that as the boy began reading, there appeared to be increasing tension in his body, to a point where the boy actually experienced pain. The therapy in this instance was quite direct. The boy was taught to return himself to a state of relaxation when he became aware of tension. He was very bright and had no difficulty learning this. On his third day at the clinic he sat and read aloud for half an hour. The boy has not experienced any "reading" difficulty since. The difficulty was primarily a reaction to stress.

Efficient movement is not possible without relaxation. Relaxation is necessary for the development of kinesthetic awareness during the early years and later for the use of kinesthetic awareness. Too much tension can result in fatigue, hyperactivity, or emotional distress. Children (and adults) who do not know how to relax, or who experience physical tension in certain types of situations, can be taught to relax themselves and recognize the state of relaxation. Relaxation, like kinesthetic awareness, is a desirable goal for education to maximize the child's efficiency of operation.[6]

Symptoms and Causes of Learning Problems

When children have difficulty in school, some behavior *symptoms* are generally observed by the teacher. The child's behavior may be disruptive; he may seem to be overactive or underactive; he may day-

6. Teachers and parents should be cautioned that relaxation problems are frequently a reaction to stress. A teacher or parent who yells at a child, "Relax!" is not going to help a child to relax.

dream a lot; he may seem tired all the time. Sometimes the symptoms are not the *causes* of the learning problem. My point of view is that many causes can lead to the *same* behavior symptom. Skilled diagnosis is necessary for the proper identification and treatment of the cause rather than the symptom. Treating symptoms instead of causes frequently does not lead to a correction of the child's problem, although this is a controversial issue. Two symptoms associated with learning and performance problems are viewed here in terms of *some* of their possible causes.

Hyperactivity

Hyperactivity is frequently observed in schools. Hyperactivity may result from body-chemistry imbalance, emotional problems, poor motor control, boredom, poor vision, sensitivity to sound, and learned behavior (one can learn to be hyperactive). Medication is thought to be the most appropriate treatment *when* the cause of hyperactivity is a body-chemistry imbalance, although there is no clear research evidence on this point. It is doubtful that this treatment is appropriate for all cases of hyperactivity even though medication seems effectively to suppress hyperactive behavior in many cases.

A child with poor motor coordination is frequently seen as a "bull in the china shop." Such a child may appear hyperactive, but the underlying problem is frequently a lack of motor control. Appropriate treatment in these cases may involve motor training or kinesthetic awareness training. Again, medication may suppress the hyperactive behavior, but it may not fundamentally improve motor control.

Children can learn to be hyperactive. Children raised in households that tolerate considerable motor activity may not acquire certain "socially desirable" skills such as sitting quietly for long (or even short) periods of time. These children can acquire a general behavior pattern that is viewed as hyperactive by teachers. Higher percentages of minority-group children (blacks, Puerto Ricans, Mexican-American) than white children are labeled hyperactive in elementary school. I know of no evidence that the discrepancy in frequency of hyperactivity between ethnic groups is due to body-chemistry factors. The motor activity of many minority-group children is probably due to an environment that reinforces "hyperactive" behavior. Appropriate treatment in these cases would be to learn more "socially acceptable" behavior. Again, medication may suppress socially unacceptable behavior but is unlikely to establish desired behavior. Since this type of hyperactivity in part reflects cultural patterns that differ from the norm, the desirability of changing the behavior may involve conflict between white middle-class and minority-group values. If schools are going actively to pursue modification of behavior of this type, it is probably best carried out with the consent and cooperation of the child's family.

Friedland and Shilkret (1973) have proposed that some cases of hyperactivity reflect what they call "defensive hyperactivity." Children with histories of traumatic experiences with adults may use excessive movement, talking, and other symptoms of hyperactivity as a coping device for keeping others, particularly adults, at a distance. In this sense, hyperactive behavior can be seen as adaptive.

Many factors may produce the symptoms of hyperactivity. Diagnosis of the underlying causes is essential if remedial efforts are to be successful.

Handwriting

Symptoms of difficulty in handwriting include poor letter or number formation, reversal of letters (*p, q; b, d*), inversion of letters (*p, b; q, d*), reversal of words (*was* for *saw, tac* for *cat*), and general slowness and illegibility. The causes of handwriting difficulties are as numerous as the causes of hyperactivity. Children who have poor fine-motor control may write very slowly and illegibly because they lack kinesthetic awareness of finger and hand movements. When writing, they may exert excessive pressure on a pencil, making very dark lines on the paper (and sometimes etching the desk top). In these cases, remedial efforts frequently should begin with training in kinesthetic awareness.

Some children who have adequate motor control may not have enough experience to generalize kinesthetic skills to letter formation. They need to build up the "feeling" of letters and numbers. This is probably best accomplished through tracing or similar techniques, where the consistency of kinesthetic signals can be maximized (see Chaney and Kephart 1968).

Reversals and inversions in handwriting are fairly common among children as old as eight years and need not be a concern at earlier age levels. Some children reverse and invert letters, not because they cannot write them properly, but because their thinking is topological

206 · TEACHING PRINCIPLES AND PRACTICES

instead of Euclidean (see pp. 139–40). They see no difference between *b* and *d* or between *p* and *q* because the letters are the same shape topologically. With young children this may reflect a general slow rate of development or a specific lack of development in some aspects of spatial knowledge rather than being a visual discrimination problem. A "wait-and-see-if-it-develops" approach may be appropriate in these cases. If a child is still committing reversal and inversion errors when thought has become Euclidean with respect to space, then visual-discrimination training may be needed (see Shilkret and Friedland 1974).

Slow, laborious writing may result from excessive muscular tension that hampers control of the pencil and also results in fatigue. A child writing at a desk needs only to activate the muscles in the fingers, hand, arm, and shoulder. But some children have their whole bodies knotted up from excessive muscular activity while writing. The legs are tight, the neck is tight; arms, hands, and fingers are tight. Children who cannot relax during a performance task such as writing *sometimes* lack kinesthetic awareness, although a child can have adequate kines-thetic awareness and still not relax at motor tasks. This frequently calls for some type of relaxation training.

Some slow and/or sloppy writers may lack motor *rhythm*, or fluidity of movement. They may be able to draw ⎍⎍⎍ easily, which requires a series of independent movements, but they may have difficulty with ∿∿∿ or *llllllll* or *nmnmnmn* , which are most efficiently ex-ecuted through rhythmic movement (see Roach and Kephart 1966, Grzynkowicz and Kephart 1975). Some children may have to be taught rhythm, although a lack of rhythm in kindergarten and first-grade children is not unusual.

Some children may have difficulty with *sequencing* or ordering tasks, which can result in their placing letters in incorrect series (*hta* for *hat, banna* for *banana, siwn* for *swim*). This may indicate that the child has not yet *developed* seriation or ordering concepts, which is not uncommon among preoperational children. The same child who cannot repeat "5-9-6-1-3" may not be able to copy a word accurately from the blackboard. The child may have to take one look at the board for each letter and may still make errors because of sequencing (or memory). Children who evidence sequencing difficulties should be given a developmental assessment to determine whether the difficulty lies in their level of thinking or other possible factors.

Some causes of handwriting difficulties can be quite bizzare. Kephart relates a story about a boy who was sent to a clinic because of a "writing problem." The boy read well and could read his own handwriting, but no one else could read it. It was totally unrecognizable as English script, although the formation of his "letters" was excellent. When asked to write something like *the boy hit the ball*, he wrote:

He could identify every word and every letter, and he seemed to wonder why no one else could read his writing. The diagnosis eventually arrived at was that this boy identified letters and words by looking only at *part* of each letter or word, roughly the upper half. When he wrote, he did the same thing; he wrote only the top half of letters and words. Thus he was able to read his handwriting, but no one else could figure out what he was doing!

Difficulty in handwriting is a *symptom* that can have multiple causes. As with other symptoms of learning and performance problems, the teacher must look beyond the symptom to the cause if remedial efforts are to be effective. That there can be many causes for a given symptom (or similar symptoms) should be clear. To treat all children who have similar symptoms in the same way is educationally unsound. Only a small percentage of children can possibly benefit under such conditions. Those children for whom a particular treatment is inappropriate will not be helped, and chances for negative consequences are increased. The problems of children who do not respond to inappropriate treatment will come to be viewed as increasingly less retractable.

Diagnosis of Learning Problems

An accurate assessment of learning problems is a demanding task requiring training, thought, and experience. Any simplistic approach to learning problems or their diagnosis is highly suspect. Any methodology that recommends a general treatment for a particular symptom or similar symptoms is going to fail to help large numbers of children. Methods that treat symptoms (e.g., medication for all hyperactive children) are helpful to some, but on a chance basis only; they may not help others. A "cookbook" approach to learning problems is to be avoided! Methods that fail to help children only deepen the belief of everyone—teacher, parent, and child—that the child cannot be helped.

Proper diagnosis requires that teachers, school psychologists, educational specialists, administrators, and parents look at children's learning and behavior from a variety of different conceptual positions.[7] A pair of sunglasses with interchangeable lenses make the world look a little different with each change of the lens; so it is with different conceptual positions or ways of looking at a particular child and his functioning. Each way of conceptualizing a child's learning and behavior suggests different possibilities. Thorough diagnosis requires looking at children's functioning from many different perspectives.

Armed with an array of ways to conceptualize the child's learning and behavior, the educator can begin testing hypotheses about the child and his performance. Good evaluation and diagnosis, as Piaget has repeatedly indicated, is a form of hypothesis testing: trying to figure out what makes the child work the way he does. If the teacher is interested in why a child's handwriting is so poor, she might first look at the child's posture and muscle tension while writing. If there is a lot of tension in legs, neck, or chest, the teacher might obtain an evaluation of the child's kinesthetic awareness in those muscles necessary for writing and the rest of the body muscles. If the initial hypothesis about kinethetic awareness proves unhelpful, the teacher might want to look at the child's eye control (see Roach and Kephart 1966). If eye control seems adequate, the teacher might evaluate the child's visual discrimination skills to determine how well the child can differentiate between shapes.

Proper diagnosis is a form of hypothesis testing. When a diagnosis

7. The conceptual position presented in the part of this book that deals with Piagetian principles is basically a developmental conception of learning and behavior. Developmental conceptions are one set of ways to look at a child. While Piagetian and developmental conceptions are not incorporated into educational practice as much as they should be, developmental conceptions are not the only way to look at the child. The educator with *only* developmental conceptions is as limited conceptually as a behaviorist with only behavioristic conceptions. There *is no one way* of conceptualizing the child and his learning and performance that will *always* be the most useful. Most conceptions of the child have some utility in certain situations. Effective diagnosis requires an intellectually unbiased diagnostician who can select appropriate hypotheses and look for evidence to support or reject them.

is thought to be accurate, it can be confirmed only after attempts are made to remediate the child's problem. If remedial efforts do not result in improvement fairly quickly, then the diagnosis may need revision. New hypotheses need to be explored. If none of the examiner's hypotheses proves helpful, other ways of looking at the child are necessary, including the possibility of referral to specialists.

Some Principles for Working with Children with Learning Problems

The correction of learning problems is a topic larger in scope than this book can handle. My purpose has been primarily to give the reader an *idea* of the *scope* of learning problems; to suggest the difference between *symptoms* and *causes*; and to indicate what form proper diagnosis should take. These have been related to Piagetian theory wherever possible. What has been covered here is general and only scratches the surface of the topic of learning problems. The reader who is interested in any of the ideas presented here can find much more to read and assimilate (see Myers and Hammill 1976). A few principles of conceptualizing and dealing with learning problems have enough generality and/or are crucial enough to warrant mention in an abbreviated presentation.

Adaptation

Piaget has repeatedly stressed that intellectual development is a form of adaptation in the biological sense. The symptoms that children work out to learn and do things, even if they are very inefficient from an adult perspective, generally have some adaptive value to the child *at the time* of their incorporation. For example, a child without kinesthetic awareness will develop visual techniques for controlling movement. This is inefficient but better than nothing. It is adaptive in the sense that the child is less efficient without any control than with visual control. Similarly, every teacher has observed some of the strange systems that children frequently work out to solve arithmetic problems. If the system works better than what the child used before, it is adaptive *to the child* at the time it is acquired even though it may not be the most efficient system.

Methods that work for children some of the time, but not regularly enough to be efficient, tend to persist (Nolen 1975). The strongest reinforcement schedule (i.e., most difficult to extinguish) is intermittent or variable reinforcement. Things that work once in a while are reinforced on this principle. Thus, children (and adults) are frequently reluctant to change of their own accord as long as their efforts meet with periodic success. Sunday golfers and fishermen frequently maintain poor habits because of periodic reinforcement. A fish is occasionally caught or a ball is occasionally well hit, and so the behavior is maintained.

In trying to correct learning problems, it may be necessary to remove the value of the child's inefficient adaptation during the remediation process, so that it cannot be used. For example, in teaching kinesthetic awareness and control of movement, it is necessary to *remove* the possibility of visual control during remediation. This is typically done by initially blindfolding the child during training sessions.

Strengths and Weaknesses

Invariably, a child with learning problems has strengths and weaknesses in learning and performance. For example, a child may learn most efficiently if information is received visually but have great difficulty if information is received auditorily.[8] Such a child may be able to learn by reading but not be able to learn from a lecture or verbal presentation. A visual learner learns best through visual methods. Remediation of auditory difficulties can go on separately. Similarly, some children learn most efficiently through auditory methods, and

---

8. Many people seem to have a dominant learning modality. Some people learn best through visual, auditory, or kinesthetic-tactile methods. In young children development and learning proceed primarily through the motor system while the visual and auditory functions are simultaneously developing. For most adults and older children, the modality of reception is of little importance. It does not matter if information is heard or seen; the same meaning comes through. This is because most people have sufficient *intersensory integration*, which permits information from different modalities to be interpreted in the same way. Some children do not develop intersensory integration. Reception through one modality may be fine, while reception through the other modality may add nothing but "static" and "noise." For children without adequate intersensory integration, one popular innovation in education, multisensory stimulation, can be a disaster. Multisensory stimulation is an approach to teaching that presents learning through as many different sensory channels as possible. A story may be read, acted out, and listened to. For children who are strictly visual, auditory, or kinesthetic learners, multisensory stimulation adds a lot of distraction to instruction.

some beyond early childhood learn best through kinesthetic-tactile methods. If children are expected to learn, they should be taught through their strengths.

Structure in the Classroom

Piaget's theory of cognitive development argues in favor of "active" education. Objects and events must be manipulated, acted on and transformed, and correspondences sought out by the child in order for learning and development to proceed. Activity can be physical or mental. The general principles of the open classroom, the traditional nursery and kindergarten, and *some* aspects of Montessori educational programs are generally consistent with Piaget's theory.[9] All these programs have definite structure although they may appear "unstructured." There is considerable self-selection of learning activities, and there is a lot of movement in the classroom. Typically, desks and chairs are not lined up in rows, and the teacher is not a full-time lecturer. An educational program run on Piagetian principles *is* as structured as a traditional program although the structure permits and encourages active and spontaneous learning by the child.

The *problems* of children with learning difficulties are not automatically helped by a Piagetian or open environment. The difficulties that these children have may require highly structured programs, structured in specific ways to help their problems. A child without kinesthetic awareness needs to be put through a highly controlled program in which movement and control of movement are manipulated in a specifically structured way by another person. A child without adequate visual discrimination needs a specifically structured training. This does not mean that the teacher should abandon progressive educational techniques when working with children with learning problems. It simply means that children with specific problems require more consideration than children who do not have such problems.

The Need for Success

Learning problems usually come to light after a period of failure or inability to perform school work adequately. Children who do their

9. Piaget criticizes Montessori materials as being too restrictive. Piaget believes that structured materials of the Montessori type are unnecessary and probably do not maximize conceptual development because they limit possibilities. Montessori materials do not reflect the structure of the real world but of a contrived structure.

work satisfactorily are not usually considered to have learning problems although many children who appear to perform well in school have severe problems. The difference frequently is that children who *get by* in school have typically worked out more effective means for compensating for their learning inefficiencies than children who do not get by. These compensations often come at very high cost, for which the child later pays. A resourceful child can put off the effects of inefficiency for a long time; some survive until college before they discover their inefficiencies.

Failure and poor grades can be destructive experiences (Glasser 1968). Children who fail habitually frequently become convinced that they are incapable of learning; they begin to hate themselves and to hate school and everything associated with it. Learning problems are invariably accompanied by emotional overlays, although these need not be overt. The child who withdraws into silence is in as much pain as his counterpart who screams out his resentment and is destructive.

Children who have experienced the inability to perform well frequently have to be "conditioned" to view themselves as capable of success. They need to learn that they *can* learn. Success must be guaranteed for these children. This means, among other things, that in the initial stages of remediation, children should be asked to do only those things that they can do successfully. They need lots of encouragement and praise. Attempts to stretch the child's capabilities should not occur before a measure of self-assurance has returned to the child. This may take time, but successful remediation usually cannot take place without the cooperation *of the child*.

How Soon Should Results Be Evident?

In remediation of learning problems, if *some signs* of success are not quickly forthcoming, the teacher is probably doing something wrong. There is a need to revise the hypothesis about the child's difficulty and what to do about it. Kephart (1971b) once said that when he began working with children he thought that if you did not see some improvement in a year or two, you were doing something wrong or had not diagnosed the problem properly. Several years later he concluded that if you did not see some improvement after several months, you were doing something wrong. A few years ago he felt that if you did not see improvement in a few days, you were on the wrong track. His last position was that if you did not see improvement in a *few minutes*, you were probably approaching the problem incorrectly and needed to revise your thinking.

The point is not that children's problems can be solved quickly but that, if an educational method is going to work, some signs of its working should be apparent relatively early on. If a child has poor handwriting (letter formation) and is diagnosed as lacking fine-motor control, and the prescribed method of correction employs tracing, then some improvement in letter formation should quickly become apparent with tracing. If improvement is not noted after a few minutes of tracing, then the level at which the child can effectively learn has not been reached. One has to "go back a step" and try a simpler approach. In this case it might be having the child trace with his or her fingers large sandpaper letters or some other more elementary letter-form task.

Splinter Skills

Splinter skills are skills developed in isolation that have no generality and are consequently inefficient. For example, I once examined a junior high school student who was awkward physically and had laborious handwriting. Yet he excelled at building little ships in bottles, which certainly required fine motor control. His was a classic case of a splinter skill—he could build ships in bottles but not generalize his skill to other behaviors.

Splinter skills are often misleading because they can infer more competence and efficiency than really exists. Regardless of how satisfactory a performance is, if it is accomplished only under highly restricted conditions, it is probably inefficient. Skills that can be used in a variety of situations are more useful than those that can be used only under restricted conditions.

Children with learning problems frequently develop splinter skills in an effort to compensate for their problems. Also, in remediation efforts, teachers have to be careful to *avoid teaching* children splinter skills. Ideally, they should provide opportunities for correct generalizations to occur.[10] Efficient learning is learning that can be used in a variety of situations, not in one restricted situation.

Summary

This chapter has attempted to convey the conception that learning problems can have a variety of causes, some of which may be related to development. Any two children can have what seems to be the same learning difficulty for different reasons. Each cause implies a different form of remediation. The different causes for similar symptoms can be diagnosed.

Children who have evolved inefficient processes can usually be helped to develop more efficient processes. Even brain damage, which has been traditionally viewed fatalistically, may not always prohibit improvement in impaired capabilities. More often than not, if children are not helped by remedial efforts (assuming they are cooperative), the teacher is doing something wrong.

Educators do not know all the answers to helping children with learning problems. As no two people are never exactly alike, the causes of their problems are never exactly alike. The successful worker with children with learning problems must have a range of conceptions and must generate and test hypotheses. Educators who attempt to use a "cookbook" approach to working with children with learning problems will frequently do more harm than good.

10. An exception to the practice of avoiding teaching splinter skills may, at times, be necessary. Frequently with children of high school age whose problems are so ingrained and whose compensations so well-established, to "break down" their methods of functioning and "rebuild" may be too traumatic for them. In these cases the best approach may be to try to make the adolescents' compensations (frequently splinter skills) as efficient as possible.

COGNITIVE-
DEVELOPMENTAL

PART IV

ASSESSMENT

Assessment of

19

Intellectual Development

We live in a time when test scores play a major role in decisions about people—particularly students in school. Test results and school grades in large part determine how students move through the educational maze, who gets "certified" at different levels, and what our self-concepts are. Some persons become persuaded that they are bright, successful, and talented. Other persons become persuaded that they are dull, failures, and without promise. Failure to perform well on tests and subsequent poor grades are viewed by many as the major problem in education today (Glasser 1968).

This is a test-crazy society. One of the areas of greatest confusion and ignorance is IQ testing. Intelligence is a concept surrounded by mystery, mysticism, anxiety, and above all, ignorance. Intelligence is a psychological *construct*.[1] We infer the existence of intelligence from *behavior*. The behavior we typically look at in determining intelligence is test performance because testing is assumed to be the most organized, systematic, valid procedure available for determining intelligence. We cannot look at intelligence directly and make judgments about it because it does not exist as an object. Like all constructs, intelligence is subject only to indirect observations. Is it any wonder that so much confusion surrounds the word "intelligence" and many other psychological and educational constructs?

1. A construct is a concept whose existence is inferred. Unlike some concepts, constructs do not exist as physical objects. We have concepts of trees, cars, books, people, etc., all of which have physical referents. But concepts such as intelligence, creativity, aptitude, instincts, genius, motivation, love, are all inferred to exist, their real characteristics determined only by *inference*. Education and psychology abound with constructs. Their existence, characteristics, and how they should be thought of are subject to interpretation.

Assessment of intelligence starts with a conception of intelligence based on assumptions and inferences. Conceptions are like sunglasses. If you insert red lenses, the world looks red. If you insert blue lenses, the world looks blue. Similarly, if your conception of intelligence is that it is inherited and fixed, you will come to conclusions that are different from those derived from conceptualizing intelligence as developed, acquired, or changeable. *How* one conceptualizes places constraints on what one sees and thinks. The teacher who sees intelligence as inherited, fixed, etc., is unlikely to try to help the ten-year-old who has been left back two times and is a poor performer in school. The teacher who sees intelligence as developed, acquired, etc., *might* try to figure out why the child has been learning inefficiently.

Herein lies the injustice that surrounds intelligence and similar conceptions. As teachers, we know that how we conceptualize things such as intelligence directly affects how we behave toward our students. How does one decide how to conceptualize things, and in particular, how is one to decide how to conceptualize intelligence? This chapter deals with assessment of intellectual (or mental, cognitive, etc.) development. The primary purpose is to present the Piagetian approach to looking at children and their "intelligence."[2] Piagetians feel that this approach makes a lot of sense for many reasons. The advantages and disadvantages of several testing procedures (psychometric or standardized testing), observational procedures, and Piagetian techniques are here outlined and compared.

Group Versus Individual Testing

There are basically two formats for testing in education: group and individual testing. The advantages and disadvantages of each procedure are fairly obvious. Group testing permits testing of large numbers of people at one time, while individual testing limits the number of persons that can be tested at one time. From the standpoint of numbers and time, group testing is more efficient. Thus we

2. Most of Piaget's ideas presented here come from one of his earliest books, *The Child's Conception of the World* (1963a), originally published in English in 1929. The strength of these early ideas is evident when one considers that thousands of psychologists have used Piaget's methods of assessment and the technique has remained intact since 1929.

have tests like the College Boards and the Scholastic Aptitude Tests and the Graduate Record Exam, which are administered to tens of thousands of students throughout the United States at the same time. In public schools, tests such as the Iowa Test of Basic Skills, the Metropolitan Achievement Test, the California Test of Mental Maturity, and the Stanford Achievement Test similarly permit testing of classes of students rather than one student at a time.

Individual testing presumably permits the examiner to evaluate more carefully and thoroughly an individual's performance. In education, tests are presumed to be used when information about ability, learning, personality, and so forth is needed. Of course, regardless of whether the method is group or individual testing, the interpretation of the test results by educators, psychologists, or parents always is determined by their conceptions of what the test measures.

This chapter deals exclusively with individual testing procedures. Much can be said in criticism of group paper-and-pencil tests; for example, they are often tests of reading and writing skills and not necessarily pure tests of what they claim to be. Within the framework of individualized intelligence testing, three approaches are here examined: (1) the psychometric or standardized approach to testing, (2) testing by observation, and (3) the clinical-interview approach to testing exemplified by Piagetian methods.

Standardized Testing

Standardized tests include the individually administered intelligence tests such as the Wechsler Intelligence Scale for Children (WISC), the Wechsler Adult Intelligence Scale (WAIS), the Stanford-Binet, and the Peabody Picture Vocabulary Test. There are also many group-administered and individual intelligence, achievement, aptitude tests. In the United States today, the WISC and the Stanford-Binet are probably the individual intelligence tests used most frequently in schools. Indeed, in some states the Wechsler tests and the Stanford-Binet are the only tests that seem to be used to *legally* determine intelligence.[3]

3. The WISC and the Stanford-Binet are the tests most frequently used to assess mental retardation. Children are placed in institutions for the retarded, special education classes, and similar programs on evidence gleaned primarily from this one way of looking at children.

These two individual intelligence tests were derived largely from sampling techniques and normative comparisons according to psychometric principles. In brief, a pool of verbal and performance test items was constructed. These items were given to a large number of children at different age levels. Selected were items that differentiated between age levels and also resulted in a range of scores within an age level. Obviously the test had to be one on which the average older child did better than the average younger child. Once the item pools were sufficiently narrowed so that the test would not take too long (about one hour), the items forming a test were administered to another large number of children. From this sample of children, norms were created. That is, the means and standard deviations (spread of scores) for the test for each age range were developed. In a manner similar to this, a psychometric test is derived that provides the user with a set of norms against which to compare a child's performance and make some statement about the child's performance relative to that of the norm group. Generally there is some attempt to establish the reliability[4] and validity[5] of the test.

Testing is always carried out in a standardized procedure, otherwise interpretation in terms of the norms is invalid. Generally one is interested *only* in the correctness of children's answers. The reasoning behind answers, for instance, is of no interest in standardized procedure. Piaget (1963a) compares the three methods of investigation under discussion here: tests of the standardized conventional type, pure observation, and the clinical method. According to Piaget, the primary characteristics of standardized tests are that the questions put to children and the conditions of testing remain the same for each child, as much as possible. In addition, a child's responses can be compared with a set of norms for his age. The

4. Reliability refers to the "consistency" with which the test measures. A reliable test would be one in which the results were about the same for persons tested several times (without any recall of previous testings). If results for individuals were very different, the consistency of the test, or reliability, would be in doubt.

5. Validity refers to whether or not a test really measures what one thinks it measures. Does the WISC really measure intelligence, or does it primarily measure verbal skills, specific learnings, and visual-motor skills (which are presumably different from intelligence)? There is no precisely adequate way to determine validity of tests, even though people talk about the validity of tests. For psychological tests, validity is basically determined by the judgments of experts. The problem with this is that experts are afflicted by the same limitations as the rest of us. Test validity is always, in the end, a judgment.

major defects of standardized tests is that they do not allow a "sufficient analysis of the results" and do not "take into account the natural mental inclination" of the child being tested (Piaget 1963a, p. 3). Piaget illustrates:

> . . . in trying to find out how a child conceives the movement of the sun and moon the question may be asked, "What makes the sun move?" The child perhaps answers, "God makes it move," or "the wind blows it," etc. Such answers are not to be neglected, even if they be only the result of "romancing," that is of that peculiar tendency of children to invent when embarrassed by a given question. However, even had this test been applied to children of all ages, no real advance would have been made, since it may well be that a child would never put the question to itself in such a form or even that it would never have asked such a question at all. The child may quite possibly imagine the sun to be a living being moving of its own accord. In asking "What makes the sun move?" the suggestion of an outside agent occurs at once, thus provoking the creation of a myth. Or in asking the question, "How does the sun move?" one may be suggesting the idea of "how." . . . The only way to avoid such difficulties is to vary the questions, to make *counter-suggestions*, in short, to give up all idea of a fixed questionnaire . . .
>
> In short, the test method [standardized testing] has its uses, but for the present problem it tends to falsify the perspective by diverting the child from his natural inclination. It tends to neglect the spontaneous interests and primitive [but important] reactions of the child as well as other essential problems. (pp. 3–4)

Standardized individual tests typically provide the examiner with a set of norms against which a child's performance can be compared. Such comparisons are justified only if the examining procedure and conditions are "standard." From a Piagetian perspective, such tests, relying on the child's response to set questions within a rigid testing situation, provide little useful information about the child's thinking, reasoning, and so on. Whether a child's responses are a consequence of thinking or rote memory is of little concern under standardized procedures. Thus, these two forms of assessment should be viewed as performing different functions, both having limitations and both being useful if used properly. Whether the abilities measured by the WISC and similar tests reflect accurately what people mean when they use the word "intelligence" or whether Piagetian measures come closer to doing this is a separate question.

Observation

Observation includes recording or taking note of children's spontaneous statements and questions. Pure observation usually proceeds without *any* questioning of the child by the observer. The major value of observation is that what you get from the child is structured by the child, not by the observer (as in standardized testing). For Piaget (1963a), observation of children's reasoning as reflected in children's spontaneous questions is of primary importance:

> The detailed study of the contents of these questions reveals the interests of children at different ages and reveals to us those questions which the child is revolving in its own mind and which might never have occurred to us, or which we should never have framed in such terms. Further, a study of the exact form of the questions indicates the child's implicit solutions, for almost every question contains its solution in the manner in which it is asked. For example, when a child asks "Who made the sun?" it is clear he thinks of the sun as the product of an act of creation. Or again, when a child asks why there are two Mount Saleves, the big Saleve and the little Saleve, when there are not two Matterhorns, he evidently imagines mountains as arranged according to a plan which excludes all chance. (pp. 4–5)

". . . the child neither spontaneously seeks nor is able to communicate the whole of his thought" (p. 6).[6] Children's thinking is not as socialized as adults' and that which could be explained in words is not always so explained. Thus, questions of some sort from the observer frequently are necessary to elicit certain types of thought from the child.

Another drawback of the method of pure observation cited by Piaget (1963a)

6. The theme of egocentricity and the nature of the child's communications is detailed in *The Language of the Thought of the Child* (1955).

is the difficulty of distinguishing a child's play from his beliefs. Take the example of a child, who imagining himself to be alone, says to the roller: "Have you flattened out all those big stones?" Is he playing or does he really personify the machine (the roller)? In a particular case it is impossible to judge with conviction. Pure observation is inadequate for distinguishing belief from romancing. (p. 7)

Thus, according to Piaget, pure observation is a productive way of getting information about children and their thinking. Productive as it is, however, it remains fairly inefficient for many purposes including most educational uses that seek to determine a child's particular reasoning and thinking capabilities.

Clinical Method

The Piagetian conception of intelligence has been elaborated extensively.[7] A second source from the Genevan group is Inhelder (1968). Inhelder's work demonstrates the application of Piagetian techniques to diagnosing retardation and "pseudo-retardation."[8]

Piaget considers both the standardized test method and pure observation inadequate for making assessments of children's reasoning. A method that utilizes the advantages of the method of pure observation but avoids the drawbacks of the standardized test method is necessary. To this end, Piaget has elaborated his interpretation of the clinical method, which has become associated with his name:

The clinical examination is . . . experimental in the sense that the practitioner sets himself a problem [determine the child's reasoning], makes hypotheses, adapts the conditions to them and finally controls each hypothesis by testing it against reactions he stimulates in conversation. But the clinical examination is also dependent on direct observation, in the sense that a good practitioner lets himself be led,

7. Piaget originated many of his measurement ideas while working in Binet's laboratory in France, presumably standardizing items on the original Binet test of intelligence. Piaget became fascinated by the wrong answers children gave and the reasoning behind their answers. From this experience in trying to evaluate children's intelligence using a standardized procedure grew the Piagetian principles for his clinical method.

8. Pseudo-retardation results from a lack of adequate experience rather than from a physiological defect.

> though always in control, and takes account of the whole of
> the mental context, instead of being the victim of "syste-
> matic error" as so often happens to the pure experimenter.
> (1963a, p. 8)

Piaget's clinical interviews, then, have specific goals, as do psychometric tests. But, like observation, the route to the goal is not through
a series of rigid, prestructured questions. The clinical examiner
observes carefully the child's behavior and statements and lets his
(the examiner's) questions follow and evolve from the child's
statements.

> The good experimenter must, in fact, unite two often in-
> compatible qualities; he must know how to observe, that is
> to say, to let the child talk freely, without ever checking or
> side-tracking his utterance, and at the same time he must
> constantly be alert for something definitive, at every moment
> he must have some working hypothesis, some theory, true or
> false, which he is seeking to check. . . . (Piaget 1963a, p. 9)

While much of the Piagetian philosophy makes intuitive sense
to people, making assessments of development from a Piagetian
framework is neither an easy nor an obvious business. It requires a
basic understanding of Piagetian theory and its principles for investigation of the reasoning of the child. The goal of the clinical
interview is to determine the nature of the child's reasoning—
whether it is about a specific content (e.g., number, area, life) or
more general or more inclusive in scope. There are children who are
"easy" to work with and others who are "hard." The practitioner
must be thinking all the time, changing with the responses of the
child to get at his thinking, not telling the child what to say (suggestion) but giving him enough clues to what to think about. There
are no set rules for this type of diagnosis. It comes with practice.
Critical to the proper use of the clinical-interview technique is an
understanding of Piaget's theory.

Like children, adults learn best when they are active. Mastery of
the clinical interview can be achieved only by actively using the
procedure. The more thoroughly one assimilates Piaget's theory and
the more practice one has trying out Piagetian tasks with children,
the more complete will be one's understanding of both the theory
and the clinical-interview procedure.

One may be very discouraged by the prospect of a year of daily practice necessary to become proficient in the Piagetian clinical interview. A teacher's purpose for comprehending the clinical-interview procedure may be other than sophisticated diagnosis. Comprehension of Piagetian theory and assessment techniques can help improve a teacher's understanding of students. The more *active* experience one has, the better the comprehension will be.

Features of the Piagetian Clinical Interview

The clinical interview of Piaget is a theory-based technique. With an outline of Piaget's developmental stages and the primary characteristics of each *in mind*, the interviewer is ready to examine a child's reasoning and thinking and to begin *experimenting* with the clinical interview. Indeed, the word "experiment" best describes the clinical interview as Piaget conceives it. The interviewer asks questions of a child, listens, observes, makes a hypothesis about the child's conceptual ability, and proceeds to ask more questions *based on the hypothesis* he has formed. There is a constant testing and reformulating of hypotheses until the interviewer is persuaded that the Piagetian criteria for assessment have been met and the child's thought and reasoning is clearly revealed. In this procedure the child's responses are accepted as valid by the interviewer. "Wrong" answers are of as much interest as "correct" answers. Every attempt is made to avoid leading or cueing a child's response.

Criteria for Assessment

There are four criteria for assessment using the clinical interview. In order to be considered at a specific reasoning level the child must: (1) make a "correct" judgment, (2) logically justify that judgment, (3) successfully resist a verbal counter-suggestion, and (4) produce a successful performance on a related behavioral task (Strauss 1972). With respect to the first criterion, making a correct judgment means simply giving what we know as the right answer by adult standards. For example, we present a child with the classic conservation-of-number problem (see p. 250). We then ask the child *why* the rows have (or do not have) the same number of elements. We ask the child to justify the answer logically (whether or not it was correct). This is the second criterion, which is *always* employed when children give responses.

The third criterion, successful resistance to a counter-suggestion, is employed if the preceding response and justification suggest that the child understands the concept. For example, one might remove an element from one of the rows in the conservation-of-number problem while the child is observing and say, "The rows still have the same number of elements, don't they?" or "Now this row [the longer one] has more elements than this one [the shorter one]." If the conservation response is maintained, we *may be* persuaded that the child can conserve number. If we are not certain, other questions can be improvised until the criteria are met.[9] Because children sometimes are apparently able to do things in one situation and not in another, one looks for successful performance on a related task, the fourth criterion. We might ask the child to bring a box of pencils that has more (or fewer pencils) where one box has less than the other.

Without meeting all the criteria, it is possible for children to give apparently correct answers that are devoid of any comprehension on the child's part. An inexperienced interviewer might assume that the child "has the concept" on the basis of a "correct response." This clearly is not always the case. Children can give correct responses for a number of reasons: (1) they know the answer and understand it; (2) they guess at the answer; (3) they are cued to an answer by the examiner; or (4) they remember something that cues them to the answer, but with no real understanding (rote memory). It is not always important that the child have the correct answer, but it is important to learn the child's reasoning and whether or not the child changes his convictions in the face of counter-suggestion.

A second possibility not to be overlooked is that children may "have the concept" but not give a correct response. Reasons for this may include: (1) not understanding the question (e.g., poor hearing); (2) lack of motivation to answer, lack of interest; (3) fear or anxiety as a consequence of the novelty of the situation; or (4) preoccupation with something else.

9. The significance of the counter-suggestion both in testing and teaching cannot be overlooked (see Elkind 1972).

Characteristics of Piagetian Testing

Piagetian testing as presented in this volume measures something different from traditional IQ tests such as the Wechsler Intelligence Scale for Children. Traditional tests measure a wide range of abilities, including verbal skills, specific facts acquired, visual skills, motor skills, and combined visual/motor skills. Piagetian tasks primarily assess reasoning ability (logical thought) with respect to those concepts children have learned more or less on their own without direct instruction (Elkind 1971). One could argue that traditional tests measure a wider range of abilities than Piagetian tasks and are thus of greater value to the educator, but the arguments against this are many. Both types of assessment procedures have value.

One distinct advantage of a Piagetian-type assessment is that the interpretation of results is always reasonably clear. Piagetian tasks evolved out of theory. The interpretation of results based on these tasks is always in terms of Piaget's theory. Thus, if a child cannot conserve number and cannot perform adequate classifications and seriations, Piagetian theory suggests that the child does not yet have stable number concepts or is prenumerical. Such a child is not going to *comprehend* formal arithmetic instruction. This interpretation holds even if the child can arrange elements in 1:1 correspondence with trial and error, can count, and can tell you that $1 + 1 = 2$.

The most frequently used IQ tests are not based on a particular theory. The items on these tests were selected to discriminate between different age levels. This can make for difficult interpretation. For example, if a child is asked, "Who discovered America?" and responds, "Columbus," what does this mean? Does the child comprehend that Columbus discovered America? Is there any reasoning involved in the response? Is this something the child recalled or memorized? What interpretation does this lead to? What if the child's response to the question was "I don't know"? Does this mean there is no intelligence involved? Sigel (1969) writes:

> The child's correct contextual use of a term is not necessarily indicative of his comprehension of that term or an accurate reflection of the child's ability to understand the logical basis of a concept. (p. 475)

Traditional tests do not permit the range of exploration of a Piagetian clinical interview. They are concerned almost exclusively with whether a child's answers are correct or not. In Piagetian assessment, the correctness or incorrectness of responses is much less important. The examiner is as interested in incorrect answers as correct answers. One also is interested in the child's reasoning behind an answer, and in the durability of the response, whether the child "sticks with his answer" under counter-suggestion. In this sense, traditional tests seem to be almost exclusively concerned with *content*, while Piagetian measures are concerned with *reasoning* and the dynamics of thought.

Sex Differences

One intriguing phenomenon in the assessment of intellectual development using Piagetian clinical-interview techniques is that one finds few sex differences among students. There are, to be sure, considerable differences in performance within each sex at any age or grade level, but on the average, a boy performs as well as a girl (Wadsworth 1968; Wadsworth et al. 1975; Gollishian, Hinkelman, and Wadsworth 1971). It is well known that in elementary school girls on the average perform better than boys on conventional IQ tests, achievement tests, and teacher-made tests, the difference usually holding into early adolescence. These overall differences are not found in Piagetian-type assessment, which is difficult to explain. If one tries to account for the sex differences found on traditional tests through maturation, i.e., that girls mature physiologically earlier than boys on the average, then why is there not a difference between the sexes on Piagetian scales? Other explanations fall to a similar fate. One wonders whether the standardized tests measure how much specific content learnings students have acquired that are relevant to the tests. If this is the case, then IQ tests are measuring *the same thing* as achievement tests and teacher-made tests. In any event, Piagetian tests reveal no sex differences among boys and girls in general and suggest that the development of logical thought proceeds at about the same rate in both sexes.

Verbal Requirements in Testing

In conventional IQ and achievement tests verbal abilities account for a large portion of a child's performance. On a test such as the

WISC or the Stanford-Binet, a full one-half of the subscales require vocabulary and verbalization on the part of the child. On group-administered tests (e.g., Iowa Test of Basic Skills, Stanford Achievement Test) reading ability, speed of reading, and the like clearly contribute to the nature of one's performance.

One's ability to read or verbalize is not necessarily indicative of one's ability, knowledge, or logical reasoning. A Piagetian scale in some respects acts to minimize the dependence on verbal skills (listening, speaking, reading) and maximize dependence on reasoning ability. The child must still listen and speak, but care is taken under Piagetian methods to ensure that the child *understands* what the examiner is getting at. One is more interested in the child's *reasoning* than in his answers, and one is not interested in the elaborateness of a child's vocabulary for assessing reasoning. A Piagetian scale minimizes the dependence on verbal skills.

Culture-free Tests

The search for tests that are not biased in favor of or against cultural groups is probably a fruitless quest. Tests such as the WISC and Stanford-Binet are clearly "biased" in favor of children from middle-class, educationally oriented families.[10] They are clearly biased against lower-class whites, lower-class blacks, and lower-class Puerto Ricans. It would be absurd to take a test used in our public schools to a remote Eskimo community and administer it to Eskimo children (in English or Eskimo), then try to compare their performance to that of white children in the *typical* American school. Nevertheless, to a lesser extent this practice is carried out in our schools when testing children other than "normal" middle-class cultural groups. Tests *are not* culture-free.

A Piagetian scale is not entirely culture-free either. But research has shown (Bruner, Olver, and Greenfield 1966) a remarkable consistency across very different cultures in the ages at which children attain levels

10. WISC revised (1974) takes into account social-class differences by using as its norm group a representative sample of the population of children. That is, middle-class, lower-class, white, black, and Puerto Rican children are included in the norm group in numbers proportionate to their percentage in the general population. This *does not erase* cultural differences because it does not permit comparison of lower-class black children against other lower-class black children, etc.

and types of logical thought. There is almost perfect consistency in the *sequence* or order in which structural concepts are acquired. While there are some cultural differences, these seem to be minimized when compared to other types of tests. Piaget (1971a) writes:

> In some social environments the stages are accelerated, whereas in others they are more or less systematically retarded. This differential development shows that stages are not purely a question of the maturation of the nervous system but are dependent upon interaction with the social environment and with experience in general. The order, however, remains constant. (p. 7)

Within American society, the research literature shows a small relationship between performance on Piagetian scales and social-economic class. I found a small but significant relationship between father's occupation (taken as a measure of social-economic class) and performance on conservation of number tasks in 222 kindergarten children (Wadsworth 1968).

While the idea of a culture-free test is probably a fantasy, some procedures are less affected by cultural differences than others. Piagetian scales seem to be one of these procedures. Comparisons of children in schools is less likely to be influenced by cultural or class differences using Piagetian measures than by using standardized tests.

Summary

Piagetian measures can be used to assess a child's level of cognitive development and reasoning capabilities. This *cannot* be done as readily using traditional intelligence tests. The two types of assessment procedures measure different things. Educational assessments in a Piagetian manner can be very useful in education.

For those educators interested in evaluating a child's comprehension, cognitive structure, and mental processes instead of specific content learnings, Piagetian procedures offer a viable alternative. They help to avoid the deceptions of the very verbal child and the nonverbal child as well. Some readers may construe Piagetian assessments as a more desirable and more valid measure of "intelligence" than traditional intelligence tests. It would be inaccurate to argue that all there is to intelligence is reasoning; but it is equally absurd to argue that reasoning has nothing to do with intelligence. In any event, Piagetian assessments and traditional intelligence and achievement tests measure *different* things.

The confirmation that Piagetian tasks measure something different from conventional intelligence and achievement tests makes intuitive sense. If one examines carefully a test such as the Wechsler Intelligence Scale for Children (WISC), one finds the test largely measures acquired or learned *content* and perceptual skills. There is very little reasoning involved on the test. Six subscales on the WISC are verbal tasks. The first is called "Information" and is a series of content questions. One of the simpler ones is, "How many legs does a dog have?" Another is, "Who discovered America?" Yet another is, "Who was Genghis Kahn?" The items in this section of the test are clearly content items. They do not measure skills of logical thought; they measure specific bits of memorized or "learned" information. To be able to say that "Columbus discovered America" does not require logical thinking and does not reflect any underlying cognitive structure.

The second subscale on the WISC, "Comprehension," is similar in not requiring reasoning skills. Some of the questions are: "What is the thing to do if you cut your finger?" "Why are criminals locked up?" and "What should you do if you see a train approaching a broken track?" The items on this subscale do not require reasoning; answers primarily reflect a child's awareness of normal social expectations. One of the subscales on the WISC, "Similarities," does to some extent reflect children's thinking. It contains questions like: "In what way are a cat and a mouse alike?" and "In what way are a mountain and a lake alike?" The items on this scale require verbal classification skills and can reflect qualitative differences in thinking. Nevertheless, this subscale alone provides a limited amount of information about children's thinking because there are no opportunities for exploring children's reasoning. The test administrator is never certain whether the responses reflect reasoning or rote memory or associations. Indeed, there is no concern for *how* the child arrives at an answer on this test; the concern is solely for whether the child's first response is correct.

The last six subscales on the WISC are called "performance scales." "Picture Completion" requires putting together four sets of puzzle pieces, one at a time, to form figures such as a horse and a car. "Block Design" requires arranging blocks in a given pattern. "Coding" is primarily a writing and reading task that requires writing down as quickly as possible the figures associated (coded on the test) with the letters of the alphabet. One can argue that some aspects of these tasks can reflect thinking, though the performance tests primarily reflect general visual and motor capabilities.

If one becomes familiar with Piagetian assessments and standardized intelligence tests such as the WISC, it becomes clear that they measure different things, as Stephen's (1972) study makes clear. Elkind (1971) suggests that traditional intelligence tests sample a much wider and probably less in-depth range of abilities than do Piagetian tasks. Thus Piagetian scales can be seen as revealing a profile of logical reasoning abilities, while conventional tests produce a broader profile of individual performance. Piagetian tasks primarily assess the cognitive *structures* the child has available, while tests such as the WISC assess cognitive *content*, verbal skills, and perceptual and motor skills.

Because these two types of tests, based on different conceptions of intelligence, measure different things, they cannot be viewed as sub-

stituting for one another. Both forms of assessment can be very useful in the hands of skilled examiners and skilled interpreters. The Piagetian method can give one information about a child's level of cognitive development and reasoning skills that is not available from the WISC. The WISC can give one information about a child's general store of information, verbal skills, and some aspects of visual and motor performance that is not directly available through Piagetian methods.

Assessing Cognitive Development

20

Using Piagetian Techniques

This section presents a description of how to conduct a Piagetian interview. The clinical method and features of a Piagetian clinical interview are described in the previous chapter and should be reviewed while reading this section. We can become more appreciative of Piaget's work if we try to assess children's reasoning. Like the child, we must be active in order to comprehend fully the objects we wish to know. We can never fully comprehend Piaget's theory merely by reading books.

The Assessment

There is no quick way to become a skilled clinical interviewer or assessor of children's reasoning. Piaget estimates a year of training, practice, and supervision to develop these skills. Probably the best way to begin to learn the techniques is to work with people who use them, or in a college testing course where the techniques are taught. While making full-scale developmental assessments of reasoning cannot be learned quickly, practicing and trying out tasks with children will enhance one's understanding of Piaget and of the children one works with.

Assessment of children, by any procedures, is fraught with danger. On the basis of test results you can fixate your thinking about a child. Test results tend to lead to conclusions. Piagetian assessment results are not immune to the misuses of test results. Piagetian techniques can be used to determine a child's level of reasoning about a particular concept or to assess a child's general level of reasoning with respect to his or her agemates. Currently there are no standardized Piagetian "tests" that permit one to classify school-age children in the same manner as standardized IQ and achievement tests. What a proficient examiner can do is make a relatively accurate determination of what stage of development a child is in, or approaching, and determine whether there is any degree of stage mixture. Also, the examiner can determine a child's level of reasoning with respect to a particular concept.

A Piagetian assessment is not a set of tasks or test items. It is primarily a *method* and a *philosophy* of assessment. A set of assessment tasks is provided in this chapter primarily as a "starter." After you understand the assessment method and philosophy, you can begin to create your own tasks and procedures. A major aspect of a Piagetian assessment is that the particular questions an examiner asks are determined by the child's answers to previous questions and his reasoning. Thus the procedure is *never* a set of fixed questions but a dynamic interchange between the examiner and the child. Of course, if you wish to determine how eight-year-old children reason about a particular concept, then you have to standarize the procedure sufficiently to ascertain that reasoning. But in that case the focus is on groups of children rather than individual children.

Where materials are called for, materials that are familiar to the child can be interchanged. For example, instead of using blocks for the term-to-term correspondence task in this chapter, you could use checkers, bottle caps, pennies, or stones. Or, for assessing conservation of liquid, you do not have to use standard laboratory beakers; glasses or plastic containers that are the same size and shape can be substituted. The materials can be improvised from what is available as long as they are familiar to the child. Many materials, such as standard one-inch colored blocks, can be used in several different tasks.

A Sample Interview

The following interview uses the term-to-term correspondence task found on page 251. Note that questions must be asked by the examiner in a way that avoids suggesting answers. Thus, one *does not* ask only, "Which row has more blocks?" which implies that one row has more blocks than the other. Questions should always include the possibility of equivalence *and* difference.

The examiner arranges a row of nine blue blocks, each about an inch apart, between himself and the child. *Examiner:* "Will you make a row of blocks using the red ones just like my row, and right in front of you?" The child makes a row below the examiner's row by first placing two end blocks in position, then placing eight blocks between those two without any careful comparison.

EXAMINER: Does one row of blocks have more blocks than the other, or do they both have the same number?
CHILD: They're the same.
E: Are you sure?
C: Yes.
E: How do you know they're the same number of blocks? (*request for reasoning*)
C: I can count them. (*Child proceeds to count the blocks in each row. He counts nine for the blue row and ten for the red row.*) They're different. There are more reds.
E: Can you make them so they have the same number?
(*Child removes one of the red blocks from the middle of the row and lines the other red ones up corresponding to the blue ones.*)
E: Now both rows have the same number of blocks?
C: Yes.
E: Okay, I'm going to move my blue blocks together like this. (*The row of blue blocks is collapsed so that they are about one-half inch apart.*) Now, are there more blocks in my row or in your row, or do we both have the same number of blocks?
C: I have more.
E: How can you tell?" (*request for reasoning*)
C: My row sticks out more (*preoperational reasoning*).
E: Okay, I'm going to make my row just like your row again. Who has more blocks now, or do we have the same number of blocks? (*Examiner makes his row of blocks as long as Child's.*)
C: Same.
E: How do you know? (*request for reasoning*)
C: See, they both come out to here and here. (*The child points to the ends of each row.*)
E: Now if I move your blocks closer together (*Child's row of blocks is collapsed the way Examiner's row was previously*),

do we both have the same number of blocks or does one of us have more blocks than the other?

c: You have more.

e: How do you know I have more? (*request for reasoning*)

c: Same as before; your row is bigger.

e: Why don't you count the number of blocks in each row? (*suggestion is made to determine whether counting influences reasoning*)

(*Child counts nine blocks for each row*)

e: How many blocks in your row?

c: Nine.

e: How many blocks in my row?

c: Nine.

e: Which row has more blocks or do they both have the same number of blocks?

c: You have more.

e: Tell me why I have more blocks than you have. (*request for reasoning*)

c: You have more blocks. They come out more (*pointing to the ends of Examiner's row*).

At this point the interview could have been terminated, and one would conclude that the child had not yet developed, or was still preoperational with respect to, term-to-term correspondence. The interview was extended in the following way to assess number concepts further.

e: Okay, I'm going to take one block out of my row like this (*see figure*)

Who has more blocks now, or do we still have the same number?

c: Same.

e: How do you know? (*request for reasoning*)

c: I can see it.

e: Why don't you count the number in each row again?

(*Child counts both rows. For Examiner's row Child counts*

*eight. For Child's row Child counts nine. After finishing
counting, Child looks puzzled.*)
c: I have more!
e: How do you know you have more? (*request for reasoning*)
c: I counted. I have nine and you have eight.
e: Is nine more than eight?
c: Yes!
(*Examiner then moves his row of eight blocks so the blocks
are about 1½ inches apart, forming a longer row than Child's
blocks* [see figure].)

E □ □ □ □   □ □ □   □

C   □□□□□□□□□

e: Do we have the same number of blocks now, or does one
of us have more blocks than the other?
c: You have more blocks.
e: Can you tell me why? (*request for reasoning*)
c: Your row has more. I see it.
e: Why don't you count the number of blocks in each row
once again?
(*Child counts eight for Examiner's row and nine for Child's
row.*)
e: Which row has more blocks or do we have the same number of blocks?
c: You have more.
e: Tell me why I have more blocks. (*request for reasoning*)
c: You've got more; your row is bigger.

At this point the interview was terminated. It was reasonably clear
that the child did not yet conserve number. The child was probably
close to being in transition from nonconservation to conservation;
at one level the child "knows" that nine is more than eight, but his
knowledge is incomplete. When faced with a conflict between perception and reasoning, the child still made a perceptual judgment,
and reasoning was not logical with respect to number. A child who
could conserve number would have gone through all the questions and
given "correct" answers followed by logical reasoning.

The reader should note the *way* in which the examiner asked questions. Equivalence questions were *always* asked to include the notion

of difference and similarity. Reasoning was requested after each answer the child gave to an equivalence question, whether the answer was correct or incorrect. One evaluates the child's reasoning as well as the child's answer. Counter-suggestions were not employed because the child did not give any "correct" answers to questions. Counter-suggestions would have been employed to test the resistance of the child's answers to suggestions if the child had given correct answers. Counter-suggestions are always illogical in their conclusion (see p. 226).

Assessment Tasks

I developed the following set of twenty-nine tasks to *introduce* the reader to the process of assessing children's reasoning. While the tasks have been designed to reflect accurately the fixed sequence in which children acquire knowledge according to Piaget, the tasks should not be thought to comprise a standardized test.[1] The tasks have come directly from the work of Piaget and his co-workers. Many of the tasks have been suggested by Stephens (1972) and are in line with the developmental sequence for achievement of Piagetian reasoning initially developed by Stephens, Mahoney, and McLaughlin (1972).[2]

The twenty-nine tasks selected for inclusion in the current set include tasks in classification (8), conservation (7), concrete reasoning (4), symbolic imagery (3), spatial orientations (2), and formal reasoning (5). The tasks cover the range of thought found in the preoperational period through the period of formal operations. Thus the tasks are appropriate for use with most elementary and secondary school children. Table 5 lists the tasks in the order in which reason-

1. Protocols for all tasks were written from descriptions provided in Stephens (1972) and from the other sources noted. I attempted throughout to preserve the validity of the tasks. The reader is cautioned that the assessments as they are presented here have not been completely validated in the usual manner, although I am experienced in using Piagetian methods for assessing children's reasoning. Thus, the assessments presented do not at this time meet the usual requirements for standardization.

2. Beth Stephens, Head of the Special Education Program at the University of Texas at Dallas, reports that the protocols for Piagetian assessments that she has been developing for several years are being readied for publication and may be in print now. To date, Stephens has been developing normative information on the sequence in which both normal and retarded children acquire reasoning skills. I anticipate that Stephens' publication will be of great interest to those interested in Piagetian assessments of school-age children.

ing is thought to develop, the approximate *average* mental ages at which each develops, and the *major* type of reasoning involved in each task. The reader will note that in several instances two or more levels of reasoning (assessments) are evaluated in one set of protocols. For example, Assessments 10, 18, and 19 deal with three different aspects of reasoning about the dissolution of sugar in water (substance, weight, and volume). The three assessments are all carried out at the same time and are contained within one set of protocols. Scoring of tasks has been limited to determining whether a child has or has not acquired a particular type of reasoning (dichotomous scoring).[3] Our experience to date has been that if one gets consecutive "failures" on two tasks that the child's level of development has been identified and further evaluation is usually not called for.

You should be able to assess a child's level of reasoning using five to ten assessments around what is thought to be a child's level of development. You should also be able to assess a child's reasoning relevant to a particular concept. With young children in particular, a lack of comprehension of relational terms such as "same," "more," or "less" may be a factor in a child's response to an examiner's questions. If there is any doubt about a child's understanding of any relational terms used in interviews, the child's comprehension should be checked in the following manner suggested by the work of Griffiths, Schantz, and Siegel (1967). Present the child with a set of four blocks and a set of three blocks, all of the same color. Questioning proceeds in the following manner:

1. "Tell me about the two piles of blocks." This is an effort to get a *spontaneous* use of relational terms.
2. "Does this pile of blocks [point to one] have more, less, or the same number of blocks as the other?"
3. "Point to the pile of blocks that has more blocks."
   "Point to the pile of blocks that has less blocks."
   "Point to the pile of blocks that has the same number of blocks."

If a child does not understand the relational terms used in the assessment questions, then his responses to questions cannot be assumed to

3. Stephens (1972) has developed methods for evaluating children's reasoning that result in more refined differentiations of children's reasoning abilities than a dichotomous score. Such scoring procedures will be of interest to persons wishing to make more sophisticated interpretations of children's reasoning than current procedures permit.

reflect his reasoning. A child's comprehension of the relational terms employed is an essential prerequisite to an effective interview.

A word of caution in interpreting the results of any assessment: I have included *approximate* mental ages when children typically develop the different reasoning abilities described in the assessments. These mental ages are approximations and *must* be treated as such. The tasks as they are described here do not constitute a valid "test." The primary purpose of these tasks is to introduce the reader to conducting Piagetian-type interviews of children. Mental ages cannot be derived from assessments using these tasks. Properly used, these assessments can determine a child's dominant stage of functioning and his or her reasoning regarding a particular concept. Children who appear to perform irregularly with respect to the sequence of tasks may do so for a variety of reasons, including:

1. *Normal stage mixture.* Some children will be more advanced with respect to one type of content than another. For example, a child *can* have an operational understanding of brother-sister relationships (Assessment 17) and not have an operational understanding of right-left (Assessment 15), due to considerably more experience with one concept over another.

2. *Inadequate assessment.* The person beginning to assess children's reasoning using the procedures described here (or any other procedures) is going to make some mistakes. Skill at interviewing requires time, practice, and adequate supervision. It is very easy to lead children into giving certain responses. The beginner must anticipate that his or her assessments will not be perfect at the outset.

3. *Age variations.* The ages at which children acquire particular concepts may vary from social group to social group because of their different experiential backgrounds. The evils of testing reside largely in the *interpretation and use of test results,* not in the instruments themselves. Unwarranted conclusions that lead to rigid classification of children and limited expectations must be guarded against. If Piaget tells us anything, it is that *all* children learn. Results of assessments can be constructively used in education only if they are directed toward facilitating learning.

TABLE 5

Developmental Sequence and Mental Ages for Achievement of Piagetian Reasoning Assessments[a]

Assessment Number	Name of Task	MA	Cognitive Ability
1	Intersection of classes	6	Classification
2	Rotation of beads	6	Symbolic imagery
3*	Euclidean space	7	Spatial reasoning
4	One-for-one exchange	7	Concrete reasoning
5	Term-to-term correspondence	7	Concrete reasoning
6	Conservation of length	7	Conservation
7	Conservation of liquids	7	Concrete reasoning
8	Conservation of length— rod sections	7	Concrete reasoning
9	Conservation of substance	7	Conservation
10	Dissolution of sugar— substance	7	Concrete reasoning
11	Conservation of weight	7	Conservation
12	Class inclusion—beads	7	Classification
13	Class inclusion— animals (1)	7	Classification
14	Relationships—right and left	7	Classification
15	Class inclusion— animals (2)	8	Classification
16	Relationships—brothers and sisters	8	Classification
17*	Spatial coordinates	9	Spatial reasoning
18	Dissolution of sugar— weight	9	Concrete reasoning
19	Dissolution of sugar— volume	10	Concrete reasoning

TABLE 5 (continued)

Assessment Number	Name of Task	MA	Cognitive Ability
20	Changing perspectives—stationary	11	Symbolic imagery
21	Changing perspectives—mobile	12	Symbolic imagery
22	Conservation of volume—solids	12	Formal reasoning
23	Combination of liquids	12	Formal reasoning
24*	Probability	12	Formal reasoning
25	Dissociation of weight and volume	13	Formal reasoning
26	Conservation of volume (1–3)	14	Conservation
27	Conservation of volume (4)	15	Conservation
28	Class inclusion—animals (3)	15	Classification
29	Class inclusion—animals (4)	16	Classification

ᵃ This table is adapted from Stephens (1972); the starred assessments I have added. Mental ages (MA) were determined for the nonstarred items by the Wechsler Intelligence Scale for Children (WISC) and the Wechsler Adult Intelligence Scale (WAIS). Mental ages for the starred items and some of the nonstarred items have been established through a research program at Mount Holyoke College (Heard and Wadsworth 1977).

Assessment 1
Intersection of Classes
(Stephens 1972)

PURPOSE OF TASK: To assess a child's comprehension of the intersection of classes; that an object can be in two different classes at the same time.

MATERIALS: 10 pictures; 5 of the same object, each picture of a different color (A); 5 of the same color, but of different objects (B). An assortment of other pictures (C) one of which is the intersect of A and B.

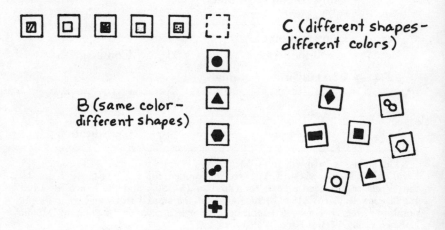

A (same shape-different colors)

B (same color - different shapes)

C (different shapes - different colors)

Arrangements of Materials

PROCEDURE: The rows of pictures are presented to the child as shown in the diagram. The child is then instructed to pick the single picture from the assorted array (C) that relates appropriately to both rows and to place it at the intersection of both rows. "Find the picture that goes with both the rows and put it in the corner where they meet" [pointing to the intersect]. Request reasoning for the picture selected. Give counter-suggestions if appropriate.*

COUNTER-SUGGESTION: Select a non-intersect picture, put it at the intersect, and say: "This picture fits in both rows just as well as yours, doesn't it?"

LEVELS OF PERFORMANCE: The child's understanding that an object can be a member of two classes or sets at the same time is acquired, on the average, around age six.

* A counter-suggestion is given by the examiner when a child gives a correct answer and correct reasoning for an answer. The purpose is to test the resistance of a child's beliefs to suggestion.

Assessment 2
Rotation of Beads

(Piaget 1952b, Stephens 1972)

PURPOSE OF TASK: To assess a child's ability to maintain an image through a transformation.

MATERIALS: Three different-colored beads (or small balls). These are attached to a stiff wire (A). An opaque tube wide enough to hold the beads or balls (B).

PROCEDURE: The beads are placed in the tube (C), and the child is asked to judge which bead will emerge first from the bottom of the tube. The beads are permitted to emerge, then placed back into the tube in the same order. The tube is rotated 180° (D). The child is again asked to predict which bead will emerge first from the bottom of the tube. Reasoning is asked for; the beads are permitted to emerge. Counter-suggestions are made when appropriate. The procedure can be repeated with the beads in different sequences.

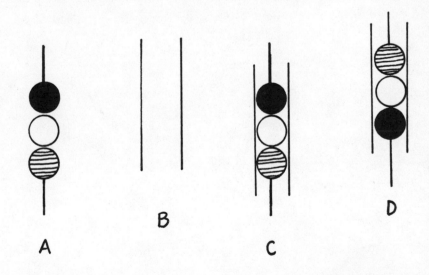

A

B

C

D

COUNTER-SUGGESTION: "If I turn the tube like this [rotate it], the red bead [incorrect color] will come out the bottom first, right?"
LEVELS OF PERFORMANCE: Children usually become capable of maintaining an image through a transformation around age six. Prior to acquisition, the child will typically predict that the colored bead that entered the tube first will exit the bottom first, regardless of whether the tube is rotated or not.

Assessment 3
Euclidean Space

(Piaget and Inhelder 1967)

PURPOSE OF TASK: To determine whether a child views space from a topological or Euclidean perspective.

MATERIALS: The following topological and Euclidean drawings; several pieces of paper and a pencil or crayon.

Topological Drawings

Euclidian Drawings

PROCEDURE: The child is shown the cards one at a time and asked to draw a picture just like the one on the card. The topological cards are presented first. Spontaneous "corrections" are permitted. After each drawing is completed the child is asked whether his drawing is just like the examiner's.

LEVELS OF PERFORMANCE: Children do not typically develop accurate Euclidean representations of space before age seven. They can recognize Euclidean shapes before this age but cannot represent them even though they have adequate motor control to do so. The typical child of 3½–4 years will draw topological representations with accuracy (they place the dot inside, outside, or on the line of the closed figure)

248

though they typically draw the different geometric shapes all as irregular closed figures. From the ages of 4½–5½, children typically become capable of representing circles and squares, although a rhombus and shapes with acute and obtuse angles are not differentiated in representation for another year.

Assessment 4
One-for-one Exchange
(Piaget 1952b, Stephens 1972)

PURPOSE OF TASK: To assess a child's comprehension of the equivalence of corresponding sets.

MATERIALS: Basket or box with 12 small packages; 8 pennies.

PROCEDURE: Inform the child that examiner has a "store" (the basket with 12 packages). Give the child the 8 pennies and instruct him to exchange with the examiner a coin for each package he "buys." At the conclusion of eight purchases, ask the child the equivalence question: "Do you have more packages or do I have more pennies or do we both have the same number?" The pennies are then spread in a row as shown. The packages are bunched close together. The equivalence question is repeated. Reasoning is requested. A counter-suggestion is given if the child's answer is "correct."

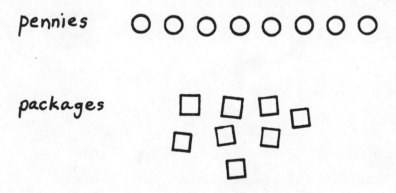

COUNTER-SUGGESTION: "If I put another package in the pile, then you still have the same number of packages as I have pennies, right?"

LEVELS OF PERFORMANCE: Understanding of the principle of one-to-one exchange and lasting equivalence is usually acquired around age seven. Prior to that, children make correct one-for-one exchanges of pennies for objects but do not conclude that the two sets exchanged are equivalent. Correct one-to-one exchange does not ensure understanding of equivalence.

Assessment 5
Term-to-term Correspondence

(Piaget 1952b, Stephens 1972)

PURPOSE OF TASK: To assess a child's comprehension of one-to-one correspondence and number.

MATERIALS: 16 blocks, 8 each of two different colors.

PROCEDURE: Arrange 8 blocks of one color in a row between the examiner and the child, placing the blocks about an inch apart. Ask the child to place blocks of the second color in front of each of the blocks that the examiner set out. After the child agrees that there are the same number of blocks in each row (A), collapse one row of blocks so that the row is shorter in length than the other row (B).

A

B

Ask the equivalence question: "Does one row of blocks have more blocks than the other, or do both rows have the same number of blocks?" Request reasoning for the answer. Make a counter-suggestion if the answer and reasoning are "correct." Move the collapsed row of blocks back to the original position (A). Ask the equivalence question again. Collapse the row not previously collapsed and repeat the procedure.

COUNTER-SUGGESTION: "If, I remove one block from this row [the longer row], each row will still have the same number of blocks, right?"

LEVELS OF PERFORMANCE: Equivalence in one-to-one correspondence is not attained until around age seven on the average. Prior to this, children may be able to place objects in one-to-one correspondence, but, as in the above problems, equivalence is not assured. For the preoperational child, the longer row has more elements than the shorter row even though they have been placed in correspondence.

Assessment 6
Conservation of Length
(*Piaget, Inhelder, and Szeminska 1964; Stephens 1972*)

PURPOSE OF TASK: To assess a child's reasoning as to whether the length of objects changes as a result of their movement or displacement.

MATERIALS: One 6-inch, one 10-inch, and two 8-inch wooden rods or dowels.

PROCEDURE: The child is asked to select two rods that are the same length. After equivalence of two rods is established, the two rods (8-inch) are placed parallel to one another and a few inches apart (A). The equivalence question is asked: "Are the two rods the same length, or is one rod longer than the other?" One rod is then moved approximately four inches to the right of the other rod (B). The

equivalence question is repeated. Reasoning is requested for the response. A counter-suggestion can be given at this time if the answer and reasoning are "correct." The rod that was moved is returned to the parallel position. The equivalence question is repeated. The same procedure is repeated, moving the rod to the left (C), then moving the rods, one left and one right (D).

COUNTER-SUGGESTION: After the movement (A), "If I move this one farther this way [to the right], it will be longer than the other one, right?" Demonstrate.

LEVELS OF PERFORMANCE: Conservation of length is usually attained around age seven. Prior to this, children see displacements of lengths as resulting in changes in lengths.

Assessment 7
Conservation of Liquids
(Piaget 1952a, Stephens 1972)

PURPOSE OF TASK: To assess a child's comprehension that a quantity of liquid does not change with a change in its shape.

MATERIALS: 2 beakers or glasses of same size and shape; 2 other containers, one wider and one taller and narrower than the first two containers; 4 containers that are smaller than the two beakers; plain or colored water.

PROCEDURE: The two beakers are filled with the same amount of water (A). Equivalence of the quantity of water in each is established. The water from one beaker is poured into the taller and narrower cylinder (B). The equivalence question is asked: "Is there more water in this container or that container, or do they both have the same amount of water?" Reasoning is requested for the answer. A

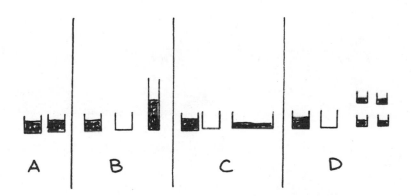

counter-suggestion is given if the answer and reasoning are correct. The water is returned to the original container (as in A). The equivalence question is repeated. The procedure is repeated with the widest container (C), and then with the four smallest containers (D).

COUNTER-SUGGESTION: "If I add some water to this container [the beaker in B], they will both still have the same amount of water, right?"

LEVELS OF PERFORMANCE: Conservation of liquid is usually acquired around age seven. Prior to acquisition, the typical child reasons that a change in the shape of the container results in a change in the quantity of liquid.

Assessment 8
Conservation of Length—Rod Sections
(Piaget, Inhelder, and Szeminska 1964; Stephens 1972)

PURPOSE OF TASK: To assess a child's reasoning about length when changes in configuration occur.

MATERIALS: One 16-inch rod and four 4-inch rods.

PROCEDURE: The procedure is essentially the same as in the conservation-of-length task (Assessment 5). The rods are arranged as in (A). Equivalence of length is established. The four short rods are displayed to form a W shape (B). The equivalence question is asked: "Which line of sticks is longer now, or are they both the same length?" Reasoning is requested and a counter-suggestion is given if appropriate. The sticks are returned to their original position (A). Transformations to an M shape (C) and a ── ── V shape (D) are executed following the same procedure.

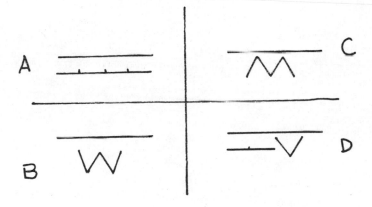

COUNTER-SUGGESTION: The W shape is collapsed even further, and the child is asked: "Now this rod [16-inch] is longer than the other ones, right?"

LEVELS OF PERFORMANCE: Conservation of length with rod sections is attained around age seven. Prior to this acquisition, children reason that a change in the configuration of the four 4-inch rods results in a change in their total length.

Assessment 9
Conservation of Substance
(Piaget and Inhelder 1941, Stephens 1972)

PURPOSE OF TASK: To assess a child's reasoning as to whether amount of a substance changes when its shape changes.

MATERIALS: Two balls of clay approximately 3 inches in diameter.

PROCEDURE: Obtain equivalence of the two balls of clay, taking some clay from one ball if necessary. Transform one ball of clay into a "hotdog" shape. Ask the equivalence questions: "Is there more clay in one of the pieces of clay now, or do they both have the same amount of clay?" Request reasoning for answer and give counter-suggestion if appropriate. Return the transformed clay (hotdog) to its original shape. Repeat the equivalence question. Repeat the above procedure with transformations to a "pancake" shape, then break one ball into several (10–12) small pieces.

COUNTER-SUGGESTION: "If I stretch the hotdog piece longer, now it has more clay than the other piece, doesn't it?"

LEVELS OF PERFORMANCE: Conservation of substance is usually acquired around age seven. Prior to conservation, the transformation of a shape results in a change in quantity in the child's reasoning.

Assessment 10*
Dissolution of Sugar—Substance

(*Inhelder 1968, Stephens 1972*)

PURPOSE OF TASK: To assess a child's reasoning about dissolved substances:

1. Substance: After sugar dissolves in water, is there still sugar in the glass? (Assessment 10)
2. Weight: Is weight unchanged as sugar dissolves? (Assessment 18)
3. Volume: After the sugar dissolves, is there as much sugar as before? (Assessment 19)

MATERIALS: Two identical beakers or jars filled to the same level with water (preferably warm water); several sugar cubes or packets of

PROCEDURE: Equivalence of the amount and weight of water in each container is established. A cube of sugar is placed in one container and dissolved. Three questions are asked:

1. "Do the two containers of water still weigh the same or is one heavier than the other?" (purpose 2)
2. "Is there the same amount of sugar in the water as there was in the cube, or is there less or more?" (purpose 3)
3. "Are the water levels of the two containers the same, or is one higher than the other?" (purpose 1)

Each answer to each question is followed by a request for reasoning and a counter-suggestion if appropriate.

COUNTER-SUGGESTIONS:

1. "If I put a sugar cube in the other glass, this one will still be heavier, right?"
2. "If I put some more water in the glass with the sugar cube, there will be less sugar; is that right?"
3. "If I put two more cubes of sugar in this one, this one will still have the same amount as the other one, right?"

LEVELS OF PERFORMANCE: Understanding the dissolution of sugar problem is attained around age seven for substance, age nine for weight, and age ten for volume.

* Assessment 10 includes the procedures for Assessments 10, 18, and 19. These three assessments deal with the same content and are lumped together for that reason.

260

Assessment II
Conservation of Weight
(Piaget and Inhelder 1941, Stephens 1972)

PURPOSE OF TASK: To assess a child's reasoning about whether the weight of a substance changes when its shape changes.

MATERIALS: Two balls of clay approximately 3 inches in diameter; a scale or balance.

PROCEDURE: Obtain equivalence of weight of the two balls of clay, subtracting some clay from one ball if necessary. The child is encouraged to use the scale to confirm the equivalence. Remove the clay balls from the scale. Transform one ball of clay into a "hotdog" shape. Ask the equivalence question for weight: "Does one piece of clay weigh more than the other now or do they both weigh the same?" Ask for reasoning. Permit the use of the scale. Give a counter-suggestion if appropriate. Return the transformed shape to a ball and repeat the equivalence question. Repeat the same procedure transforming one ball of clay into a "pancake" shape, then into 10 or 12 small pieces.

COUNTER-SUGGESTION: "If I stretch the hotdog piece out even more [demonstrate], it will weigh more than the ball of clay, right?"

LEVELS OF PERFORMANCE: Conservation of weight is usually acquired around age seven. Prior to attainment, the transformation of the shape of an object is reasoned to result in a change in its weight.

Assessment 12
Class Inclusion—Beads
(Piaget 1952b, Stephens 1972)

PURPOSE OF TASK: To assess a child's comprehension of the addition of classes (when objects are members of two classes at the same time).
MATERIALS: 10 or more wooden beads, so that 2 beads are of one color and the remainder of another color.
PROCEDURE: The child is shown the beads, either in containers or in piles on a table. The ability of the child to classify the beads by color and material is determined. The following questions can be used: "How many white beads are there?" "What are the white beads made of?" "How many black beads are there?" "What are the black beads made of?"

When it is clear that the child can classify all the beads by color and material, the class inclusion question is asked: "Are there more wooden beads or are there more black beads?" Reasoning is requested. A counter-suggestion is given if the child's answer and reasoning are "correct."
COUNTER-SUGGESTION: "If the white beads are taken away, there are more wooden beads than black beads, right?"
LEVELS OF PERFORMANCE: Class inclusion is usually developed around age seven. Prior to this, children have difficulty reasoning using two classifications (color and material) at the same time. Perceptually, it looks like there is more of one than the other, so a perceptual response is made.

Assessment 13[*]
Class Inclusion—Animals (1)
(Inhelder and Piaget 1969, Stephens 1972)

PURPOSE OF TASK: To assess a child's comprehension of the relationship of subcategories of animals to categories of animals.

MATERIALS: 13 small pictures: 4 of ducks, 3 of birds other than ducks, and 6 of wingless animals.

PROCEDURE: The child is presented with the 13 cards and asked to make 3 piles, putting together the cards that go together. After the collections of ducks, birds, and animals are completed (the examiner may have to help sort the cards into the three desired collections and ask whether the ones put together go together), the following questions are asked:

1. "How many ducks are there?" "How many birds are there?" "How many animals are there?"
2. "In the whole world are there more birds or more animals? Why?" (Assessment 28)
3. "Suppose that the Indians laughed and said, 'We are going to kill all the ducks.' Would any birds be left?" (Assessment 13)
4. "Can we put this pile [ducks] with this pile [birds]?" "Can we put all three piles together [ducks and birds and animals]?" (Assessment 15)
5. Separate into two piles the ducks (4 cards) and the birds (3 cards). Ask the question "Are there more ducks or more birds?" (Assessment 29)

After responses to the questions, ask for reasoning and offer counter-suggestions if appropriate.

COUNTER-SUGGESTION [Question 4]: "If I had three cards with fish on them, I could put them with the birds too, couldn't I?" and "My fish cards wouldn't fit with the animals, would they?"

LEVELS OF PERFORMANCE: Question 1 merely establishes whether the child can differentiate and accurately identify the number of ducks, birds, and animals. Question 2 (Assessment 28) requires the

---

[*] Assessment 13 includes the procedures for Assessments 15, 28, and 29 because these deal with the same content and are most easily presented together.

manipulation of abstract categories and correct reasoning is attained around age fifteen. Question 3 (Assessment 13) requires the analysis and synthesis of categories and appropriate reasoning is also acquired around age seven. Question 4 (Assessment 15) requires class-inclusion reasoning, and such reasoning is usually acquired around age eight. Question 5 (Assessment 29) was found by Stephens (1972) not to be solved correctly until about age sixteen. This task requires hierarchical classification while dealing with conflicting pictorial cues.

Assessment 14
Relationships—Right and Left
(Piaget 1964b, Stephens 1972)

PURPOSE OF TASK: To determine the child's understanding of right/left relationships.

MATERIALS: Four different objects (e.g., pencil, key, coin, piece of paper).

PROCEDURE: The child is asked: (1) to identify his or her own right and left limbs, (2) to identify the examiner's right and left limbs while the examiner is opposite the child. Place three objects in a row on the table (Set 1). While the child is facing the row of objects, ask the child: "Is the pencil to the left or right of the key? Is the

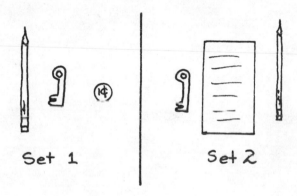

Set 1   Set 2

penny to the left or right of the key?" "Is the key to the left or right of the penny? Is the pencil to the left or right of the penny?" "Is the penny to the left or the right of the pencil? And the key, is it to the left or right of the pencil?" (six questions and answers).

Show the child the arrangement of three items as in Set 2. Tell the child to look at them carefully because you are going to cover them up soon. After about half a minute, cover the Set 2 items. Ask the child to recall the position of the items using the six questions previously used.

COUNTER-SUGGESTION: "If we move to the other side of the table, the key [object 2] will still be on the left of the penny [object 3], right?"

LEVELS OF PERFORMANCE: Stephens (1972) reports that children demonstrate an understanding of left-right relations about age seven. Prior to that time, children may correctly identify their own right and left hands but do not use the terms in a relational sense.

Assessment 15
Class Inclusion—Animals (2)

See Assessment 13 for procedure.

Assessment 16
Relationships—Brothers and Sisters
(Piaget 1964b, Stephens 1972)

PURPOSE OF TASK: To determine the child's comprehension of brother-sister relationships.

MATERIALS: None.

PROCEDURE:

1. Ask the child: "Are you a brother [or sister]? What is a brother [or sister]?"
2. Ask the child to relate the concepts of brother and sister to his own family; e.g., "How many brothers have you? How many sisters have you?" Ask how many brothers and sisters each other child in the family has. For example, in the case of one sister, Joan, ask: "How many brothers does Joan have? How many sisters does Joan have?"
3. "How many brothers are there in your family? How many sisters? How many brothers and sisters altogether?"
4. Ask the child to apply the concept to a hypothetical family. For example, "There are three brothers in a family: Peter, Bob, and David. How many brothers does Peter have? and Bob? and David?"
5. "Judy has three sisters: Sarah, Betty, and Ruth. How many sisters has Betty? How many sisters are there in the family?"

COUNTER-SUGGESTION [For (2)]: "Your sister has one brother, so you must have one brother too, right?"

LEVELS OF PERFORMANCE: The relationship of brother and sister is not well developed until around age eight. Prior to that time, children typically do not consider themselves as being brothers or sisters, though they may know how many brothers and sisters they have. Children may report that they are a brother (or sister) around age four or five. A correct definition employing the idea that to be a brother or sister one must have a brother or sister is not acquired until around age eight. Early definitions are that a brother is a "boy" and a sister a "girl." There appear to be little differences between only children and those with siblings in their responses to these questions.

Assessment 17
Spatial Coordinates

PURPOSE OF TASK: To coordinate the world around him, the child must develop a spatial reference system which has a stable vertical and horizontal axis. This task is used to assess the child's understanding of spatial coordinates.

MATERIALS: Two 1-quart bottles, one of which is ½ full of colored water; 5 sheets of paper with a bottle represented in the different positions shown; a crayon or pencil.

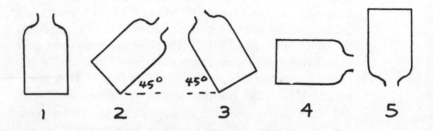

PROCEDURE: The child is shown the bottle half full of water in the different positions illustrated. The child is asked to observe the water levels in these positions. The bottle with water in it is removed from view and the empty bottle is shown in the vertical position (1). The child is given a sheet of paper with the bottle so represented that the bottle is vertical to the child and asked to draw a line where the water level would be if the bottle were half full of water. The child is asked to color in or shade in the portion of the bottle where the water is. The procedure is repeated through the five bottle positions. At the conclusion, reasoning for drawing the water level in certain ways is requested. Counter-suggestions are made where appropriate.

COUNTER-SUGGESTION: "I can draw the water level this way [incorrect], can't I?"

LEVELS OF PERFORMANCE: Until the age of approximately nine years, children typically draw the water level as parallel to the bottom of the bottle regardless of the orientation of the bottle. The coordination of external and internal reference systems is not stable. Young children will frequently be seen to draw the water level correctly in number five, but will place the water in the upper half of the bottle.

Assessment 18
Dissolution of Sugar—Weight

See Assessment 10 for procedure.

Assessment 19
Dissolution of Sugar—Volume

See Assessment 10 for procedure.

Assessment 20*
Changing Perspectives—Stationary

(Piaget and Inhelder 1967, Stephens 1972)

PURPOSE OF TASK: To assess a child's ability to change perspectives.
MATERIALS: A tower, a house, and a tree made of cardboard or other materials so they can stand; 4 pictures of four different perspectives, as shown on page 271.

---

* Includes procedures for Assessment 21.

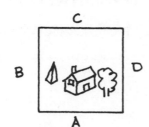

Initial arrangement on table.

Pictures of perspectives

PROCEDURE: The tower, house, and tree are placed on a table as shown in the initial arrangement.

1. Changing perspectives, mobile: The child is asked to move around the table and view the collection from the four different sides of the table or perspectives (A–D). After moving through the different positions, the child is seated and asked to select the drawing which represents the complex when viewed from each of the four perspectives.

2. Changing perspectives, stationary: The child is seated at (A) and shown a drawing (B, C, or D). The child is asked where a person would have to stand in order to see the perspective corresponding to a drawing shown to the child. Repeat with one or two other drawings.

LEVELS OF PERFORMANCE: Not until about age eleven for perspectives, stationary, and about age twelve for perspectives, mobile, are children able to coordinate perspectives as they are viewed from other positions. Children typically do not distinguish between the viewpoint they see and other possible perspectives. Thus the arrangement viewed from other sides of the table (B, C, D) are thought to be the same as from where the child is (A).

Assessment 21
Changing Perspectives—Mobile
See Assessment 20 for procedure.

Assessment 22
Conservation of Volume—Solids
(Piaget, Inhelder, and Szeminska 1964)

PURPOSE OF TASK: To assess a child's understanding of solid volumes, and the conservation principle that a change in shape does not result in a change in volume.

MATERIALS: 80 or 90 one-inch wooden blocks.

PROCEDURE: The child is shown a building 4 blocks high with a base of 3 × 3 blocks as shown (1). It is explained that each block is a room. The child is asked to build a building that will have the same

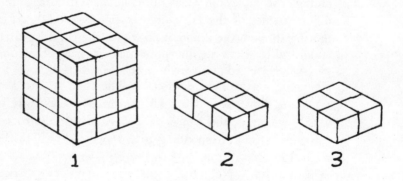

number of rooms as the model (1), but on a base of 2 × 3 blocks (2), and then on a base of 2 × 2 blocks (3). At the end of each construction the child is asked if his building has the same number of rooms as the model. Reasoning is requested. Counter-suggestions are offered if appropriate.

272

COUNTER-SUGGESTION: When the 2 × 3-block base construction is correct, ask: "If I add six more rooms on top of your building [demonstrate], it still has the same number of rooms as mine, right?"

LEVELS OF PERFORMANCE: Correct constructions reflecting conservation of solid volumes are not attained until age twelve on the average. Children four to six years of age typically will not build their buildings higher than the model regardless of the base. At ages eight and nine they begin measuring correctly using cubes as units. Around age twelve, children discover (invent) the relationship between area and volume, and this is apparent in their reasoning.

Assessment 23
Combination of Liquids
(Inhelder and Piaget 1958, Stephens 1972)

PURPOSE OF TASK: To assess a child's comprehension of combinatorial logic (reasoning) using chemical substances.

MATERIALS: Five identical bottles each filled with a different colorless liquid: (1) diluted sulphuric acid, (2) water, (3) oxygenated water, (4) thiosulphate (a bleach), and (5) potassium iodide; 4 beakers or jars; an eyedropper.

PROCEDURE: The child is shown two containers, one containing acid and oxygenated water (1 + 3); the second containing plain water (2). Several drops of potassium iodide (5) are added to each glass. The reaction is noted: (1 + 3 + 5) yield a yellow-colored liquid; (2 + 5) result in a clear liquid. The child is asked to reproduce the yellow color and determine which liquids, when combined, produce the yellow-colored liquid.

LEVELS OF PERFORMANCE: The systematic exploration of all possible combinations of liquids until a correct solution is achieved is not attained until about age twelve. Prior to this age, children's combinations are less systematic and result in limited combination of liquids. At the preoperational level, children typically try only combinations of two liquids at a time. At the concrete operational level, children frequently combine potassium iodide with all the other liquids one at a time and sometimes try some combination of three liquids, but not systematically, and so achieve a correct solution only by chance.

Assessment 24
Probability
(Piaget and Inhelder 1969)

PURPOSE OF TASK: To assess the child's comprehension of probability.
MATERIALS: 96 one-inch wooden blocks of four different colors; the distribution by color should be 36, 36, 20, 4; a paper bag or box.
PROCEDURE: Separate the blocks into groups by color. Divide each color group in half. Half the blocks of each color are given to the child and set aside to be used as a reference set. The rest of the blocks are placed in the paper bag and mixed up. Make sure that the child is aware that the reference set of blocks is identical to the set of blocks in the bag. Tell the child you are going to pull two blocks out of the paper bag without looking at them. Ask the child to guess what the colors of the two blocks will be. Continue this procedure until all the blocks are pulled from the bag. Periodically ask "Why?" after predictions and before draws. As blocks are drawn, place them on the table but separate from the child's reference set. Permit the child to organize the drawn blocks if he wishes to do so. Note the strategy that the child uses for predicting. Counter suggestions can be made before draws (e.g., "I think the next two blocks will be yellow and green [low-probability colors]. What do you think?")
LEVELS OF PERFORMANCE: The ability to make predictions based on probability is not well established until formal operations are developing. While I am not aware of any adequate mental age norms for this task, typical children do not seem to use systematic probability on these types of tasks until about age twelve (Piaget and Inhelder 1969). Probability is reflected in those judgments where the child's predictions are based on the number of blocks of each color that remain in the bag. This can be determined throughout the task by comparison of the number of blocks already drawn with the child's reference set. Children without formal operations generally respond by guessing which color blocks will be drawn. Preoperational children are prone to make "perceptual" responses. They frequently predict the next colors to be drawn to be the same as the color of the previous block drawn. Children sometimes guess their favorite color.

Concrete operational children frequently use a clear strategy, but it is not based on probability. Piaget and Inhelder (1969) write:

> . . . the child must be capable of at least two operations characteristic of this level. He must be able to apply a combinational system that enables him to take into consideration all the possible combinations of the given elements; and he must be able to calculate proportions, however elementary, so that he can grasp the fact (which eludes subjects on the previous levels) that probabilities like 3/9 and 2/6, etc., are equivalent. It is not until the age of eleven or twelve that the child understands combinatorial probabilities. . . . (p. 144)

Assessment 25
Dissociation of Weight and Volume
(Stephens 1972)

PURPOSE OF TASK: To assess a child's understanding of the relationship between weight and volume.

MATERIALS: Two identical beakers or glasses containing the same amount of water; a number of sinking cylinders varying in height and density, some of which are of equal height, but different density. Two cylinders of the same height and density but of different diameter.

PROCEDURE:

1. Obtain agreement of the equivalence of the amount of water in each container. Place the cylinders two by two (one in each container) in the containers in succession until all combinations are tried. Prior to each immersion, ask the child to predict whether the water level after immersion will be the same or different in the two containers. Request reasoning for answers. Make counter-suggestions when appropriate.

2. Place a cylinder in one container. Ask the child to select a cylinder or cylinders that will raise the water level in the other container to the same level as the water level in the container with a cylinder in it. Request reasoning. Make counter-suggestion if appropriate. Some children will begin to make judgments based on the height of cylinders. In this case, ask the child to predict using the two cylinders of the same height and density but of different diameters.

COUNTER-SUGGESTION: Suggest that two weights will raise the water levels the same when they will not.

LEVELS OF PERFORMANCE: Reasoning that sinking objects displace their volume is attained around age thirteen. Prior to that time, children typically believe that water level is influenced by the weight of the object immersed.

Assessment 26*
Conservation of Volume (1–3)
(Piaget and Inhelder 1941, Stephens 1972)

PURPOSE OF TASK: To assess a child's reasoning about whether the volume of liquid a sinking object displaces changes when the shape of the object is changed ("Does density of an object change with a change in shape?"); and to assess a child's understanding of relationship between weight of sinking objects and volume displaced.

MATERIALS: Two small balls of clay; a metal ball or stone the same size as a ball of clay; 2 beakers or jars of the same size, each filled about half full of water.

PROCEDURE: Obtain equivalence of size (volume) of the two balls of clay and the metal ball. Obtain equivalence of the amount of water in the two containers.

1. Transform one ball of clay into a "hotdog" shape. Ask the equivalence question: "Will the water level be the same if I put the ball of clay in this container and I put the "hotdog" in this other container, or will the water levels be different?" Ask for reasoning. Give counter-suggestion if appropriate. Return the "hotdog" to its original shape and repeat the equivalence question.
2. Transform one ball of clay into a "pancake" shape and repeat the procedure in (1) above.
3. Break one ball of clay into 10 or 12 pieces and repeat the procedure in (1) above.
4. Substitute the heavy ball for one of the balls of clay. Ask the equivalence question. Request reasoning.

COUNTER-SUGGESTION: [For (1)]: "If I make the hotdog longer [demonstrate], it will make the water level go higher than the ball of clay will, right?"

LEVELS OF PERFORMANCE: Conservation of volume (1–3), or the reasoning that sinking objects displace their volume, conservation of formation in their shape, is usually attained around age fourteen. The reasoning that sinking objects displace their volume, conservation of

---

* Includes procedure for Assessment 27.

volume (4), is usually attained around age fifteen. Prior to these levels of development, changes in shape are predicted by children to affect the amount of water displaced, and heavy sinking objects are predicted to displace more water than lighter sinking objects.

Assessment 27
Conservation of Volume (4)

See Assessment 26 for procedure.

Assessment 28
Class Inclusion—Animals (3)

See Assessment 13 for procedure.

Assessment 29
Class Inclusion—Animals (4)

See Assessment 13 for procedure.

Concluding

21

Thoughts

From a cognitive-development perspective, education should be directed to help the child maximize his intellectual, social, and ethical development and to structure educational programs so as to encourage the acquisition of skills in ways that are consistent with development. Piaget (1973) writes:

> The proposition "every person has the right to education" . . . means . . . every person has the right to be placed in a scholastic environment during his formation which will enable him to build until completion the basic tools of adaptation which are the processes of logic. . . .
> Affirming the right of all human beings to education is to take on far greater responsibility than simply to assure to each one reading, writing, and arithmetic capabilities; it is to guarantee fairly to each child the entire development of his mental faculties and the acquisition of knowledge and of ethical values corresponding to the exercise of these faculties until adaptation to actual social life. (pp. 50, 53–54)

A central thesis of this book is that the contribution of education to the development of advanced intellectual and social reasoning is best fostered in an educational and social environment aligned with principles of development. All species strive to adapt to their environment. Education is an aspect of man's environment designed by man. The environment that children are provided with is the reality with which they will try to come to grips. The question for society and educators is: "To what experiences are we going to try to make children adapt?"

Everyone agrees that children should acquire adequate skills in reading, mathematics, and other academic disciplines *by the time* they graduate from *high school*. Much of this book has suggested that the skills and contents we wish children to acquire by the end of high school are not things that children can really begin to develop and learn much before the period of formal operations (age eleven or so). In some ways, *this* is when first grade as it is conceived in most schools should begin!

What, then, should the goals of preschool and elementary school education be? I would like to suggest a few affective goals that are frequently overlooked. In my view it is *most* important during the early formative years that children: (1) come to like themselves and view themselves as capable learners, (2) come to like school, (3) come to like teachers, and (4) come to believe that teachers like them. Children need to develop positive attitudes about themselves, about learning, and about education.

Other goals are important too, but it is doubtful that it is necessary for a six- or seven-year-old to be "reading" close to "second-grade level" at the end of first grade. Cramming high school goals into the elementary school years makes little sense, given what is known about children and development. In the early years, one needs to be *more concerned* with *developing concrete concepts* and *positive attitudes*. The elementary school child who learns to hate himself, hate school, and hate learning is poisoned at the outset, possibly for life. The child who comes to like learning and to like himself is more apt to go forward on a positive footing, both emotionally and developmentally.

Piaget shows us that *all* children develop and learn. One can say, as Smith (1975) does, that children are learning devices, the most efficient ones ever made. We need to make better use of what we know about how children develop and learn, and what we know about the individual differences between children. If a more appropriate match between children's development and their educational experiences can be made, classrooms and schools can become more productive, more enjoyable, and more supportive places for everyone involved—children, teachers, and parents.

Piaget's developmental perspective argues for an increase in children's self-selection of activities at all educational levels to permit spontaneous interest to activate the efficient learning mechanisms in all children. An active learner is more likely to be a motivated and happy learner, and children in schools should enjoy what they do a large part of the time. One does not have to be unhappy to learn! Children need to be encouraged to interact in school, to discuss, argue, consult, and exchange views about knowledge in orderly but not stifling ways. Children can learn and be taught by one another. The largest source of untapped assistance for the teacher are students themselves. Teaching *is* a valid learning experience. More use of students as teachers should be encouraged, as is the practice in many informal classrooms.

It has been argued that in addition to an increase in spontaneous activity and active learning, elementary schools need to deemphasize symbolic activities. Symbols and signs should not be eliminated. Written words and numbers should be put in proper perspective in relation to the development of concepts and introduced to children when they are meaningful, spontaneously of interest, or have some clear adaptive value. Ashton-Warner's (1963) program is an example of a meaningful, individualized, positive, and nurturant reading, writing, and spelling program designed to bring children into the world of written words in a sane way. Dienes (1971) in a similar manner suggests how written mathematics can be made meaningful. Children can be "pushed" intellectually, but the pushing should be done largely by the *structure* of the educational environment the teacher creates. The pushing should be done by the many options for action on objects that the environment offers.

Piaget's view of the child has suggested many new ways of looking at children and the mental processes we infer children to have. Piaget has outlined for us a view of intelligence as a construction of the child: a dynamic system continuously subjected to revision by contact with the environment. It is a view primarily of the effects of active experience on the development of knowledge. While Piaget has described the course of *normal* development, by implication he has told us about developmentally related learning problems as well. The child whose intellectual development is delayed, regardless of the factors, typically is unable to "learn" contents that his nondelayed agemates can learn. Piaget has made it clear that many concepts cannot be acquired with comprehension unless prerequisite concepts have been acquired. He has also suggested that education too frequently tries to get average and advanced children to learn things they cannot learn (comprehend). These children can no more learn the impossible than their developmentally delayed peers can.

A major concern for education remains motivating children to learn. Piaget has shown that children *do not* have to be motivated to learn. Neither the carrot nor the whip are necessary. If children are provided with opportunities to act on objects in prepared environments, to undertake activities that challenge them spontaneously, motivation will not be lacking, and "discipline problems" will be minimized. What children have to be motivated and bribed to "learn" are things that make no sense to them and things that they cannot learn.

Discipline problems frequently reflect the child's conscious or unconscious awareness that what he is asked to learn is impossible for him to learn, meaningless to him, or of no "real" value (in the adaptive sense). Of course there are other reasons for discipline problems. Going to school is compulsory under the law. If adults were required to go to school, to sit quietly in rows, to learn things they could not comprehend, and to learn things they could not see any reason for learning, what would their reaction be? Somehow we have persuaded ourselves that such treatment is good for children, and by implication, good for society. Is it any wonder that so many children dislike school at such an early age? It is not the end goals of education that are askew, but the *means*. Some traditional views, ignorance of the developing child, and the politicalization of education have imposed on educational practice. Education is presumably for the benefit *of the child* and of society. From a Piagetian view, society has selected means that do not appear best for the child; it is also hard to figure out how they can be best for society!

The transformation of psychological theory into teaching practice is at best an experimental process. Any idea must be tried out in the local school context and adapted to local conditions. Any school faction (parents, teachers, administrators, school boards, etc.) can easily relegate any new program to the scrap heap. Over the years, various innovations in curriculum and teaching methods have come down the road. Most of these have failed to be successfully incorporated into educational practice, and this has produced considerable cynicism on the part of everyone involved. What needs to change is how people think about children and learning. Change does not always require massive outlays of taxpayers' money. A change in thinking does not cost money. What does cost a great deal more than money is the waste in human resources; society along with the child pays this price.

A school is a social system. Like Piaget's egocentric adolescent, the idealistic teacher without a realistic orientation to the social pressures within school systems is in for an adaptive experience in a school system permeated by a philosophy of education opposed to his or her views. These schools are not always "bad" (although some schools are criminal), but they operate on different collective assumptions. My purpose here is not to tell the reader how to teach or what to teach. My purpose is simply to relate what Piaget has said that is relevant to education—and my interpretation of what this means for education. I hope the reader will try out, experiment with, and eventually use Piagetian concepts to add to and modify his or her present teaching.

I think a kindergarten-through-high-school program that incorporates the best of Piaget and other educational and developmental knowledge can result in positive change in education—if it is given a chance. But the reality of change involves several factors:

1. All factions within the school system must be sympathetic to the proposed change and *truly* willing to give it a try.
2. Teachers must understand the proposed change in sufficient depth to implement it effectively.
3. Transition problems from one system to another always exist and must be endured.
4. There are always pressures against change; "no change" represents security for many people.

The British Infant School model, which is based in part on Piagetian concepts, cannot be transmitted across the Atlantic and set down intact to "work" in Harlem, Denver, South Hadley, or Kingsville. In the same way, no program can be implemented without planning, revision, evaluation, and modification to meet the unique needs of the local school system. But it must be done. Where does it start? It starts with a concept—a new or different way of looking at the world—or an intuitive way formalized and reinforced by thoughts of others. Like the child's concepts, our concepts do and can develop. Like the child, we must actively construct and use our concepts; we must test them, revise them. We must develop.

Bibliography

Almy, M. "Piaget and Early Childhood Education." Fifth Annual Symposium of the Jean Piaget Society, Philadelphia, June 1975.

Ashton-Warner, Sylvia. *Teacher*. New York: Simon & Schuster, 1963.

——. *Spearpoint*. New York: Knopf, 1972.

Ayers, D. J. "Assessing Cognitive Development via Measures of Optimal Performance." In *Measurement and Piaget*, edited by D. Green, M. Ford, and G. Flamer. New York: McGraw-Hill, 1971. Pp. 245–55.

Balikci, A. *The Netsilik Eskimo*. Garden City, N.Y.: Natural History Press, 1970.

Barsch, R. *Achieving Perceptual-motor Efficiency: A Space-oriented Approach to Learning*. Seattle: Special Child Publications, 1967.

Bearison, D. J. "The Role of Measurement Operations in the Acquisition of Conservation." *Developmental Psychology* 1 (1969): 653–60.

——. "The Comparative Development of Social and Physical Knowledge." Paper presented at the annual meeting of the Jean Piaget Society, Philadelphia, June 1975. Mimeographed.

Bereiter, C., and Engelmann, S. *Teaching Disadvantaged Children in the Preschool*. Englewood Cliffs, N.J.: Prentice-Hall, 1966.

Birns, B., and Golden, M. "The Implications of Piaget's Theory for Contemporary Infancy." In *Piaget in the Classroom*, edited by M. Schwebel and J. Raph. New York: Basic, 1973. Pp. 114–37.

Brearley, Molly. *The Teaching of Young Children*. New York: Schocken, 1970.

Bruner, J. R. "Nature and Uses of Immaturity." *American Psychologist*, August 1973, pp. 687–708.

Bruner, J. S.; Olver, Rose R.; and Greenfield, Patricia M., eds. *Studies in Cognitive Growth*. New York: Wiley, 1966.

Carnegie Quarterly 23, no. 3 (Summer 1975).

Chaney, C., and Kephart. N. *Motoric Aids to Perceptual Learning*. Columbus, Ohio: Merrill, 1968.

Charlesworth, W. "The Role of Surprise in Cognitive Development." In *Studies in Cognitive Development*, edited by D. Elkind and J. Flavell. New York: Oxford University Press, 1969. Pp. 257–314.

Copeland, R. *How Children Learn Mathematics*. 2nd ed. New York: Macmillan, 1974a.

——. *Diagnostic and Learning Activities in Mathematics for Children*. New York: Macmillan, 1974b.

Cruickshank, W. *The Teacher of Brain-injured Children*. Syracuse, N.Y.: Syracuse University Press, 1966.

DeMao, Vicki L. "A Piagetian Interpretation of Reading in Early Childhood." In *Piagetian Theory and the Helping Professions*, edited by M. Paulsen, J. Magary, and G. Lubin. Los Angeles: University of Southern California Press, 1976. Pp. 138–52.

deMeuron, M. "The Uses of Clinical and Cognitive Information in the Classroom." In *Piaget in the Classroom*, edited by M. Schwebel and J. Raph. New York: Basic, 1973. Pp. 231–57.

DeVries, R. "Relationship among Piagetian, Achievement, and Intelligence Assessments." Paper presented at the annual meeting of the American Educational Research Association, New Orleans, 1973a.

———. "The Two Intelligences of Bright, Average, and Retarded Children." Paper presented at the annual meeting of the Society for Research in Child Development, Philadelphia, 1973b.

Dewey, J. "The Primary-educational Fetish." *The Forum*. Washington, D.C.: Government Printing Office, May 1898.

———. *Experience and Education*. New York: Collier, 1970.

Dienes, Z. P. *Building Up Mathematics*. London: Hutchinson Educational, 1971.

———. *An Experimental Study in Mathematics Learning*. London: Hutchinson, 1963.

———. "Some Basic Processes Involved in Mathematics Learning." In *Research in Mathematics Education*, edited by Joseph M. Scandura. Washington, D.C.: National Council of Teachers of Mathematics, 1967. Pp. 21–34.

———, and Golding, E. W. *Modern Mathematics for Young Children*. New York: McGraw-Hill, 1966, 1973.

Duckworth, E. In *Piaget Rediscovered*, edited by R. Ripple and O. Rockcastle. Ithaca, N.Y.: Cornell University Press, 1964. Pp. 1–15.

———. "Language and Thought." In *Piaget in the Classroom*, edited by M. Schwebel and J. Raph. New York: Basic, 1973. Pp. 132–54.

———. "The Having of Wonderful Ideas." *Harvard Educational Review* 42 (May 1972): 217–31.

Dunn, S., and Wadsworth, B. "An Investigation of the Relationship Between Children's Conceptions of Space and Reading Reversals." Mount Holyoke College, May 1974. Manuscript.

Elkind, D. "Quantity Conceptions in College Students." *Journal of Social Psychology* 57 (1962): 459–65.

———. "Piaget and Montessori." *Harvard Educational Review* 37 (Fall 1967): 535–45.

———. "Reason, Logic and Perception: An Approach to Reading Instruction." In *Educational Therapy*, vol. 2, edited by J. Hellmuth. Seattle: Special Child Publications, 1969. Pp. 195–208.

———. "Two Approaches to Intelligence: Piagetian and Psychometric." In *Measurement and Piaget*, edited by P. Green, M. Ford, and G. Flamer. New York: McGraw-Hill, 1971. Pp. 12–28.

———. "What Does Piaget Say to the Teacher?" *Todays Education* 61, no. 8 (November 1972): 47–48.

Engel, B. *Arranging the Informal Classroom.* Newton, Mass.: Education Development Center, Inc., 1973.

Eson, M. *Psychological Foundations of Education.* 2nd ed. New York: Holt, Rinehart & Winston, 1972.

Evans, Richard I. *Jean Piaget: The Man and His Ideas.* Translated by Eleanor Duckworth. New York: E. P. Dutton, 1973.

Flavell, J. *The Developmental Psychology of Jean Piaget.* Princeton, N.J.: Van Nostrand, 1963.

————. "The Uses of Verbal Behavior in Assessing Children's Cognitive Abilities." In *Measurement and Piaget,* edited by P. Green, M. Ford, and G. Flamer. New York: McGraw-Hill, 1971. Pp. 198–204.

————, and Wohlwill, J. "Formal and Functional Aspects of Cognitive Development." In *Studies in Cognitive Development,* edited by D. Elkind and J. Flavell. New York: Oxford University Press, 1969. Pp. 67–120.

Friedland, S., and Shilkret, R. "Alternative Explanations of Learning Disabilities: Defensive Hyperactivity as a Case in Point." Paper presented at the second annual International Symposium on Learning Disabilities, Miami Beach, October 1972. Also in abbreviated form in *Exceptional Children* 40 (1973): 213–15.

Frostig, M. *Movement Education: Theory and Practice.* Chicago: Follett, 1970.

Furth, H. G. *Thinking Without Language: Psychological Implications of Deafness.* New York: Free Press, 1966.

————. *Piaget and Knowledge.* Englewood Cliffs, N.J.: Prentice-Hall, 1969.

————. *Piaget for Teachers.* Englewood Cliffs, N.J.: Prentice Hall, 1970a.

————. "On Language and Knowing in Piaget's Developmental Theory." *Human Development* 13 (1970b): 241–57.

————. "Reply to Piaget's Paper on the Problems of Equilibration." In *Piaget and Inhelder on Equilibration,* edited by C. Nodine, J. Gallagher, and R. Humphreys. Philadelphia: Jean Piaget Society, 1971. Pp. 21–29

————, and Wachs, H. *Thinking Goes to School.* New York: Oxford University Press, 1974.

Gagné, R. *Conditions of Learning.* 2nd ed. New York: Holt, Rinehart & Winston, 1970.

Gallagher, J. "Equilibration: Sources for Further Study." In *Piaget and Inhelder on Equilibration,* edited by C. Nodine, J. Gallagher, and R. Humphreys. Philadelphia: Jean Piaget Society, 1972. Pp. 60–78.

Geschwind, N. "The Organization of Language and the Brain." *Science* 170, no. 27 (November 1970): 940–44.

Glasser, W. *Schools Without Failure.* New York: Harper & Row, 1968.

Goldschmid, M. "The Role of Experience in the Rate and Sequence of Cognitive Development." In *Measurement and Piaget,* edited by D. Green, M. Ford, and G. Flamer. New York: McGraw Hill, 1971. Pp. 103–10.

Goodglass, H., and Kaplin, E. *The Assessment of Aphasia and Related Disorders.* Philadelphia: Lea & Febiger, 1972.

Goolishian, H.; Hinkelman, S.; and Wadsworth, B. "A Study of the Effects of Grouped Stimuli on the Ability of Young Children to Conserve Number." Mount Holyoke College, May 1971. Manuscript.

Gray, W. M. "Children's Performance on Logically Equivalent Piagetian Tasks and Written Tasks." *Educational Research Monographs.* Dayton, Ohio: University of Dayton, 1970.

————. "Development of a Piagetian-based Written Test: A Criterion Referenced Approach." Paper presented at the annual meeting of the American Educational Research Association, 1973. Mimeographed.

Griffiths, J.; Schantz, C.; and Siegel, I. "A Methodological Problem in Conservation Studies: The Use of Relational Terms." *Child Development* 38 (1967): 841–48.

Gruber, H. "Courage and Cognitive Growth in Children and Scientists." *Piaget in the Classroom,* edited by M. Schwebel and J. Raph. New York: Basic, 1973. Pp. 73–108.

Grzynkowicz, W. M. *Teaching Inefficient Learners.* Springfield, Ill.: Charles C Thomas, 1971.

————, and Kephart, M., eds. *Learning Disabilities: Last Lectures of Newell C. Kephart.* Romeoville, Ill.: WGMK Publishers, 1975.

Hall, E. "A Conversation with Jean Piaget and Barbel Inhelder." *Psychology Today* 3, no. 12 (1970): 25.

Hall, M. *Teaching Reading as a Language Experience.* Columbus, Ohio: Charles E. Merrill, 1970.

Hallam, R. "Piaget and the Teaching of History." *Educational Research* 12 (1969): 3–12.

Hamlyn, D. "Epistemology and Conceptual Development." In *Cognitive Development and Epistemology,* edited by T. Mischel. New York: Academic, 1971.

Hawkins, D. "Messing about in Science." *Science and Children* 3 (February 1965): 5–9.

Heard, S., and Wadsworth, B. "The Relationship Between Cognitive Development and Language Complexity." Mount Holyoke College, May 1977. Manuscript.

Hess, J. *New York Times,* 19 October 1972, p. 49.

Howes, V. M. *Informal Teaching in the Open Classroom.* New York: Macmillan, 1974.

Hunt, J. *Intelligence and Experience.* New York: Ronald Press, 1961.

————. *The Challenge of Incompetence and Poverty.* Urbana, Ill.: University of Illinois Press, 1969a.

————. "The Impact and Limitation of the Giant of Development Psychology." In *Studies in Cognitive Development,* edited by D. Elkind and J. Flavell. New York: Oxford University Press, 1969b. Pp. 3–66.

Incel, P., and Jacobsen, L. *What Do You Expect?* Menlo Park, Calif.: Cummings, 1975.

Inhelder, B. *The Diagnosis of Reasoning in the Mentally Retarded.* New York: John Day, 1968.

―――. "Memory and Intelligence in the Child." In *Studies in Cognitive Development,* edited by P. Elkind and J. Flavell. New York: Oxford University Press, 1969.

―――. "Developmental Theory and Diagnostic Procedures." In *Measurement and Piaget,* edited by P. Green, M. Ford, and G. Flamer. New York: McGraw-Hill, 1971.

―――. "Information Processing Tendencies in Recent Experiments in Cognitive Learning." *Piaget and Inhelder on Equilibration,* edited by C. Nodine, J. Gallagher, and R. Humphreys. Philadelphia: Jean Piaget Society, 1972. Pp. 32–51.

―――, and Piaget, J. *The Growth of Logical Thinking from Childhood to Adolescence.* New York: Basic, 1958.

―――, and Piaget, J. *The Early Growth of Logic in the Child.* New York: Norton, 1969.

―――, and Piaget, J. "Closing Remarks." In *Measurement and Piaget,* edited by D. Green, M. Ford, and G. Flamer. New York: McGraw-Hill, 1971. Pp. 210–13.

―――; Sinclair, H.; and Bovet, M. *Learning and the Development of Cognition.* Cambridge, Mass.: Harvard University Press, 1974.

Jacobsen, E. *Progressive Relaxation.* Chicago: University of Chicago Press, 1938.

Jensen, Arthur. "How Much Can We Boost I.Q. and Scholastic Achievement?" *Harvard Educational Review* 30, no. 1 (1969): 1–123.

Kamii, C. "Pedagogical Principles Derived from Piaget's Theory: Relevance for Educational Practice." In *Piaget in the Classroom,* edited by M. Schwebel and J. Raph. New York: Basic, 1973a. Pp. 199–215.

―――. "Piaget's Interactionism and the Process of Teaching Young Children." In *Piaget in the Classroom,* edited by M. Schwebel and J. Raph. New York: Basic, 1973b. Pp. 216–30.

―――, and Derman, L. "Comments on Englemann's Paper: The Englemann Approach to Teaching Logical Thinking: Findings from the Administration of Some Piagetian Tasks." In *Measurement and Piaget,* edited by D. Green, M. Ford, and G. Flamer. New York: McGraw-Hill, 1971. Pp. 127–46.

―――, and DeVries, R. "Piaget-based Curricula for Early Childhood Education: The Kamii-DeVries Approach." Part of a pre-symposium paper presented at the biennial meeting of the Society for Research in Child Development, Philadelphia, April 1973a.

―――, and DeVries, R. "Piaget-based Curricula for Early Childhood Education: Three Different Approaches." 1973b. Mimeographed.

―――, and Radin, N. L. "A Framework for a Preschool Curriculum Based on Some Piagetian Concepts." In *Educational Implications of Piaget's Theory,* edited by I. Athens and D. Rubadeau. Waltham, Mass.: Ginn-Blaisdell, 1970. Pp. 89–100.

Kamin, Leon. *The Science and Politics of I.Q.* Potomac, Md.: Lawrence Erlbaum, 1974.

Kaplan, S.; Kaplan, J.; Madsen, S.; and Taylor, B. *Change for Children: Ideas and Activities for Individualizing Learning.* Pacific Palisades, Calif.: Goodyear, 1973.

Kelley, G. A. *The Psychology of Personal Constructs*, vol. 1, A *Theory of Personality.* New York: Norton, 1955.

Kellogg, Rhoda. *Analyzing Children's Art.* Palo Alto, Calif.: National Press Books, 1970.

Kephart, N. *The Slow Learner in the Classroom.* 2nd ed. Columbus, Ohio: Charles E. Merrill, 1971a.

————. Intensive Training Workshop at Glen Haven Achievement Center, 2–25 June, 1971b.

Kessen, W. "Early Cognitive Development: Hot or Cold?" In *Cognitive Development and Epistemology*, edited by T. Mischel. New York: Academic, 1971. Pp. 288–309.

Kohlberg, L. "Early Education: A Cognitive Developmental View." *Child Development*, December 1969a, pp. 1013–62.

————. *Stages in the Development of Moral Thought and Action.* New York: Holt, Rinehart & Winston, 1969b.

————, and Mayer, R. "Development of the Aim of Education." *Harvard Educational Review* 42, no. 4 (November 1972).

Kubie, Lawrence S. "Loss of the Freedom to Change through Acquisition of the Symbolic Process." Address presented at the biennial meeting of the Society for Research in Child Development, Philadelphia, 1973.

Langer, J. *Theories of Development.* New York: Holt, Rinehart, & Winston, 1969.

Lavatelli, C. *Piaget's Theory Applied to an Early Childhood Curriculum.* Boston: American Science of Engineering, 1970.

————. "A Piaget-derived Curriculum for Early Childhood Education." Mimeographed, 1973.

Lee, D. M., and Allen, R. V. *Learning to Read Through Experience.* New York: Appleton-Century-Crofts, 1963.

Lovell, K. *The Growth of Basic Mathematical and Scientific Concepts in Children.* London: University Press, 1961.

————. "Some Problems Associated with Formal Thought and Its Assessment." In *Measurement and Piaget*, edited by D. Green, M. Ford, and G. Flamer. New York: McGraw-Hill, 1971a. Pp. 81–93.

————. *The Growth of Understanding in Mathematics: Kindergarten through Grade Three.* New York: Holt, Rinehart & Winston, 1971b.

————. "Intellectual Growth and Understanding Mathematics." *Journal for Research in Mathematics Education* 3 (May 1972): 164–82.

Lyons, John. *Noam Chomsky.* New York: Viking, 1970.

Maier, H. *Three Theories of Child Development.* New York: Harper & Row, 1969.

Makita, K. "The Rarity of Reading Disabilities in Japanese Children." *American Journal of Orthopsychiatry* 38, no. 4 (July 1968): 599–614.

Mar, C.; de la Vega, M.; and Wadsworth, B. "The Relationship Between Spatial Conceptions and Reversals in Reading and Writing." Mount Holyoke College, May 1975. Manuscript.

Mays, W. "Translator's Introduction." In *Principles of Genetic Epistemology* by Jean Piaget. New York: Basic, 1972. Pp. 1–9.

McCarthy, J., and Kirk, S. *Illinois Test of Psycholinguistic Abilities*. Urbana, Ill.: University of Illinois Institute of Research for Exceptional Children, 1966.

McLaughlin, G. "Psycho-logic." *British Journal of Educational Psychology* 33 (1963): 61–67.

Mischel, T. "Piaget: Cognitive Conflict and Motivation of Thought." In *Cognitive Development and Epistemology*, edited by T. Mischel. New York: Academic, 1971. Pp. 311–55.

Mokinnen, J., and Renner, J. "Are Colleges Concerned with Intellectual Development?" *American Journal of Physics* 39 (1971): 1047–52.

Montessori, M. *The Montessori Method*. New York: Schocken, 1964. Originally published 1912.

Myers, P., and Hammill, D. *Methods in Learning Disorders*. 2nd ed. New York: Wiley, 1976.

Neisser, V. *Cognitive Psychology*. New York: Appleton-Century-Crofts, 1967.

Nichols, E. D., et al., eds. *Holt School Mathematics*. New York: Holt, Rinehart & Winston, 1974.

Nolen, P. "Piaget and the School Psychologist." In *Piagetian Theory and the Helping Professions*, edited by G. Lubin, J. Magary, and M. Paulsen. Los Angeles: University of Southern California, 1975. Pp. 287–99.

O'Hara, Ethel. "Piaget, the Six-Year-Old, and Modern Math." *Todays Education*, September–October 1975, pp. 33–36.

Olson, D. "What Is Worth Knowing and What Can Be Taught?" *School Review* 82, no. 1 (1974): 27–43.

Phillips, J. *The Origins of Intellect: Piaget's Theory*. San Francisco: Freeman, 1969.

Piaget, J. *The Origins of Intelligence in the Child*. New York: International Universities Press, 1952a.

———. *The Child's Conception of Number*. London: Humanities Press, 1952b.

———. *The Language and Thought of the Child*. New York: World, 1955.

———. "The Language and Thought of the Child." In *Classics in Psychology*, edited by T. Shipley. New York: Philosophy Library, 1961. Pp. 994–1031.

———. *Play, Dreams and Imitation in Childhood*. New York: Norton, 1962a.

————. *Comments on Vtgotsky's Critical Remarks.* Cambridge, Mass.: MIT Press, 1962b.

————. "Will and Action." *Bulletin of the Menninger Clinic* 26, no. 3 (1962c): 138–45.

————. *The Child's Conception of the World.* Paterson, N.J.: Littlefield, Adams, 1963a.

————. *Psychology of Intelligence.* Paterson, N.J.: Littlefield, Adams, 1963b.

————. "Development and Learning." In *Piaget Rediscovered,* edited by R. Ripple and U. Rockcastle. Ithaca, N.Y.: Cornell University Press, 1964a. Pp. 7–20.

————. *Judgement and Reasoning in the Child.* Paterson, N.J.: Littlefield, Adams, 1964b. Originally published in translation, 1928, Harcourt, Brace & Co.; Translated by Marjorie Warden.

————. *The Moral Judgement of the Child.* New York: Free Press, 1965.

————. *Six Psychological Studies.* New York: Vintage, 1967.

————. *Science of Education and the Psychology of the Child.* New York: Viking, 1969a.

————. *Mechanisms of Perception.* New York: Basic, 1969b.

————. *Genetic Epistemology.* New York: Columbia University Press, 1970.

————. "The Theory of Stages in Cognitive Development." In *Measurement and Piaget,* edited by D. Green, M. Ford, and G. Flamer. New York: McGraw-Hill, 1971a. Pp. 1–11.

————. *Biology and Knowledge.* Chicago: University of Chicago Press, 1971b.

————. "Problems in Equilibration." *Piaget and Inhelder on Equilibration,* edited by E. Nodine, J. Gallagher, and R. Humphreys. Philadelphia: Jean Piaget Society, 1972. Pp. 1–20.

————. *To Understand Is to Invent.* New York: Viking, 1973.

————. "On Correspondence and Morphisms." Translated by Mlle. Eleanor Duckworth. Address at fifth annual symposium of the Jean Piaget Society, Philadelphia, June 1975.

————, and Inhelder B. *Le developement des quantities physiques chez l'enfant.* Neuchatel: De lachaux et Niestle, 1941.

————, and Inhelder, B. *The Child's Conception of Space.* New York: Norton, 1967.

————, and Inhelder B. *The Psychology of the Child.* New York: Basic, 1969.

————; Inhelder, B.; and Szaminska, Alina S. *The Child's Conception of Geometry.* New York: Harper & Row, 1964.

Pinard, A., and Laurendeau, M. " 'Stage' in Piaget's Cognitive-Developmental Theory: Exegesis of a Concept." In *Studies in Cognitive Development,* edited by D. Elkind and J. Flavell. New York: Oxford University Press, 1969. Pp. 121–70.

Presseisen, B. "Individualizing the Social Studies: An Application of

Piaget's Theory." Paper presented at the annual Piagetian Theory and Helping Professions Conference, Los Angeles, February 1973. Mimeographed.

――――, and D'Amico, J. "A Functional Social Studies Curriculum Emphasizing Piagetian Operations." *Educational Forum* 34, no. 2 (January 1975): 163–75.

Pribram, K. "Education: An Enterprise in Language Learning." In *Psychology and the Process of Schooling in the Next Decade: Alternative Conceptions*, edited by M. Reynolds. Washington, D.C.: Leadership Training Institute, U.S. Office of Education, 1970. Pp. 141–46.

Roach, E., and Kephart, N. *The Perceptual Motor Survey*. Columbus, Ohio: Charles E. Merrill, 1966.

Rosenthal, R., and Jacobsen, L. *Pygmalion in the Classroom*. New York: Holt, Rinehart & Winston, 1968.

Schwebel, M. "Formal Operations in First Year College Students." *Journal of Psychology* 91 (1975): 133–41.

Shilkret, R. Personal communication, 1976.

――――, and Friedland, S. "Alternative Conceptualizations of Space: Implications for Educational and Clinical Practice." *Perceptual and Motor Skills* 39 (1974): 451–59.

Shore, M., and Massimo, J. "Mobilization of Community Resources in the Outpatient Treatment of Adolescent and Delinquent Boys: A Case Report." *Community Mental Health Journal* 2, no. 4 (Winter 1966): 329–32.

Shuell, H. *Differential Diagnosis of Aphasia with the Minnesota Test*. Minneapolis: University of Minnesota Press, 1965.

Sigel, I. E. "The Piagetian System and the World of Education." In *Studies in Cognitive Development*, edited by D. Elkind and J. Flavell. New York: Oxford University Press, 1969. Pp. 465–90.

――――. "Developmental Theory: Its Place and Relevance in Early Intervention Programs." *Young Children* 27 (August 1972): 364–72.

Simpson, B. Mimeographed, n.d.

Simpson, D. M. *Learning to Learn*. Columbus, Ohio: Charles E. Merrill, 1968.

Sinclair, H. "Recent Piagetian Research in Learning Studies." In *Piaget in the Classroom*, edited by M. Schwebel and J. Raph. New York: Basic, 1973. Pp. 57–72.

Sinclair, H. "From Preoperational to Concrete Thinking and Parallel Development of Symbolization." In *Piaget in the Classroom*, edited by M. Schwebel and J. Raph. New York: Basic, 1973. Pp. 40–56.

Sinclair-de-Zwart, H. "Developmental Psycholinguistics." In *Studies in Cognitive Development*, edited by D. Elkind and J. Flavell. New York: Oxford University Press, 1969. Pp. 315–36.

Skeels, H. M., and Dye, H. B. "A Study of the Effects of Differential Stimulation of Mentally Retarded Children." *Proceedings of the American Association of Mental Deficiency* 44 (1939): 114–36.

Smedslund, Jan. "Internal Necessity and Contradictions in Children's Thinking." In *Piaget Rediscovered*, edited by R. Ripple and O. Rockcastle. Ithaca, N.Y.: Cornell University Press, 1964. Pp. 92–94.

Smith, F. *Understanding Reading*. New York: Holt, Rinehart & Winston, 1971.

———. *Psycholinguistics and Reading*. New York: Holt, Rinehart & Winston, 1973.

———. *Comprehension and Learning*. New York: Holt, Rinehart & Winston, 1975.

Stauffer, Russel G. *The Language-experience Approach to the Teaching of Reading*. New York: Harper & Row, 1970.

Stephens, W. B. "The Development of Reasoning, Moral Judgment, and Moral Conduct in Retardates and Normals: Phase II." Philadelphia: Temple University, May 1972.

———; Mahoney, E.; McLaughlin, J. "Mental Ages for Achievement of Piagetian Reasoning Assessment." Mimeographed, 1972.

———. "Stephen's Response to Barbel Inhelder's Discussion of Information Processing in Children's Thinking." In *Piaget and Inhelder on Equilibration*, edited by C. Nodine, J. Gallagher, and R. Humphreys. Philadelphia: Jean Piaget Society, 1972. Pp. 52–59.

Strauss, S. "Inducing Cognitive Development and Learning: A Review of Short-term Training Experiments—The Organismic-developmental Approach." *Cognition* 1, no. 4 (1972): 329–57.

Taylor, J. *Organizing the Open Classroom: A Teachers Guide to the Integrated Day*. New York: Schocken, 1972.

Tisher, R. P. "A Piagetian Questionnaire Applied to Pupils in Secondary School. Mimeographed, n.d.

Tuddenham, R. D. "The Nature and Measurement of Intelligence." In *Psychology in the Making*, edited by L. Postman. New York: Knopf, 1962. Pp. 459–529.

———. "Comments on Elkind's Paper." In *Measurement and Piaget*, edited by D. Green, M. Ford, and G. Flamer. New York: McGraw-Hill, 1971. Pp. 28–31.

Turiel, E. "Developmental Processes in the Child's Moral Thinking." In *Trends and Issues in Developmental Psychology*, edited by P. Mussen, J. Langer, and M. Covington. New York: Holt, Rinehart & Winston, 1969. Pp. 92–133.

Uzgiviz, I. "Patterns of Cognitive Development in Infancy." *Merrill Palmer Quarterly* 19, no. 3 (1973): 181–204.

Voight, R. *Invitation to Learning*. Vol. 2. Washington, D.C.: Acropolis Books Ltd., 1974.

Von Senden, Marius. *Space and Sight: The Perception of Space and Shape in the Congenitally Blind Before and After Operation*. Glencoe, Ill.: Free Press, 1960.

Voyat, G. "The Development of Operations: A Theoretical and Practical Matter." In *Piaget in the Classroom*, edited by M. Schwebel and J. Raph. New York: Basic, 1973.

Wadsworth, Barry J. "The Effect of Peer Group Social Interaction on the Conservation of Number Learning in Kindergarten Children." Ed.D. dissertation, State University of New York at Albany, 1968.
———. *Piaget's Theory of Cognitive Development*. New York: McKay, 1971.
———; Banks, L.; and Kraemer, L. "The Use of Numerical Operations to Train Kindergarten Children in Length Conservation and the Investigation of Transfer of Acquired Conservation Ability to Other Areas of Conservation." Paper presented at the annual meeting of the Jean Piaget Society, Philadelphia, June 1975. Mimeographed.
Wapner, S., and Werner, H. eds. *The Body Percept*. New York: Random House, 1965.
Webster, N. *A Collection of Essays and Figurative Writings*. 1790.
Webster's New Collegiate Dictionary. Springfield, Mass.: Merriam, 1956.
Wechsler, David. *Wechsler Intelligence Scale for Children*. New York: Psychological Corporation, 1949.
———. *The Measurement of Adult Intelligence*. Baltimore: Williams & Wilkens, 1944.
Weikart, P.; Rogers, L.; Adcock, C.; and McClelland, P. *The Cognitively Oriented Curriculum: A Framework for Preschool Teachers*. Washington, D.C.: National Association for the Education of Young Children, 1971.
Wiener, M., and Cromer, W. "Reading and Reading Difficulty: A Conceptual Analysis." *Harvard Educational Review*, Fall 1967, pp. 620–43.
Williams, F. A., and Stephens, W. B. "Formation of Individual Piagetian Profiles and Their Translation into Educational Practice." Mimeographed, n.d.

Index

DeVries, R., 52, 73, 100–3, 104, 106, 110, 113, 114, 115, 119, 120
Dewey, J., 4, 6, 10, 55, 82–83, 132
Diagnosis, 207–9; see also Assessment, Testing
Dienes, Z. P., 55, 162, 172–75, 177, 283
Disequilibrium, 78–85, 89, 90, 93, 107, 146, 176, 186
Duckworth, E., 73, 75, 92, 102, 158–60
Dunn, S., 140
Dye, H. B., 25

Educational technology, 10
Egocentrism, 19, 21, 107, 115
Elkind, D., 20, 78, 118, 226, 227, 232
Emotional stress, 203
Equilibration, 79–83, 176
Equilibrium, 6, 79–81, 176
Eson, M., 6
Euclidean space, 139–40, 249–50
Experience, 6, 22–27, 194–96

Failure, 154–55
Feedback, 148–49
Figurative knowledge, 40–42
Flavell, J., 13, 23
Formal operations, 12, 116, 171, 188–89
Friedland, S., 139, 205, 206
Frostig, M., 116
Furth, H. G., 68, 71, 120, 133, 135, 136, 155, 197

Gagné, R., 50
Genetic factors. See Maturation
Glasser, W., 212, 217

Glen Haven Achievement Center, 201
Golding, E. W., 173
Goolishian, H., 228
Gordon, S., 157
Greenfield, P. M., 229
Griffiths, J., 240
Grzynkowicz, W. M., 191, 199, 201, 206

Hallam, R., 183
Hamlyn, D., 5
Hammill, D., 209
Handwriting, 205–7
Hawkins, D., 177–79
Heard, S., 243
Heredity. See Maturation
Hinkelman, S., 228
Historical knowledge. See Knowledge
Holt School Mathematics Program, 170–71
Hunt, J., 4, 25, 26, 46, 89, 116, 194
Hyperactivity, 202, 204–5

Images, 64
Imitation, 63, 68, 187
Inclusion, 59, 88, 193
Individual differences, 145, 154, 183, 190, 282
Initial teaching alphabet, 135
Inhelder, B., 13, 26–27, 30, 83–88, 93, 118, 119, 223, 253, 257, 259, 260, 261, 263, 270, 276, 278
Instruction, inappropriate, 195
Intelligence, 36–37; see also Cognitive development
Intelligence tests, 111